T0210671

Human–Computer Interaction Series

Editors-in-chief

Desney Tan
Microsoft Research, USA

Jean Vanderdonckt
Université catholique de Louvain, Belgium

HCI is a multidisciplinary field focused on human aspects of the development of computer technology. As computer-based technology becomes increasingly pervasive—not just in developed countries, but worldwide—the need to take a human-centered approach in the design and development of this technology becomes ever more important. For roughly 30 years now, researchers and practitioners in computational and behavioral sciences have worked to identify theory and practice that influences the direction of these technologies, and this diverse work makes up the field of human–computer interaction. Broadly speaking it includes the study of what technology might be able to do for people and how people might interact with the technology. The HCI series publishes books that advance the science and technology of developing systems which are both effective and satisfying for people in a wide variety of contexts. Titles focus on theoretical perspectives (such as formal approaches drawn from a variety of behavioral sciences), practical approaches (such as the techniques for effectively integrating user needs in system development), and social issues (such as the determinants of utility, usability and acceptability).

Titles published within the Human–Computer Interaction Series are included in Thomson Reuters' Book Citation Index, The DBLP Computer Science Bibliography and The HCI Bibliography.

More information about this series at http://www.springer.com/series/6033

Georgios Paliouras · Symeon Papadopoulos
Dimitrios Vogiatzis · Yiannis Kompatsiaris
Editors

User Community Discovery

Springer

Editors
Georgios Paliouras
Aghia Paraskevi, Attiki
Greece

Dimitrios Vogiatzis
Aghia Paraskevi, Attiki
Greece

Symeon Papadopoulos
Thermi, Thessaloniki
Greece

Yiannis Kompatsiaris
Thermi, Thessaloniki
Greece

ISSN 1571-5035
Human–Computer Interaction Series
ISBN 978-3-319-35456-9   ISBN 978-3-319-23835-7 (eBook)
DOI 10.1007/978-3-319-23835-7

Springer Cham Heidelberg New York Dordrecht London
© Springer International Publishing Switzerland 2015
Softcover re-print of the Hardcover 1st edition 2015

Printed on acid-free paper

Springer International Publishing AG Switzerland is part of Springer Science+Business Media
(www.springer.com)

Preface

This book aims to introduce the reader to concepts and methods of user community discovery on the social Web. It does so by presenting the evolution of online user communities from the early days of the Web to the complex online social networks that we have formed today. On this basis it explains how state-of-the-art methods for web community discovery can be adapted to address new challenges. It also presents opportunities for research in the new setting and provides examples of new methods that have appeared in the literature.

The basis for current research on community discovery methods is the early work on Web community discovery. Since the wide adoption of Internet-based services and applications, the users' digital traces on Web sites allowed the segmentation of users into communities of "like-minded" individuals. Such communities supported the provision of personalized services to Web users.

Subsequently, the emergence of online social networks and media sharing services allowed users to post information and media content, and to establish explicit social relations with other users. Detecting communities in this context poses various new challenges, in terms of computational complexity and community representation. It also provides a wealth of new opportunities for discovering truly social groups and facilitating both personalization and social interaction among users.

In this fascinating new environment, the current book emphasizes the complexity and richness of social networks, i.e., networks with multiple types of nodes, and multiple types of relation between their nodes, while also examining the issues of scalability, time, and geolocation. It also touches upon the important issue of user privacy and its relation to community discovery.

The editors would like to acknowledge the high-quality contributions of the authors in this volume, which will make it an important read in the field of social network analysis and data mining. We are also indebted to the reviews provided by researchers and practitioners as they made possible the production of a high-quality volume.

Contents

List of Reviewers

Abstract We would like to express our gratitude to the reviewers of the chapters of this book. Their contribution in ensuring a high-quality book is really significant. The following researchers have contributed their reviews to this book:

- Marco Balduzzi, International Secure Systems Lab
- Fosca Giannotti, Institute of Information Science and Technologies (ISTI)
- Maria Giatsoglou, Aristotle University of Thessaloniki
- Aristides Gionis, Aalto University
- Konstantinos Konstantinidis, Centre for Research and Technology Hellas
- Aleksandra Kuczerawy, Katholieke Universiteit Leuven
- Andrea Lancichinetti, Umeå University
- Yuhong Liu, University of Rhode Island
- Radu Negoescu, Robert Kennedy College
- Dimitris Pierrakos, NCSR "Demokritos"
- George Rizos, Centre for Research and Technology Hellas
- Panagiotis Symeonidis, Aristotle University of Thessaloniki
- Lei Tang, Clari Inc.
- Charalampos Tsourakakis, Harvard University
- Julita Vassileva, University of Saskatchewan
- Dingming Wu, Hong Kong University
- Wu Zhiang, Nanjing University of Finance and Economics
- Bin Zhou, University of Maryland, Baltimore County

Contributors

Luca Maria Aiello Yahoo Labs, London, UK

Zhan Bu School of Information Engineering, National Center for International Joint Research on E-Business Information Processing (NECC), Nanjing University of Finance and Economics, Nanjing, China

Jie Cao National Center for International Joint Research on E-Business Information Processing (NECC), School of Information Engineering, Nanjing University of Finance and Economics, Nanjing, China

David Fuhry Department of Computer Science and Engineering, The Ohio State University, Columbus, OH, USA

Isaac Jones Arizona State University, Tempe, USA

Jiongqian Liang Department of Computer Science and Engineering, The Ohio State University, Columbus, OH, USA

Huan Liu Arizona State University, Tempe, USA

Georgios Paliouras Institute of Informatics and Telecommunications, NCSR "Demokritos", Aghia Paraskevi, Attiki, Greece

Symeon Papadopoulos Information Technologies Institute, Centre for Research and Technology Hellas (CERTH), Thessaloniki, Greece

Srinivasan Parthasarathy Department of Computer Science and Engineering, The Ohio State University, Columbus, OH, USA

Yiye Ruan Department of Computer Science and Engineering, The Ohio State University, Columbus, OH, USA

Lei Tang Head of Data Science, Clari Inc., Mountain view, CA, USA

Dimitrios Vogiatzis Institute of Informatics and Telecommunications, NCSR "Demokritos", Aghia Paraskevi, Attiki, Greece; The American College of Greece, Athens, Greece

Yu Wang Department of Computer Science and Engineering, The Ohio State University, Columbus, OH, USA

Zhiang Wu School of Information Engineering, National Center for International Joint Research on E-Business Information Processing (NECC), Nanjing University of Finance and Economics, Nanjing, China

Bin Zhou Department of Information Systems, University of Maryland, Baltimore County, Baltimore, MD, USA

Yi Zhuang College of Computer and Information Engineering, Zhejiang Gongshang University, Hangzhou, China

Chapter 1
Discovery of Complex User Communities

Georgios Paliouras, Symeon Papadopoulos and Dimitrios Vogiatzis

Abstract This chapter serves as an introduction to the book on *User Community Discovery*, setting the scene for the presentation in the rest of the book of various methods for the discovery of user communities in the social Web. In this context, the current chapter introduces the various types of user community, as they appeared in the early days of the Web, and how they converged to the common concept of *active user community* in the social Web. In this manner, the chapter aims to clarify the use of terminology in the various research areas that study user communities. Additionally, the main approaches to discovering user communities are briefly introduced and a number of new challenges for community discovery in the social Web are highlighted. In particular we emphasize the complexity of the networks that are constructed among users and other entities in the social Web. Social networks are typically *multi-modal*, i.e. containing different types of entity, *multi-relational*, i.e. comprising different relation types, and *dynamic*, i.e. changing over time. The complexity of the networks calls for new versatile and efficient methods for community discovery. Details about such methods are provided in the rest of the book.

Keywords User communities · Web mining · Online social networks

G. Paliouras (✉) · D. Vogiatzis
Institute of Informatics and Telecommunications, NCSR "Demokritos",
Patr. Grigoriou and Neapoleos Street, 15310 Aghia paraskevi, Attiki, Greece
e-mail: paliourg@iit.demokritos.gr

S. Papadopoulos
Information Technologies Institute, Centre for Research and Technology Hellas (CERTH),
Thessaloniki, Greece
e-mail: papadop@iti.gr

D. Vogiatzis
The American College of Greece, Athens, Greece
e-mail: dimitrv@iit.demokritos.gr

© Springer International Publishing Switzerland 2015   1
G. Paliouras et al. (eds.), *User Community Discovery*, Human–Computer
Interaction Series, DOI 10.1007/978-3-319-23835-7_1

1.1 Introduction

Nowadays, much of our social activity takes place online. Technological advances have led to the emergence of the *social Web* (also known as *Web 2.0*), which made Web users active participants, generating their own content and forming Online Social Networks (OSNs). Friendship and interaction among users lead naturally to the formation of communities either by explicit connections or by connections that can be inferred through the similarity of the users or the online trails of their interactions (implicit communities). The composition of communities and the underlying characteristics that their members share is valuable knowledge to companies that provide products and services online. As an example, taking into account the communities in which social network users participate can considerably improve the relevance of the recommended content and ultimately the engagement of users, i.e. a form of *social recommendation* [103].

The focus of this book is on the discovery of implicit communities of users,[1] i.e. beyond the explicit friendship or other types of connection that can be found in OSNs. This discovery process is data-driven and it is based on statistical and machine learning approaches. Even though it has made its appearance in user modeling research more than 20 years ago [20, 74] it has been recently revived in the context of statistical physics [27] and graph mining research [94]. Such data mining methods have supported new powerful ways of personalization, such as collaborative filtering and recommendation [40, 49, 50, 98]. However, the advent of the social Web has introduced a number of new challenges and opportunities for community discovery methods. Social media, generated primarily by the users themselves and exchanged over OSNs, make user data richer, larger in size and highly multi-dimensional [80]. In fact, user data is becoming truly social data, like the data one would collect by observing the interaction of the members of a society. Discovery methods need to be adapted to this new type of data, in order to be able to identify the complex multi-scale community structures that are formed. At the same time, the ease with which such rich social data can be collected increases the responsibility of researchers and service providers to respect the privacy of individuals and user groups.

This chapter serves as an introduction to the book, setting the scene for the presentation of various methods for discovering user communities in the rest of the book. Based on the categorization introduced in [75], the chapter starts (Sect. 1.2) by presenting the different types of user community that have been studied in the literature and how these converge into the common concept of *active user community* in the social Web. Then, in Sect. 1.3, it presents the basic characteristics of communities, as subgraphs of a larger graph of connected entities, e.g., a network of users. Section 1.4 presents briefly the main approaches to community discovery, while Sect. 1.5 explains the challenges and opportunities for community discovery in the social Web. A more thorough treatment of community discovery methods in the

---

[1]Although the term "community discovery" is more suitable to describe this process, throughout the text we adopt the term "community detection", which is the prevalent term used in the literature to refer to this problem.

social Web is provided in the rest of the book chapters. Section 1.6 highlights some example applications of community discovery in the social Web. Finally, Sect. 1.7 summarizes the main concepts introduced in this chapter and discusses some of the main open issues.

1.2 Types of Web Community

According to [75] the term "Web community" has been used with three different meanings in computer science literature:

User communities   correspond to clusters of users of a Web site, who share common interests. Typical such communities are the customers of online shops. User communities are formed on the basis of user log data, as recorded on the Web servers of the site. These data are analyzed by statistical and machine learning methods [76] in order to identify groups of users with common interests or behavior, e.g., users who buy similar products.

Web communities   correspond to subgraphs of the Web graph, i.e. clusters of Web pages, that are densely connected. Such dense subgraphs arc identified by graph mining methods [26, 52] and indicate Web sites that provide similar or related content, e.g., art museums in different countries.

Web-based communities   are associated with systems that support the formation or strengthening of real-life communities. These were typically either local communities (e.g., within a University campus) or interest-driven ones (e.g., professional associations). Early work in this field focused on *community networks* [95] and *virtual communities* [90], which then evolved into *Web community portals* [100] and finally into *Web-based communities* [10]. What makes this type of community particularly interesting is the fact that users start producing content for the community. In other words, they move from being passive consumers of content to becoming active community participants. This idea, aided by corresponding technological advances, later developed in what we now call the social Web.

The social Web has been facilitated by technological advances in the interaction of the users with Web resources (a.k.a. Web 2.0 technologies) and has facilitated, in turn, two important socio-technical developments, often referred to as social media and Online Social Networks (OSNs). Social media and user-generated content represent the widespread participation of Web users in the generation and publication of digital content, which has now become more dynamic than ever before. It is this active participation of the users in content publishing that has led to the use of the term *active user* in the social Web. On the other hand, OSNs are typically Web applications that support the active networking of users, much in the spirit of Web-based communities. OSNs can be considered the natural descendants of *Web-based communities* and community networks. As such, they bear similarities to those earlier paradigms, for instance the goal of linking people with common interests or needs. However, OSNs also have significant differences from their predecessors [11], among which are:

- Their much larger user base.
- The diversity of their user base and their detachment from particular themes or geographic locations.
- The fact that people link to each other, but do not necessarily join predefined groups. A social network is a graph, in the sense of the Web itself, rather than a group of people.
- Their participatory nature turns passive consumers into active users, who provide content and information of many new and interesting types.

Using the terminology of [75], we call communities of users in OSNs *active user communities*. These are naturally related to Web-based communities, but they are also related to the other two types of community mentioned above.

Due to the fact that OSNs are naturally mapped to graphs, active user communities are subgraphs of the larger graph, similar to *Web communities*. In contrast to the Web though, the nodes of the social graph are typically users and thus its subgraphs form *user communities*. In this manner, the three different types of community seem to converge to the common and much richer structure of the active user community in the social Web.

Beyond the fact that they bring together the three different notions of community, active user communities introduce a number of novel and interesting possibilities. In the social Web, users provide much richer information about their preferences and needs, than what the logs of a Web server could reveal. They choose their neighbors in the network, they publish their own content, they rate and tag content that other people have provided and participate in a number of online activities. Due to the variety of entities involved in the social Web, one may choose to create graphs other than those connecting users, e.g., by relating content items posted by the users, or even multi-partite graphs that relate different types of entity (see Chap. 3). Additionally, these graphs may contain different edge types, e.g., edges that represent friendship and others that represent communication among the users. This multi-relational nature of the social Web (see Chap. 4) makes the task of active community discovery particularly interesting and challenging.

1.3 Representation of Communities

1.3.1 Communities as Graphs

The common representation of a community is that of a graph $C = (V, E)$, where V and E represent the nodes and edges respectively, that connect closely-related users or other entities. Usually, this graph is a subgraph of a larger one $C \subseteq G$, e.g., all the users of a social network, and is assumed to have a dense structure, representing the close relation among its members. However, there is considerable discussion about the best choice for representing such a dense structure.

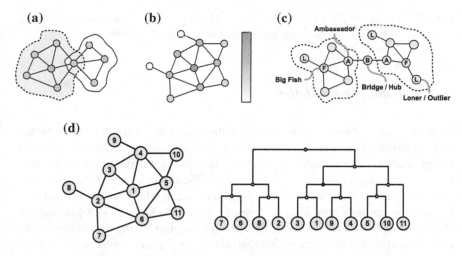

Fig. 1.1 Several attributes that may characterise community structure: **a** overlap, **b** weighted membership, **c** node (vertex) roles within/across communities, **d** hierarchical organization. Image originally presented in [80]

A large body of literature assumes that G should be partitioned into subsets (the communities), whereby each node of the graph belongs to exactly one subgraph. However, in reality, especially in the context of the social Web, community membership is more complicated. A user may well belong to more than one community and may belong to different communities in different degrees (Fig. 1.1a). The need to allow overlaps between communities was realized even in early research in community discovery (e.g., [74]). Being the most dense graph structure, cliques (i.e. fully connected subgraphs: $\forall v \in V(C) : degree_C(v) = |V| - 1$) were among the first options to be considered. Thus, in the early days of community detection research, community graphs G were required to be maximal cliques of C, i.e., cliques that are not subsumed by other cliques of C. The strictness of this definition often leads to unwanted effects, such as very low participation of nodes to communities.

In order to overcome this problem, alternative, less strict definitions were used, such as cores or k-shells (introduced in [97]). A k-shell is a subgraph C of a graph $G = (V, E)$ iff $\forall v \in V(C) : degree_G(v) \geq k$ and C is the maximum subgraph with this property. An equivalent definition is that k-shell is a maximal subset of nodes such that each is reachable from each of the others by at least k node independent paths. Two paths are defined as node independent if they share none of the same nodes, with the exception of the start and the end nodes [69, Sect. 7.8.2]. Among their other benefits, k-shells can be computed efficiently in large graphs, such as social networks. This concept of core has been expanded in [9, 92], and core-periphery structures have been studied in the context of weighted networks [29], hypergraphs [87], as well as in temporal networks [63].

Additionally, a number of other graph structures have been used in the literature to address the issue of overlapping communities, some based on cliques, e.g. Palla et al. [77], but many others as well [17, 18, 37, 58]. An extensive treatment of the problem of overlapping community detection is presented in [108].

1.3.2 Community Attributes

The assumption that communities either partition the graph or are allowed to overlap is an important differentiating attribute of community representation and discovery approaches. In addition, there are other attributes that nodes of a network may have in relation to communities. For instance, different nodes may participate with varying degrees in a community depending on their centrality[2] within it (Fig. 1.1b). Moreover, nodes may have discrete roles: for example, Xu et al. [109] define two roles (*hubs* and *outliers*) for nodes that are not assigned to any community. Hubs are connected to multiple communities and act as liaisons, thus enabling interactions among communities. Outliers are connected to a single community through a single link, therefore they are usually considered as noise. Community-based node roles are also discussed by Scripps et al. [96]. Specifically, the roles of "loners", "big fish", "bridges" and "ambassadors" are defined (Fig. 1.1c).

It is also possible to impose hierarchical (Fig. 1.1d) or multi-scale structure on communities [1]. Community organization may be defined at different scales with respect to real-world systems. For instance, a set of users of a social Web application may be organised in a community focused on a very specific topic (e.g., fans of a particular indie-rock band) and at the same time they may be considered as members of a broader community (rock music). In many cases, however, such hierarchies are not flexible enough to model the complexities of multi-level organization in social Web systems, as for instance in the case of folksonomies [15].

An orthogonal dimension concerning the characterization of communities is time. This is a significant aspect of community detection that is worth further attention especially due to the volatile and highly dynamic nature of social Web data and interactions. According to a recent survey on the topic [35], a three-layered stream of graph snapshots can be used to capture the evolution of social interactions. Graph snapshots are used at the lowest level to capture the state at specific points in time. At a higher level, these are grouped into segments, 3D tensor structures, encompassing short-term evolutions. At the top level the complete graph stream captures the history of interactions among the graph nodes. An alternative representation of graph evolution relies on an initial (base) graph that corresponds to the original state, and a stream of changes (e.g., node additions/removals, edge additions/removals). Accordingly, time-awareness can be incorporated in the underlying community structure of time-evolving graphs, either by considering a series of community structures defined at the corresponding graph snapshots and a set of pairwise community structure associations across snapshots, or by considering an initial (base) community structure and a stream of changes on this structure, or by inherently integrating time-awareness

---

[2]Centrality quantifies how often nodes belong to the paths connecting other nodes.

into the community detection process [31]. A set of basic changes (or transforma-tions) that community structures may undergo are described in the seminal work by Palla et al. [77]: Essentially, there are three types of transformation: (a) one-to-one, which involves community growth or contraction, (b) one-to-many, which involves one community splitting to many or many communities merging to one, and (c) one-to-zero (and zero-to-one), which involves the emergence or the extinction of a community.

1.4 Community Detection on Simple Graphs

Depending on the underlying methodological principles, five broad classes of com-munity detection and graph clustering methods were defined in [80]: (a) cohesive subgraph discovery, (b) vertex (or node) clustering, (c) community quality optimiza-tion, (d) divisive, and (e) model-based. Note that these classes are not mutually exclusive. For instance, spectral community detection methods [72] can be consid-ered both to perform quality optimization and be divisive.

Cohesive subgraph discovery. The methods of this class presume a specifica-tion of the structural properties that a subgraph of the network should satisfy to be considered a community. Once such a subgraph structure is chosen, methods involve the enumeration of subgraphs in the network under study. Local community defi-nitions, such as cliques, n-cliques, k-cores, LS sets and lambda sets, are examples of such cohesive structures and therefore algorithmic schemes for enumerating such structures, such as the Bron-Kerbosch algorithm [13] and the efficient k-core decom-position algorithm of Batagelj and Zaversnik [4], belong to this class of community detection methods. In addition, methods such as the Clique Percolation Method [78] and the SCAN algorithm [109], which lead to the discovery of subgraph structures with well-specified properties, fall under the same class of methods.

Vertex (node) clustering. Such techniques originate from traditional data clus-tering research. A typical means of casting a graph clustering problem to one that can be solved by conventional data clustering methods (such as k-means and hierarchical agglomerative clustering) is by embedding graph nodes in a vector space, where pair-wise distances between nodes can be calculated. Another popular method is to use the spectrum of the graph for mapping graph nodes to points in a low-dimensional space, where the cluster structure is more profound [23, 59]. Other node similar-ity measures such as structural equivalence [12] and neighborhood overlap have been used to compute similarities between graph nodes [107]. Finally, a noteworthy method, called Walktrap [81], makes use of a random-walk based similarity between nodes and between communities and uses modularity in a hierarchical agglomerative clustering scheme to derive an optimal node clustering structure.

Community quality optimization. There is a large number of methods that are founded on the basis of optimizing some graph-based measure of community quality. Subgraph density and cut-based measures, such as normalized cut [99] and conduc-tance [47], were among the first to be used for quantifying the quality of some network division into clusters. A whole new wave of research was stimulated by the measure of modularity. Approximate modularity maximization schemes abound in the literature. Apart from the seminal greedy optimization technique of Newman [70], and speeded up versions of it, such as max-heap based agglomeration [19] and iterative heuristic schemes [7], more sophisticated optimization methods have been devised, for instance, extremal optimization [24], speeded simulated annealing [61] and spectral optimization [71]. Methods aiming at the optimization of local measures of community quality, such as local and subgraph modularity [18, 58]), also belong to this category. Finally, this category includes methods that exploit the "hills" and "valleys" in the distribution of network-based node or edge functions, e.g., the ModuLand framework proposed by Kovács et al. [51] and the "reachability" measure by Chen et al. [17], and the highly popular OSLOM method [53], which performs local optimization of a fitness function expressing the statistical significance of clusters.

Divisive. These methods rely on the identification of network elements (edges and nodes) that are positioned between communities. For instance, the seminal algorithm by Girvan and Newman [36] progressively removes the edges of a network, based on some edge betweeness measure until communities emerge as disconnected components of the graph. Several measures of edge betweeness have been devised, for instance, edge, random-walk, and current-flow betweeness [73], as well as information centrality [28] and the edge clustering coefficient [85]. A similar principle is adopted by node removal methods [105]; such methods remove nodes in order to reveal the underlying community structure. Finally, min-cut/max-flow methods [26, 44] adopt a different divisive perspective: they try to identify graph cuts (i.e. sets of edges that separate the graph into pieces) of minimum size.

Model-based. This is a broad and more recent category of methods that either consider a dynamic process taking place on the network, which reveals its communities, or they consider an underlying model of statistical nature that can generate the division of the network into communities. Examples of dynamic processes are label propagation [37, 54, 86], synchronization of Kuramoto oscillators [3], diffusion flow, better known as Markov Cluster Algorithm [104], and the popular spin model by Reichardt and Bornholdt [89]. In addition, community detection can be cast as a modelling problem, such as the well-known stochastic block model [41] and its extensions [2], or a statistical inference problem [39], assuming some underlying probabilistic model, such as the planted partition model, that generates the community structure and estimating the parameters of this model. Other model-based approaches rely on the principle that a good clustering is determined by a low encoding cost and thus they perform community detection by finding the cluster structure that results in the lowest possible cluster encoding cost [16, 93].

Several of the aforementioned and other methods and are discussed in detail in the survey articles by Danon et al. [21], Fortunato [27], Porter et al. [82], and Schaeffer [94]. Also, a useful listing of a large number of community detection methods appears in the supplementary material of Kovács et al. [51]. The majority of the aforementioned methods have been designed for use with undirected graphs. A thorough treatment of the community detection problem in the context of directed networks is presented in [60].

It is worth stressing that methods such as the ones listed above, have been proposed and applied in the context of User and Web communities (as defined in Sect. 1.2, typically giving rise to graphs with a single type of node and edge. In recent years, however, there has been a tendency for increasing complexity in the structure of real-world networks with the emergence of active user communities, as discussed above. This naturally leads to more sophisticated data models, for instance networks with attributed nodes [111], networks with content-associated edges [83], as well as multi-mode and multi-relational networks. Consequently, the active user communities call for new representations and new detection methods. For instance, modern OSNs, such as Twitter and Facebook, can be modelled by means of different entities, such as users, resources, and tags, and relations, such as likes, comments, affiliations, etc. In the next section, we examine how this additional complexity has brought new developments to the research field of community detection.

1.5 Communities in the Social Web

As previously discussed, OSNs are complex systems comprising multiple entity types associated with multiple relations. Thus, there may be users connected to other users, but also users creating posts, or replying to, sharing, commenting or rating posts. Moreover, the posts could contain references to external resources such as Web pages, be associated with a theme or a geographic location and carry a timestamp.

A complete representation of an OSN would require a graph to represent users, posts, and other entities in the form of nodes, whereas replies, comments, participation in groups would be represented as relations. Moreover, the relations between entities could be binary, ternary or of higher order. In the context of this chapter we use the term *multi-dimensional graph* to refer to graphs that contain edges that comprise more than two nodes, or to graphs that contain multiple types of edge. An overview of such graphs can be found in [48]. We divide multi-dimensional graphs into two broad categories, *hypergraphs* and *multi-relational graphs*.

Hypergraphs. Multi-dimensional graphs that contain a single type of edge will be referred to as hypergraphs, formally defined as $G = (V, \mathbf{E})$, where V is the set of nodes and $\mathbf{E} \subseteq V \times V \times \cdots \times V$, is the set of hyperedges. A further distinction between hypergraphs could be made between single partite and multi-partite hypergraphs. In the latter case there are nodes of more than one type, i.e. $\mathbf{E} \subseteq V_1 \times V_2 \times \cdots \times V_k$, given k types of node (see Fig. 1.2). Despite their recent popularity in social network analysis, hypergraphs are not a novel concept, as they were already proposed by Berge in 1973 [5].

In hypergraphs, the definitions of graph properties such as node degree, path, cycle, clustering coefficient and clique have been extended to accommodate the new properties of the hyperedges. For instance, hypergraph path definitions can be found in [106], centrality in [8] and cliques in [22].

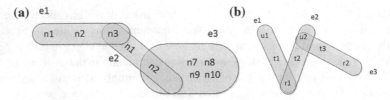

Fig. 1.2 Hypergraphs and hyperedges: **a** general hypergraph, **b** tripartite graph; e1, e2, e3 denote hyperedges. The nodes in (**a**) are of single type, whereas the nodes in (**b**) are of three types: u, t, r

Tri-partite graphs in particular, have been studied in the context of social tagging systems. They arose from the need to represent triadic relations. For instance, a seller, a buyer and a broker participating in a business transaction; or a person seeing a movie, and annotating it with tags. Thus, one partite could stand for users, another for tags and a third for movies. Hyperedges could be interpreted as tag assignments by a user to a resource. Moreover, it is often assumed that there are no connections between nodes of the same partite and each edge contains one node from each partite. In this case, i.e. if each hyperedge has a node from each partite, the result is a k-partite uniform hypergraph. Three commonly used datasets for the study of hypergraphs are excerpts from Delicious, MovieLens and LastFM.[3]

The usage of a uniform k-partite network could be extended to represent other social networks that were not originally conceived to be such; for instance in Twitter, we may consider three partites: users, named entities (such as people, places and organizations) that are referred to in the tweet text, and references to external resources such as URLs.

Multi-relational graphs. Multi-relational graphs comprise more that one relations between their nodes. These can be represented as $G = (V, \mathbf{E})$, where V is the set of nodes and $\mathbf{E} = E_1, E_2, \dots, E_l$ is a set of sets of edges, l is the number of relations, and $E_i \subseteq V \times V$. Each edge type carries certain semantics, for instance relations could denote colleagues, friends, etc. Multi-relational graphs appeared in the field of artificial intelligence as semantic networks [84], in the field of machine translation as a representational language [91] and ultimately they originate from predicate logic. Multi-relational networks are a natural way to represent the various forms of relation in OSN, but also to represent information across OSNs that could be used to unify relevant information about users. For instance, in Fig. 1.3, various users are present in both the Twitter and the LinkedIn OSNs. In the aforementioned definition of multi-relational networks we implied that the relations are binary, but this definition can be generalized to cover multi-relational hyper-graphs.

---

[3]http://grouplens.org/datasets/hetrec-2011/.

Fig. 1.3 Multi-relational
graph representing three
types of relation over two
networks. Contacts in
LinkedIn; and Followers and
Replies in Twitter. The node
labels denote the user, for
instance user 1 participates
in all relations, across all
networks

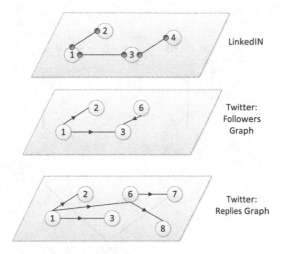

1.5.1 Definitions of Communities in the Social Web

Next, we provide definitions of the community types for the social Web that are
relevant in the current presentation. We will be making references to the diagram
of Fig. 1.4. Let $G(V, E)$ denote a social network of $|V|$ nodes and $|E|$ edges. A
set of non-overlapping communities is represented as $\{C_1, \ldots, C_k\}$, where $C_i =
\{v_{i(1)}, v_{i(2)}, \ldots, v_{i(k)}\} \in V$, and $\forall i, j \ C_i \cap C_j = \emptyset$. In the case of overlapping
communities $\exists i, j, \ C_i \cap C_j \neq \emptyset$.

Communities can also be structured, as in the case of hierarchical communities,
where $\exists i, j, \ C_i \subset C_j$. Additionally, in multi-partite networks we can discover a
complex community structure that relates communities of a single type of node.
Relations between communities are shaped by the link (or edge) pattern. That is,
$\forall i \ P_i \subset V$, where P_i are the nodes from a single partite, and $C_{P_{i,j}}$ denotes a
community j from partite i. The relation of communities from different partites

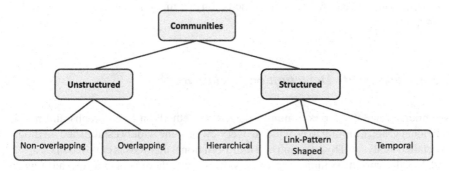

Fig. 1.4 A taxonomy of communities

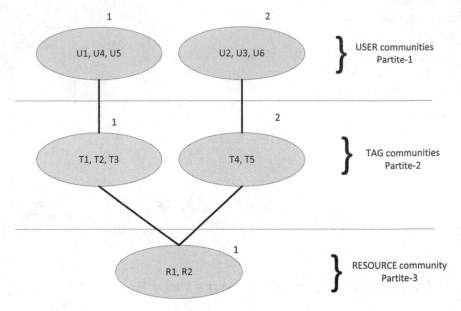

Fig. 1.5 Complex structure in multi-partite communities. Each user community is related to one tag community, and all are related to a single resource community. The numbers on the ovals correspond to community identifiers

can be expressed as: $\{C_{P_{i1,j(1)}}, C_{P_{i1,j(2)}}, C_{P_{i2,j(1)}}, C_{P_{i2,j(2)}}, C_{P_{i3,j(3)}}, \ldots\}$, where the first index denotes the partite, and j is an index to the community. For instance in Fig. 1.5, the complex community structure can be expressed as: $\{C_{P_{1,1}}, C_{P_{2,1}}, C_{P_{3,1}}\}$, and $\{C_{P_{1,2}}, C_{P_{2,2}}, C_{P_{3,1}}\}$.

Finally, in the case of temporal communities there is an ordering for each community as well as a labeling of the evolutionary phenomena that the communities undergo from time frame to time frame, i.e. $C_{t_1(i)} \prec C_{t_2(i)} \ldots$, and $e_k = f(C_{t_1(i)}, C_{t_2(i)})$, where e_k is the evolutionary phenomenon that occurred to $C_{t_1(i)}$ and transformed it into $C_{t_2(i)}$. Typically the evolutionary phenomenon can be growth, shrinking, continuation, dissolution, etc. An extensive discussion of temporal communities is included in [42, 43].

1.5.2 Community Detection on Social Graphs

We briefly review some community detection methods in hypergraphs and multi-relational graphs, aiming to provide an overview of some widely established methods. A detailed analysis of hypergraph and multi-relational methods is exposed in Chaps. 3 and 4 of the current volume respectively. Moreover, there is also a relevant review in [48].

Community detection has been applied in the context of hypergraphs broadly following two main approaches: (a) mapping the hypergraph to a simpler structure to discover communities with any algorithm for simple graphs (such as the ones discussed in Sect. 1.4), and (b) discovering communities directly on the hypergraph. Following the first approach, multi-partite graphs can be mapped to graphs, where the nodes are typically users. In this case the connections between the nodes are meant to represent the node similarity or proximity in the original hypergraph. However, in the case of bi-partite graphs it has been shown that the discovered communities in the simple graph are not always a faithful representation of the original communities under some structural measures [38].

Following the second approach, established methods of community detection in single-partite graphs have been extended to multi-partite graphs. For instance, modularity maximization, which is a widely used method in single-partite graphs has been formulated for bi-partite graphs [65]. Then it was suggested that tri-partite uniform graphs can be projected onto bi-partite graphs and the modularity of the tri-partite graph can be computed as the aggregated modularity of bi-partite graphs [68]. However, this method results in a proliferation of bi-partite structures, which makes it challenging to scale beyond more than three partites. Also, modularity maximization was subsequently formulated for tri-partite graphs [66, 67]. Moreover, spectral clustering, which can be used to embed a simple graph into the Euclidean space and then to perform clustering in that space, has been extended to multi-partite graphs [114].

Another major category of algorithms attempt to cluster links instead of nodes to detect communities; this concept has also been extended to tri-partite graphs [34]. In particular, the first step is to detect pairwise similarities between hyperedges, which is done by considering the neighbourhood of each node that is incident to a hyperedge. The result is a pairwise matrix of hyperedge similarities, on which any community detection method on simple graphs can be applied. Eventually, communities of hyperedges are obtained, and consequently the node communities can be overlapping.

In multi-relational networks there are several ways to deal with the different edge types when performing community detection. First, one could simply ignore the semantics of the edges by integrating all different edges connecting two nodes in a single one. This approach is problematic, for instance in the case that some edges denote friendship, whereas others denote animosity (as in the case of signed networks). Thus it is important to have a specific perspective on the network because this will substantiate the relations and allow their integration. A general approach is to consider each relation and the relevant nodes as a separate network, and then to proceed with some sort of integration [102]. Another approach is to focus on the discovery of relations that bind a given set of users. This results in a network with a weight matrix that is a linear combination of the various relations [14]. The resulting network is single-relational and hence communities can be discovered with standard methods.

The methods mentioned above essentially try to reduce a multi-relational network into a single-relational one. There are, however, approaches that follow a different path: they try to detect groups of consistent interactions (i.e. relations) between the entities of an OSN, and these are considered to form a community. There are two basic approaches in this line of research. The first is based on tensor factorization. The multiple relations between the entities of an OSN can be represented as the modes of a tensor. For instance, relations among users together with relations between users and visited items form a three-mode tensor. Tensor decomposition can be used for extracting latent features that are later used to build communities [57]. The second approach in community detection directly in multi-relational networks is to extend the widely used statistical measure of modularity maximization [45].

Temporal networks can also be considered as multi-relational by considering discrete time steps. Given also the fact that time is an ordinal attribute, there can be an ordering of time relationships. Thus, an email exchange network, or a co-authorship network can be subject to an analysis that discovers communities per time frame and then associates them across time frames to study their evolution [101]. This problem has also been addressed with matrix factorization [32]. Issues such as the longevity of email communities, or the forms of their evolution are important for their characterization.

1.6 Applications of Community Detection

An important application of community detection is in the domain of user-contributed multimedia mining. The majority of social Web applications offer facilities for users to upload and annotate multimedia content. Typical and popular examples of social Web multimedia sharing applications are Flickr and Instagram for images, Sound-Cloud for audio and YouTube, Vimeo and DailyMotion for video. A common application associated with multimedia sharing on the social Web is the mining of multimedia communities, i.e. communities comprising media items. Having such structure at one's disposal, one can derive user communities by translating item communities to user communities through the respective authorship/ownership (e.g., users belong to the same communities that their respective items belong to). Alternatively, to derive multimedia communities, one may take into account the rich social context (in the form of interactions or affiliations) that is associated with the respective users. Given the huge increase in the amounts of user-contributed content in social Web multimedia sharing applications, being able to perform clustering on them can help their users navigate larger parts of the content more efficiently (i.e. by looking at one representative item per cluster instead of all cluster members).

A common analysis approach for mining communities of user-generated multimedia is to first construct a similarity graph that captures the pairwise similarities between media items and then to apply a community detection approach with the goal of extracting clusters of similar media items. Moëllic et al. [64] pursue photo clustering by use of a shared nearest neighbors approach on two graphs of photos where edges between photos are computed either by use of shared tags (tag-based graph) or based on visual similarity (visual graph). The employed clustering technique is shown to achieve improved clustering performance compared with conventional clustering algorithms (k-means and one of its speeded-up variants). Also, comparing the results of their methods with the clusters available from Flickr (Groups explicitly defined by users of the application), the authors noted similar clustering quality.

A more sophisticated application of graph clustering is presented by Li et al. [55]. Their goal is to collect different representative (*iconic*) photos for popular landmarks and use the massive visual content that is associated with them in order to create 3D landmark models. They devised a multi-stage photo processing framework, in which an important task was to group iconic photos together in order to reduce the amount of photos that are processed by the computationally intensive 3D reconstruction step. They achieve photo grouping by creating a photo graph where photos are connected by edges when they are visually similar and by applying the N-cut graph clustering algorithm by Shi and Malik [99] on this graph. In that way, they managed to reconstruct the major views of three famous landmarks (Statue of Liberty, Notre Dame and San Marco).

Papadopoulos et al. [79] identified real-world landmarks and events in large tagged photo collections by use of photo cluster classification. They applied the SCAN algorithm [109] on a hybrid photo similarity graph that encodes both visual and tag similarity between photos. Subsequently, the derived photo and tag communities are classified as landmarks or events based on cluster features such as the cluster duration and number of unique users with photos in the cluster. In their analysis, manual inspection of the results reveals that most of the clusters correspond either to famous landmarks of the city or to real events (e.g., music concerts). Furthermore, the automatically selected cluster tags provide meaningful descriptions for them.

Gargi et al. [30] used community detection to perform clustering of YouTube videos. As a first step, they formed a video similarity graph using co-watch statistics (i.e., an edge between two videos is inserted if many users watch the two videos in the same session). Then, they applied a multi-step community detection approach, consisting of a local seed community detection step based on the concept of density and conductance, and a cluster refinement step, where the text similarity between videos is taken into account to ensure topical coherence between the videos. The proposed approach was designed with scalability in mind, due to the very large size of the underlying video similarity graph, and was shown to lead to meaningful and coherent clusters.

The association of content together with structure in social Web multimedia sharing applications has recently motivated the development of community detection approaches that take into account such content [83]. Edge content provides unique insights into communities because it characterizes the nature of the interactions between participants more effectively. This is because the use of purely structural information cannot easily characterize the nature of the interactions between participants effectively. Similarly, the information which is available only at the nodes may not be able to easily distinguish the different interactions of nodes that belong to multiple communities. Correspondingly, the use of edge content enables richer insights which can be used for more effective community detection.

Content recommendation is another important application of community detection in OSNs. As mentioned before, users contribute content and they may also comment, tag or vote on the content produced by them or by others. This forms the context, and indeed the context can influence users' experience. Digg[4] is a social network that allows news sharing among users. In particular users submit news stories related to a topic, and they may vote, comment or reply to stories submitted by other users. Apart from users, there are other entities such as stories, and comments. Relations among the entities can be binary such as (user, story) or ternary such as (user, story, comment), and they vary with time. A method based on online tensor factorization has been used to detect communities that comprise users voting or commenting with respect to news items [56], thus capturing the social news context. Based on this, the next step is to predict future votes of a user on stories as well as to recommend stories.

Beyond content clustering and recommendation, another application of community detection that has been increasingly attracting interest in view of the ubiquitous use of OSNs is the automatic organization of users' online connections into meaningful groups, also referred to as "social circles", e.g. family, colleagues, etc. This is particularly valuable as a user empowerment mechanism, since it enables OSN users to share different content with different groups of their connections (e.g., personal content with close friends, professional content with colleagues, etc.). Jones and O'Neill were among the first to apply community detection on this problem [46] and found out that using the SCAN algorithm [109] led to the discovery of social circles that matched well with the perceptions of users (probed with the use of a carefully designed user study). Mcauley and Leskovec defined and formulated this problem as a multi-membership node clustering problem on a user's ego network and proposed a hybrid clustering approach relying both on the network structure of the ego network (using community detection) and on the attribute similarity between the user and their connections [62].

Finally, discovering the communities in which users participate across multiple networks may be used for user profiling. For instance, discovering a user's communities in LinkedIn could reveal his/her interests, the opinion of other users on him/her, and thus it will provide useful information for a relatively recent profile or activity of the same user in Twitter. This process may require the matching of user profile information across different networks, where a variety of methods may be used [112].

1.7 Conclusions and Open Issues

This chapter laid out the basis and context for this book, which is the discovery of communities in the social Web. The emphasis was on the challenges one faces in adapting community discovery methods to the complexity of the social graph. The

---

[4]http://digg.com/.

sources of this complexity are the multitude of entities involved in the social Web, the variety of relationships that are formed among them and the sheer volume of data that need to be analyzed. The main approaches to the problem were highlighted in this chapter, but more details about the corresponding methods are provided in the rest of the book.

Most of the work on community discovery in the social Web so far involves graph mining methods that have been used in the past for discovering Web communities and Web user communities. These methods are either used on simplified versions of the social graph, e.g., the user graph of a social network, or they are extended to deal with multiple entity types or multiple relations. The latter approach leads to a number of interesting new methods, which however are commonly limited by the assumptions made by the original methods. Therefore, the need arises for novel methods that inherently tackle the complexity of communities in the social Web. Such methods require an appropriate multi-dimensional and multi-relational model of the social graph, as well as algorithms for extracting higher-order relational patterns from this graph.

The area of statistical relational learning [33] lends itself naturally to the problem of community detection in multi-relational networks. Statistical relational methods combine the expressive power of relational logic with the statistical capabilities of probabilistic graphical models. This combination facilitates probabilistic inference and statistical analysis on top of graphical representations of relational knowledge. Statistical relational learning has started being used for community discovery in the social Web (e.g., in [25, 110]) and matrix factorization approaches are often considered to belong to this area (e.g., [56, 88]). However, these methods also need considerable improvement in order to be applied to the scale of the social Web, particularly due to their computational cost. Therefore, the development of statistical relational community discovery methods is both a promising and an open area for research.

Last but not least, an increasingly important research aspect in the context of social Web communities pertains to privacy risks and issues arising from the collective nature and function of user communities. In particular, the possibility of analyzing communities of mixed public-private user profiles for conducting inferences about the attributes of the private profiles poses new research and ethical questions with respect to information sharing and data mining in the context of social networks [113]. Community membership (even when it is not explicit) and online relations and interactions can be actually considered as a latent feature that could lead to the discovery of user interests and attributes [6]. Coupled with the fact that there is an abundance of weak annotations in the social Web in the form of e.g., hashtags, membership in groups/lists, etc., one may conclude that community detection and analysis approaches can be increasingly considered as a powerful tool for mining user profiles, thus raising important considerations and risks with respect to online privacy.

References

1. Ahn Y-Y, Bagrow JP, Lehmann S (2010) Link communities reveal multiscale complexity in networks. Nature 466:761–764
2. Amini AA, Chen A, Bickel PJ, Levina E (2013) Pseudo-likelihood methods for community detection in large sparse networks. Ann Stat 41(4):2097–2122
3. Arenas A, Díaz-Guilera A, Pérez-Vicente CJ (2006) Synchronization reveals topological scales in complex networks. Phys Rev Lett 96:114102
4. Batagelj V, Zaversnik M (2003) An o(m) algorithm for cores decomposition of networks. CoRR, arXiv:cs.DS/0310049
5. Berge C, Minieka E (1973) Graphs and hypergraphs, vol 7. North-Holland Publishing Company, Amsterdam
6. Bhattacharya P, Zafar MB, Ganguly N, Ghosh S, Gummadi KP (2014) Inferring user interests in the twitter social network. In: Proceedings of the 8th ACM conference on recommender systems, RecSys'14. ACM, New York, pp 357–360
7. Blondel VD, Guillaume JL, Lambiotte R, Lefebvre E (2008) Fast unfolding of communities in large networks. J Stat Mech 2008(10):P10008
8. Bonanich P, Holdren AC, Johnston M (2004) Hyper-edges and multidimensional centrality. Soc Netw 26:189–203
9. Borgatti SP, Everett MG (1999) Models of core/periphery structures. Soc Netw 21:375–395
10. Bouras C, Igglesis V, Kapoulas V, Tsiatsos T (2005) A web-based virtual community. IJWBC 1(2):127–139
11. Boyd DM, Ellison NB (2007) Social network sites: definition, history, and scholarship. J Comput-Mediat Commun 13(1):210–230
12. Breiger RL, Boorman SA, Arabie P (1975) An algorithm for clustering relational data with applications to social network analysis and comparison with multidimensional scaling. J Math Psychol 12(3):328–383
13. Bron C, Kerbosch J (1973) Algorithm 457: finding all cliques of an undirected graph. Commun ACM 16(9):575–577 September
14. Cai D, Shao Z, He X, Yan X, Han J (2005) Community mining from multi-relational networks. Knowledge discovery in databases: PKDD 2005. Springer, New York, pp 445–452
15. Cattuto C, Baldassarri A, Servedio VDP, Loreto V (2008) Emergent community structure in social tagging systems. Adv Complex Syst 11(4):597–608
16. Chakrabarti D (2004) Autopart: parameter-free graph partitioning and outlier detection. In: Boulicaut J-F, Esposito F, Giannotti F, Pedreschi D (eds) PKDD, Lecture Notes in Computer Science, vol 3202. Springer, New York, pp 112–124
17. Chen J, Zaïane O, Goebel R (2009) A visual data mining approach to find overlapping communities in networks. Proceedings of the 2009 international conference on advances in social network analysis and mining, ASONAM'09. IEEE Computer Society, Washington, pp 338–343
18. Clauset A (2005) Finding local community structure in networks. Phys Rev E 72:026132
19. Clauset A, Newman MEJ, Moore C (2004) Finding community structure in very large networks. Phys Rev E 1–6
20. Cooley R, Mobasher B, Srivastava J (1997) Web mining: Information and pattern discovery on the world wide web. In: Proceedings of the nineth international conference on tools with artificial intelligence (ICTAI). Newport Beach, pp 558–567
21. Danon L, Guilera AD, Duch J, Arenas A (2005) Comparing community structure identification. J Stat Mech: Theory Exp 2005(9):P09008–P09008
22. Dawande M, Keskinocak P, Swaminathan JM, Tayur S (2001) On bipartite and multipartite clique problems. J Algorithm 41(2):388–403
23. Donetti L, Munoz MA (2004) Detecting network communities: a new systematic and efficient algorithm. J Stat Mech 2004:P10012
24. Duch J, Arenas A (2005) Community detection in complex networks using extremal optimization. Phys Rev E 72:027104

25. Esposito F, Ferilli S, Basile T, Di Mauro N (2012) Social networks and statistical relational learning: a survey. Int J Soc Netw Min 1(2):185–208
26. Flake G, Lawrence S, Lee Giles C (2000) Efficient identification of web communities. In: Proceedings of the sixth ACM SIGKDD international conference on knowledge discovery and data mining, KDD'00. ACM, New York, pp 150–160
27. Fortunato S (2010) Community detection in graphs. Phys Rep 486:75–174
28. Fortunato S, Latora V, Marchiori M (2004) Method to find community structures based on information centrality. Phys Rev E 70(5):056104
29. Garas A, Schweitzer F, Havlin S (2012) A k-shell decomposition method for weighted networks. New J Phys 14(8):083030
30. Gargi U, Lu W, Mirrokni VS, Yoon S (2011) Large-scale community detection on youtube for topic discovery and exploration. In: Adamic LA, Baeza-Yates RA, Counts S (eds) ICWSM. The AAAI Press, Palo Alto
31. Gauvin L, Panisson A, Cattuto C (2013) Detecting the community structure and activity patterns of temporal networks: a non-negative tensor factorization approach. CoRR. arXiv:abs/1308.0723
32. Gauvin L, Panisson A, Cattuto C (2014) Detecting the community structure and activity patterns of temporal networks: a non-negative tensor factorization approach. PLoS ONE 9(1):e86028
33. Getoor L, Taskar B (2007) Introduction to statistical relational learning. MIT Press, Cambridge
34. Ghosh S, Kane P, Ganguly N (2011) Identifying overlapping communities in folksonomies or tripartite hypergraphs. In: Proceedings of the 20th international conference companion on world wide web. ACM, pp 39–40
35. Giatsoglou M, Vakali A (2013) Capturing social data evolution using graph clustering. IEEE Internet Comput 17(1):74–79
36. Girvan M, Newman MEJ (2002) Community structure in social and biological networks. Proc Natl Acad Sci 99(12):7821–7826
37. Gregory S (2010) Finding overlapping communities in networks by label propagation. New J Phys 12(10):103018
38. Guimerà R, Sales-Pardo M, Amaral L (2007) Module identification in bipartite and directed networks. Phys Rev Lett 76(3):036102
39. Hastings MB (2006) Community detection as an inference problem. Phys Rev E 74:035102
40. Hill WC, Stead L, Rosenstein M, Furnas GW (1995) Recommending and evaluating choices in a virtual community of use. In: Proceedings of the conference on human factors in computing systems (CHI). Denver, Colorado, pp 194–201
41. Holland PW, Laskey KB, Leinhardt S (1983) Stochastic blockmodels: first steps. Soc Netw 5(2):109–137
42. Holme P, Saramäki J (2012) Temporal networks. Phys Rep 519(3):97–125
43. Holme P, Saramäki J (2013) Temporal networks. Springer, New York
44. Ino H, Kudo M, Nakamura A (2005) Partitioning of web graphs by community topology. In: WWW. ACM, New York, pp 661–669
45. Jacquin A, Misakova L, Gay M (2008) A hybrid object-based classification approach for mapping urban sprawl in periurban environment. Landsc Urban Plan 84(2):152–165
46. Jones S, O'Neill E (2010) Feasibility of structural network clustering for group-based privacy control in social networks. In: Proceedings of the sixth symposium on usable privacy and security, SOUPS'10. ACM, New York, pp 9:1–9:13
47. Kannan R, Vempala S, Vetta A (2004) On clusterings: good, bad and spectral. J ACM 51(3):497–515 May
48. Kivelä M, Arenas A, Barthelemy M, Gleeson JP, Moreno Y, Porter MA (2014) Multilayer networks. J Complex Netw 2(3):203–271
49. Konstan JA, Riedl J (2012) Recommender systems: from algorithms to user experience. User modeling and user-adapted interaction 22 (this issue)
50. Konstan JA, Miller BN, Maltz D, Herlocker JL, Gordon LR, Riedl J (1997) GroupLens: applying collaborative filtering to usenet news. Commun ACM 40(3):77–87

51. Kovács IA, Palotai R, Szalay MS, Csermely P (2010) Community landscapes: an integrative approach to determine overlapping network module hierarchy, identify key nodes and predict network dynamics. PLoS ONE 5(9):e12528
52. Kumar R, Raghavan P, Rajagopalan S, Tomkins A (1999) Trawling the web for emerging cyber-communities. Comput Netw 31(11–16):1481–1493
53. Lancichinetti A, Radicchi F, Ramasco JJ, Fortunato S (2011) Finding statistically significant communities in networks. PLoS ONE 6(5):e18961
54. Leung IXY, Hui P, Liò P, Crowcroft J (2009) Towards real-time community detection in large networks. Phys Rev E 79:066107
55. Li X, Wu C, Zach C, Lazebnik S, Frahm J-M (2008) Modeling and recognition of landmark image collections using iconic scene graphs. In: Proceedings of the 10th European conference on computer vision: part I, ECCV'08. Springer, Berlin, pp 427–440
56. Lin Y-R, Sun J, Castro P, Konuru R, Sundaram H, Kelliher A (2009) MetaFac: community discovery via relational hypergraph factorization. In: Proceedings of the 15th ACM SIGKDD international conference on knowledge discovery and data mining, KDD'09. ACM, pp 527–536
57. Lin Y-R, Sundaram H, Kelliher A (2009) JAM: joint action matrix factorization for summarizing a temporal heterogeneous social network. In: Proceedings of the third international conference on weblogs and social media, ICWSM 2009. San Jose, California, 17–20 May 2009
58. Luo F, Wang JZ, Promislow E (2006) Exploring local community structures in large networks. In: Proceedings of the 2006 IEEE/WIC/ACM international conference on web intelligence, WI'06. IEEE Computer Society, Washington
59. Luxburg U (2007) A tutorial on spectral clustering. Stat Comput 17(4):395–416
60. Malliaros FD, Vazirgiannis M (2013) Clustering and community detection in directed networks: a survey. Phys Rep 533:95–142
61. Massen CP, Doye JPK (2005) Identifying communities within energy landscapes. Phys Rev E 71:046101
62. Mcauley J, Leskovec J (2014) Discovering social circles in Ego networks. ACM Trans Knowl Discov Data 8(1):4:1–4:28
63. Miorandi D, De Pellegrini F (2010) K-shell decomposition for dynamic complex networks. In: 2010 Proceedings of the 8th international symposium on modeling and optimization in mobile, ad hoc and wireless networks (WiOpt). IEEE, pp 488–496
64. Moëllic P-A, Haugeard J-E, Pitel G (2008) Image clustering based on a shared nearest neighbors approach for tagged collections. In: Proceedings of the 2008 international conference on content-based image and video retrieval, CIVR'08. ACM, New York, pp 269–278
65. Murata T (2009) Modularities for bipartite networks. In: Proceedings of the 20th ACM conference on hypertext and hypermedia. ACM, pp 245–250
66. Murata T (2010) Detecting communities from tripartite networks. In: Proceedings of the 19th international conference on world wide web. ACM, pp 1159–1160
67. Murata T (2011) Detecting communities from social tagging networks based on tripartite modularity. In: Proceedings of the workshop on link analysis in heterogeneous information networks
68. Neubauer N, Obermayer K (2010) Community detection in tagging-induced hypergraphs. Workshop on information in networks. New York University, New York, pp 24–25
69. Newman M (2010) Networks: an introduction. Oxford University Press, Oxford
70. Newman MEJ (2003) Fast algorithm for detecting community structure in networks. Phys Rev E 69:066133
71. Newman MEJ (2006) Finding community structure in networks using the eigenvectors of matrices. Phys Rev E 74(3):036104
72. Newman MEJ (2013) Spectral methods for community detection and graph partitioning. Phys Rev E 88:042822
73. Newman MEJ, Girvan M (2004) Finding and evaluating community structure in networks. Phys Rev E 69:026113

74. Orwant J (1995) Heterogeneous learning in the doppelgänger user modeling system. User Model User-Adapt Interact 4(2):107–130
75. Paliouras G (2012) Discovery of web user communities and their role in personalization. User Model User-Adapt Interact 22(1–2):151–175
76. Paliouras G, Papatheodorou C, Karkaletsis V, Spyropoulos CD (2000) Clustering the users of large web sites into communities. In: Proceedings of the seventeenth international conference on machine learning (ICML). Stanford, pp 719–726
77. Palla G, Barabasi A-L, Vicsek T (2007) Quantifying social group evolution. Nature 446(7136):664–667
78. Palla G, Dernyi I, Farkas I, Vicsek T (2005) Uncovering the overlapping community structure of complex networks in nature and society. Nature 435(7043):814–818
79. Papadopoulos S, Zigkolis C, Kompatsiaris Y, Vakali A (2011) Cluster-based landmark and event detection for tagged photo collections. IEEE MultiMed 18(1):52–63
80. Papadopoulos S, Kompatsiaris Y, Vakali A, Spyridonos P (2012) Community detection in social media. Data Min Knowl Discov 24(3):515–554
81. Pons P, Latapy M (2005) Computing communities in large networks using random walks (long version). Computer and information sciences-ISCIS 2005, pp 284–293. arXiv:physics/0512106v1
82. Porter MA, Onnela J-P, Mucha PJ (2009) Communities in networks. Not Am Math Soc 56(9):1082–1097
83. Qi G-J, Aggarwal CC, Huang TS (2012) Community detection with edge content in social media networks. In: IEEE 28th international conference on data engineering (ICDE 2012), pp 534–545
84. Quillian MR (1968) Semantic memory. In: Minsky M (ed) Semantic information processing. MIT Press, Cambridge, pp 27–70
85. Radicchi F, Castellano C, Cecconi F, Loreto V, Parisi D (2004) Defining and identifying communities in networks. Proc Natl Acad Sci 101(9):2658
86. Raghavan UN, Albert R, Kumara S (2007) Near linear time algorithm to detect community structures in large-scale networks. Phys Rev E 76:036106
87. Ramadan E, Tarafdar A, Pothen A (2004) A hypergraph model for the yeast protein complex network. Proceedings of the 18th international parallel and distributed processing symposium, 2004. IEEE, p 189
88. Rêgo Drumond L, Diaz-Aviles E, Schmidt-Thieme L, Nejdl W (2014) Optimizing multi-relational factorization models for multiple target relations. In: Proceedings of the 23rd ACM international conference on conference on information and knowledge management, CIKM'14, pp 191–200
89. Reichardt J, Bornholdt S (2006) Statistical mechanics of community detection. Phys Rev E 74:016110
90. Rheingold H (1993) The virtual community: homesteading on the electronic frontier. Addison-Wesley, New York
91. Richens RH (1956) General program for mechanical translation between any two languages via an algebraic interlingua. Mech Transl 3(2):37
92. Rombach MP, Porter MA, Fowler JH, Mucha PJ (2014) Core-periphery structure in networks. SIAM J Appl Math 74(1):167–190
93. Rosvall M, Bergstrom CT (2008) Maps of random walks on complex networks reveal community structure. Proc Natl Acad Sci 105(4):1118–1123
94. Schaeffer SE (2007) Graph clustering. Comput Sci Rev 1(1):27–64
95. Schuler D (1994) Community networks: building a new participatory medium. Commun ACM 37(1):38–51
96. Scripps J, Tan P-N, Esfahanian A-H (2007) Node roles and community structure in networks. In: Proceedings of the 9th WebKDD and 1st SNA-KDD 2007 workshop on web mining and social network analysis, WebKDD/SNA-KDD'07. ACM, New York, pp 26–35
97. Seidman SB (1983) Network structure and minimum degree. Soc Netw 5(3):269–287

98. Shardanand U, Maes P (1995) Social information filtering: algorithms for automating "word of mouth". In: Proceedings of the conference on human factors in computing systems (CHI). Denver, Colorado, pp 210–217
99. Shi J, Malik J (2000) Normalized cuts and image segmentation. IEEE Trans Pattern Anal Mach Intell 22(8):888–905
100. Staab S, Angele J, Decker S, Erdmann M, Hotho A, Maedche A, Schnurr H-P, Studer R, Sure Y (2000) Semantic community web portals. Comput Netw 33(1–6):473–491
101. Takaffoli M, Sangi F, Fagnan J, Zäıane O (2011) Community evolution mining in dynamic social networks. Procedia-Soc Behav Sci 22:49–58
102. Tang L, Liu H (2010) Community detection and mining in social media (synthesis lectures on data mining and knowledge discovery). Morgan & Claypool Publishers, San Rafael
103. Tang J, Hu X, Liu H (2013) Social recommendation: a review. Soc Netw Anal Min 3(4):1113–1133
104. van Dongen S (2000) Graph clustering by flow simulation. Ph.D. thesis, University of Utrecht
105. Vragović I, Louis E (2006) Network community structure and loop coefficient method. Phys Rev E 74:016105
106. Wang J, Lee TT (1998) Paths and cycles of hypergraphs. Sci China 42(1):1–12
107. Wasserman S, Faust K (1994) Social network analysis: methods and applications, vol 8. Cambridge University Press, Cambridge
108. Xie J, Kelley S, Szymanski BK (2013) Overlapping community detection in networks: the state-of-the-art and comparative study. ACM Comput Surv 45(4):43:1–43:35
109. Xu X, Yuruk N, Feng Z, Schweiger TAJ (2007) Scan: a structural clustering algorithm for networks. In: Proceedings of the 13th ACM SIGKDD international conference on knowledge discovery and data mining, KDD'07. ACM, New York, pp 824–833
110. Xu Z, Tresp V, Rettinger A, Kersting K (2010) Social network mining with nonparametric relational models. Revised selected papers of the second international workshop on advances in social network mining and analysis (SNAKDD). Lecture notes in computer science, vol 5498. Springer, New York, pp 77–96
111. Yang J, McAuley J J, Leskovec J (2013) Community detection in networks with node attributes. International conference on data mining
112. Zhang H, Kan M-Y, Liu Y, Ma S (2014) Online social network profile linkage. Information retrieval technology. Springer, New York, pp 197–208
113. Zheleva E, Getoor L (2009) To join or not to join: the illusion of privacy in social networks with mixed public and private user profiles. In: Proceedings of the 18th international conference on world wide web, WWW'09. ACM, New York, pp 531–540
114. Zhou D, Huang J, Schölkopf B (2006) Learning with hypergraphs: clustering, classification, and embedding. In: Advances in neural information processing systems, pp 1601–1608

Chapter 2
Community Discovery: Simple and Scalable Approaches

Yiye Ruan, David Fuhry, Jiongqian Liang, Yu Wang
and Srinivasan Parthasarathy

Abstract The increasing size and complexity of online social networks have brought distinct challenges to the task of community discovery. A community discovery algorithm needs to be *efficient*, not taking a prohibitive amount of time to finish. The algorithm should also be *scalable*, capable of handling large networks containing billions of edges or even more. Furthermore, a community discovery algorithm should be *effective* in that it produces community assignments of high quality. In this chapter, we present a selection of algorithms that follow simple design principles, and have proven highly effective and efficient according to extensive empirical evaluations. We start by discussing a generic approach of community discovery by combining multilevel graph contraction with core clustering algorithms. Next we describe the usage of network sampling in community discovery, where the goal is to reduce the number of nodes and/or edges while retaining the network's underlying community structure. Finally, we review research efforts that leverage various parallel and distributed computing paradigms in community discovery, which can facilitate finding communities in tera- and peta-scale networks.

2.1 Introduction

Community discovery has long served as an important primitive operator in the field of network science, and the ability of identifying user communities in social networks has lead to a plethora of applications including, among others, churn prediction [42], political analytics [1], and human behavior study [56]. While it is relatively easy to directly spot community structures embedded in the smallest networks, for other networks the task quickly becomes challenging for human beings. To illustrate, there

Y. Ruan (✉) · D. Fuhry · J. Liang · Y. Wang · S. Parthasarathy
Department of Computer Science and Engineering, The Ohio State University,
2015 Neil Avenue, 395 Dreese Lab, Columbus, OH 43210, USA
e-mail: ruan.17@buckeyemail.osu.edu

© Springer International Publishing Switzerland 2015
G. Paliouras et al. (eds.), *User Community Discovery*, Human–Computer
Interaction Series, DOI 10.1007/978-3-319-23835-7_2

are 1.35 billion monthly active users on Facebook as of September, 2014.[1] If we are to plot all of those users on the computer screen, assuming each user only occupies one single pixel, we will need more than 1700 monitors of the typical 1024-by-768 resolution to just show all of them.

The rapidly-growing size of available user network data has multiple implications, all underlining the acute need for automatic community discovery algorithms that are efficient, scalable, and effective. First of all, algorithm complexity becomes a practical concern, as the improvement (or degradation) in running time is pronounced and easily perceivable. The difference between log-linear and quadratic complexities is now seconds versus years. Secondly, the RAM capacity of a single machine may be too low to fully store the underlying network in memory, let alone any auxiliary data required for the algorithm itself. Lastly, as network size grows, more noise is introduced inevitably, and this is especially true for online social networks where spammers and bots can create fake links with trivial cost, for instance. To produce results of high quality, a community discovery algorithm has to be robust and capable of differentiating between signal and noise.

In order to address these issues, many algorithms have been proposed in the literature of community discovery. In this chapter, we outline a collection of existing methods that have proven simple yet effective and scalable. Furthermore, we discuss some promising directions that deserve further investigation. In the next three sections, we focus on three respective categories:

- **Section 2.2: Multilevel community discovery methods**, which recursively *contract* a larger network into a smaller version on which a core community discovery algorithm will be run. The procedure of contraction (also known as coarsening) can follow different strategies, and they also differ on whether the core discovery algorithm is run only once or for multiple times. As a byproduct, the multilevel paradigm also produces a natural hierarchy of communities in the network.
- **Section 2.3: Sampling-based preprocessing algorithms**, which selectively keep a subset of vertices and/or edges to reduce the network size while attempting to preserve the community structure of the underlying network. The sampling process is typically guided by some quality measures, and can leverage additional information, such as vertex attributes or content.
- **Section 2.4: Parallel and distributed community discovery approaches**, which perform community identification in parallel to speed up the process.[2] Given the fact that many discovery algorithms are based on matrix/vector operations, and that many computation kernels specially designed for such operations have been developed in the parallel computing community, there is a great potential of performing community discovery in an efficient parallel environment. Furthermore, some of such algorithms also store data in a distributed fashion (e.g. HDFS), making it possible to overcome the capacity limit of one single machine.

---

[1] http://newsroom.fb.com/company-info/. Accessed in December 2014.

[2] Here, we will discuss methods based on both shared-memory and distributed-memory architectures.

Table 2.1 Table of notations used in this chapter

$G(V, E)$	An undirected graph with the vertex set V and edge set E.
Γ_u	The neighborhood of a node u, that is, $(u, v) \in E, \forall v \in \Gamma_u$ and $\nexists v \in V - \Gamma_u$ such that $(u, v) \in E$.
Γ_S	The neighborhood of a set of nodes S, that is, $\bigcup_{u \in S} \Gamma_u$.
$A \in \{0, 1\}^{|V| \times |V|}$	The symmetric adjacency matrix of G, i.e. $A(u, v) = A(v, u) = 1$ if $(u, v) \in E$, and 0 if $(u, v) \notin E$.
$D \in \mathbb{N}^{|V| \times |V|}$	The diagonal matrix of node degrees, i.e. $D(u, u) = |\Gamma_u|$ and $D(u, v) = 0, \forall u \neq v$.
N_c	The number of communities to detect.

Among existing literature, the definition of "community" itself is still open-ended and highly context-dependent, leading to various input and output specifications across different methods. Here we summarize the premise of the algorithms described in this chapter. All these algorithms can operate on unweighted, undirected networks, and some readily accept weighted/directed networks as inputs, or can be easily adapted to do so. With the exception of Louvain algorithm in Sect. 2.2, all algorithms take the desired number of communities as an additional input, either directly or indirectly (via other control parameters). In terms of output, communities generated by those algorithms are disjoint, in that no two communities will overlap with each other. Few algorithms, such as METIS (Sect. 2.2), produce communities of equal size, while most allow variation in community size. With all the distinct properties of each method in mind, one key observation from this chapter is: *Most approaches introduced here can also be viewed as meta-algorithms, and one can reuse and enhance many existing community discovery algorithms by plugging them into these frameworks.*

Before proceeding, we note that this chapter is not intended as an exhaustive survey of community discovery algorithms, and we have provided references for further reading in Sect. 2.5. Rather, we aim at simple and scalable approaches that fall into one of the three categories mentioned above. Apart from technical descriptions, we also hope to provide a systematic view of these three generic design principles, and to inspire new algorithms that follow them. Moreover, it is feasible for one to devise methods that leverage more than one of these approaches simultaneously, as they are complementary to each other.

Notations in Table 2.1 will be used throughout this chapter. Note that, we will use the terms "node" and "vertex" interchangeably, as well as "network" and "graph".

2.2 Multilevel Approach for Community Discovery

We begin with the introduction of multilevel approach, an effective scheme that has been applied in conjunction with different community detection algorithms. The key motivation behind all multilevel algorithms is to efficiently obtain a partitioning of nodes at a coarse-grained level, and then recover fine-grained communities from high-level clusters in a recursive manner. A key point to the efficacy of the multilevel paradigm is, therefore, retaining the graph's backbone structure when reducing its size, and we will discuss several principled and heuristic-driven approaches to achieve this requirement.

Aside from being efficient, the multilevel scheme also brings the benefit of flexibility since it is largely orthogonal to the underlying community detection algorithms. This enables practitioners to experiment with various community detection "kernels" with minimal change in the implementation. Moreover, multilevel approaches naturally produce a hierarchy of communities, making it easy to explore the community structure of a graph at different scales.

Here, we will showcase concrete implementations of the multilevel approach by presenting four representative algorithms: METIS, MLR-MCL, Graclus and Louvain. There are three main phases in all multilevel community discovery algorithms:

- **Contraction (Sect. 2.2.2)**: From the original network, a series of networks of decreasing size are generated. Each small network is created by contracting multiple nodes in the parent-level network into a multinode, and their edges to other nodes in the network are retained. The selections of nodes to contract and their ordering can be decided by various strategies, as we shall see below.
- **Partitioning (Sect. 2.2.3)**: This refers to running a core partitioning algorithm on the aforementioned contracted networks. The key motivation is that such an algorithm will run more efficiently on the contracted networks because their sizes are smaller. While some approaches only call the core algorithm on the smallest contracted network, others execute the core algorithm on the contracted network at each level.
- **Refinement (Sect. 2.2.4)**: To obtain community assignments on the original network, partitions on a smaller network will be projected back to the higher level by decomposing multinodes. A fast refinement procedure often follows the projection, so that the community assignments are further improved. Typically, the refinement subroutine is lightweight and only performs simple local operations. In some cases such as MLR-MCL and Graclus, however, refinement can involve the core partitioning algorithm itself, too.

2.2.1 Overview

METIS METIS [19] is a graph clustering algorithm for undirected graphs with optionally both edge weights and vertex weights. It recursively contracts the graph and partitions the smallest graph. Then the partitioning is projected to the original graph. METIS performs recursive contraction, recursive partitioning and recursive projection separately.

MLR-MCL Multilevel Regularized Markov Clustering (MLR-MCL) is another multilevel approach for graph clustering, introduced in [45]. Unlike METIS, MLR-MCL is based on Markov Clustering [49], which is a flow-based graph clustering algorithm. MCL follows the nature of flow and transition probability in graphs to conduct clustering and is able to generate clustering results in different granularities by tuning parameters. MLR-MCL goes further to improve clustering quality and the scalability of the algorithm through additional regularization and multilevel mechanism.

Graclus Graclus [9] is quite similar to MLR-MCL, except it utilizes weighted kernel k-means in the partitioning and refinement phases. Many variants of weighted kernel k-means can be derived depending on different categories of objective functions, e.g. Kernighan-Lin objective. The multilevel mechanism guarantees a desirable initial clustering at each refinement level, making the refinement step converge very fast.

Louvain Louvain [3] also adopts the multilevel framework but aims at optimizing modularity, which is a commonly-used criterion to evaluate community detection [32]. Louvain recursively optimizes modularity at each level and deals with graphs with edge weights. It alternates between contraction and partitioning while the refinement phase is mostly trivial.

2.2.2 Contraction

A series of graphs, called contracted graphs, are generated in this phase. We denote them as $G_0, G_1, \ldots, G_m$, where $G_0 = G$ is the original graph. Each $G_{i+1} = (V_{i+1}, E_{i+1})$ is obtained by contracting $G_i = (V_i, E_i)$, and hence is smaller than G_i. Correspondingly, G_i is referred to as the parent graph of G_{i+1}. If a vertex $v \in V_{i+1}$ corresponds to a group of nodes in V_i, we call v a multinode for G_i. There are two types of contraction: edge contraction and vertex contraction [39]. The former is to contract a pair of adjacent vertices into one multinode, whereas the latter is to contract a vertex and its neighbors into one. In general, vertex contraction shrinks the graph more significantly than edge contraction because the latter shrinks the graph at most by half each time.

METIS, MLR-MCL, and Graclus In the contraction phase, METIS, MLR-MCL and Graclus all follow the same procedure. Edge contraction can be done by finding a maximal matching [39]. When a maximal matching is identified, the graph is contracted in this way: Replace a matched node pair by a multinode whose weight is the sum of those of the two absorbed nodes; If parallel edges are created between the multinode and other nodes, they are replaced by one single edge whose weight is the sum of those of all parallel edges. G_{i+1} is constructed when the whole matching in G_i are replaced. An heuristic called *Heavy Edge Matching* is used to construct the maximal matching. The idea is to maximize the difference of edge weights between two consecutive contracted graphs. The motivation is to minimize the edge weight of the contracted graph and thus the upper bound of edge cut, a commonly-used partitioning criterion (Sect. 2.2.3), in the contracted graph. The contraction process recursively contracts the graph until $|V_i|/|V_{i+1}|$ is smaller than a predefined threshold, that is, the decrease in graph size is no longer significant. An alternative strategy is to terminate the process when $|V_i|$ itself, instead of the ratio, is below a threshold.

Louvain Louvain algorithm alternates between contraction and partitioning. The contraction phase itself is simple: Contract all nodes in the same community (from the parent graph) into a single multinode, and replace each group of parallel edges with one single edge of the aggregated weights. When the contraction phase ends, a new graph with fewer nodes, each of which representing a community, is constructed.

2.2.3 Partitioning

Partitioning is to partition the graph into multiple communities such that vertices within the same community are more densely connected than vertices across communities. The partitioning algorithms of all four methods here produce disjoint communities.[3] Partitioning of METIS only occurs on the coarsest graph, whereas MLR-MCL and Graclus perform partitioning in the whole process of refinement from G_m to G_0 incrementally. On the other hand, Louvain performs partitioning in the process of contraction.

METIS METIS tries to find balanced communities, i.e. communities have similar number of vertices in an unweighted graph while have similar sum of weights in a weighted graph. A bisection procedure [15, 16] is explained here while a more sophisticated k-way partition can be found in [19]. The bisection procedure works to recursively partition the graph/sub-graph into two parts until a desired number of communities are obtained. METIS can be coupled with three bisection algorithms, one using spectral bisection while the others adapting a strategy of minimizing edge-cut.

Spectral Bisection Fiedler vector [13, 36] is used for partitioning the graph. The Fiedler vector f of a network is the eigenvector corresponding to the second smallest eigenvalue of its Laplacian matrix. After computing f, let $f(v)$ be the vth element of f, the graph is bisected by a threshold t, which minimizes $|\sum_{f(v) \leq t} vw(v) - \sum_{f(v) > t} vw(v)|$, where $vw(v)$ stands for the weight of vertex v.

KL Algorithm The Kernighan-Lin (KL) algorithm [12, 21] is an iterative algorithm starting from an initial bipartition. Nodes are ranked based on their potential of edge-cut reduction. After selecting proper nodes, edge-cut is decreased in each iteration by swapping two subsets of the nodes from the two parts. KL algorithm relies on good initial partition [5]. If a good initial partition is not available, one can run KL algorithm on multiple random initial partitions and select the one with the smallest edge-cut.

---

[3]Overlapping community detection has also attracted considerable research attention [51, 53], yet existing studies have not adapted the multilevel framework discussed here. Combining the multilevel paradigm with overlapping community discovery will be an exciting future direction.

An easier implementation is to move one vertex at a time rather than swapping two subsets. The iteration terminates when no vertex can be moved or edge-cut decreases little in some consecutive moves.

Greedy Graph Growing Partitioning Algorithm This algorithm performs heuristic-guided breadth-first search from a vertex until half of the graph, in terms of number of vertices (for unweighted graphs) or the sum of vertex weights (for weighted graphs), are included. It works by growing a community from an individual vertex. The heuristic is to order the vertices on the frontier of the growing community based on their potential to decrease edge-cut and move the vertex with the highest ranking. The frontier and the ranking should be maintained dynamically. Reference [19] shows that this algorithm requires the same data structure as KL algorithm. Reaching the desired number of communities is a termination condition for this algorithm.

MLR-MCL The partitioning phase of MLR-MCL follows the Regularized Markov Clustering (R-MCL). R-MCL itself is a clustering algorithm based on stochastic matrices and flows. In graph G, let A be the adjacency matrix, where $A(i,j)$ is the weight of the edge between vertex v_i and vertex v_j. Then a column stochastic matrix M_G is the matrix of the transition probabilities of a random walk in the graph. Specifically, $M_G(j,i)$ represents the probability of transiting from vertex v_i to v_j. The column-stochastic transition matrix M_G is usually derived by normalizing the columns of the adjacency matrix A such that each column sums up to 1, i.e. $M_G(i,j) = \frac{A(i,j)}{\sum_{k=1}^n A(k,j)}$. This is usually obtained from $M_G = AD^{-1}$, where D is the diagonal degree matrix of graph G and $D(i,i) = \sum_{j=1}^n A(j,i)$. We call this matrix the *canonical transition matrix*.

R-MCL, similar to MCL [49], follows three steps. The first step is expansion, which allows flow to go to different parts of the graph. It can be done by using $M_{exp} = Expand(M) = M * M_G$, where M is the flow distribution matrix from the previous iteration (initially it is M_G). The second step is inflation, which both strengthens what is strong and weakens what is weak of the flow by using $M_{inf}(i,j) = \frac{M_{exp}(i,j)^r}{\sum_{k-1}^n M_{exp}(k,j)^r}$. The purpose of inflation is to expedite the convergence of partitioning. As long as $r > 1$, this operator will exaggerate the imbalanced distribution of each column of M_{exp}. A higher r means a more aggressive inflation and by default, it is set as 2. The third steps is pruning, which aims to eliminate those very small values in M_{inf}. Pruning will make the matrix sparser and help save memory and computation. The threshold used to prune the small values can be computed based on the average and maximum in each column (see [49] for more details) and then all the entries below the threshold will be pruned.

At the partitioning phase for a contracted graph G_i, the canonical transition matrix is built, and the expansion-inflation-pruning cycle is performed for a small number of iterations. The corresponding flow distribution M_{inf} will be projected back to the finer graph (G_{i-1}) and be treated as the initial flow distribution for R-MCL on G_{i-1}. Details of the refinement process will be discussed in the next subsection.

Graclus For Graclus, we apply a base clustering algorithm on the coarsest graph. We can use the region-growing algorithm of METIS, which is usually very efficient. Spectral clustering and bisection methods are other alternative approaches for base clustering.

However, from G_{m-1} to G_0, Graclus adopts weighted kernel k-means to perform partitioning. Weighted kernel k-means is a variant of k-means which adopts a non-linear mapping kernel function and adds a weight to each cluster. With certain objective functions (either based on association or cuts), we can use weighted kernel k-means for graph clustering. One example will be clustering a graph based on association, where we aim to partition the graph into k disjoint parts $\pi_1, \pi_2, \ldots, \pi_k$, whose union is V, such that $WAssoc(G) = \sum_{c=1}^{k} \frac{links(\pi_c, \pi_c)}{w(\pi_c)}$ is maximized. Here, $links(\pi_c, \pi_c)$ is the sum of the edge weights inside the cluster π_c and $w(\pi_c)$ is the sum of node weights inside π_c.

As [9] proved, the trace maximization formula of objectives in weighted kernel k-means and graph clustering are actually equivalent. By setting kernel matrix K as $W^{-1}AW^{-1}$, where W is the diagonal matrix of weights and A is adjacency matrix, we can run weighted kernel k-means for graph clustering without calculating its eigenvectors. In other words, graph clustering can be done by using a simple iterative algorithm.

Similar to MLR-MCL, we do not directly run weighted kernel k-means on the original graph. Instead, we run this clustering algorithm from G_{m-1} to G_0. The partitioning result from G_i is used as the initial community assignment of G_{i-1} after projection. More details of refinement will be introduced in next subsection.

Louvain Partitioning and contraction are alternately performed in the same recursion in Louvain algorithm. Each node of the current graph is treated as a community. For each node v_i, the algorithm considers each neighbor v_j of v_i and evaluates the gain of modularity by moving v_i from its community to the community of v_j. A node v_i will be moved only if there is positive gain, and it is moved to the community that yields the maximum modularity gain. Otherwise, v_i remains in the original community. This process is applied repeatedly and sequentially for all nodes until reaching a Pareto frontier, i.e. no further improvement can be achieved. Then the partitioning phase terminates. It is shown that the order of node selection may affect computation time but not the convergence of modularity.

2.2.4 Refinement

Since our goal is to perform community detection on the original graph, we need to refine the partitioning results starting from G_m to G_0. Given the communities of multinodes on the contracted graph, we need to project the communities back to the parent graph. We define P_i to be a partition on graph G_i projected from P_{i+1}. For METIS, the main task of refinement phase is projection, while MLR-MCL and Graclus also need to run partitioning techniques on the projected result. The refinement phase runs from G_m to G_0 and the final community detection results are obtained when it reaches the original graph.

METIS Let V_i^v be the set of nodes in G_i that are contracted to the node v in G_{i+1}. The recursion of P_i is defined as $P_i(u) = P_{i+1}(v)$, $\forall u \in V_i^v$. Since uncoarsening makes graphs finer, the local optimum P_{i+1} of G_{i+1} does not necessarily lead to a local optimum of G_i. Thus, it is possible for refinement to reach a local optimum on a finer graph. Recall that the KL algorithm starts with an initial partitioning and iteratively reduces edge-cut by swapping subsets. Similar ideas work in refining and uncoarsening the graph. The strategy derived from the KL algorithm is discussed below.

Boundary KL Refinement This strategy takes P_i, which is projected directly from the partitioning on G_{i+1}, as an initial partitioning and applies KL algorithm on G_i to obtain a locally optimal partitioning. One difference from the KL algorithm is that only the boundary nodes are included in the ranking to reduce redundant computation. This refinement generates a high quality partitioning due to the high quality of the initial partitioning. It is also efficient since few nodes need to be swapped given the initial partitioning is close to a local optimum. By considering the marginal decrease of edge-cut, [19] proposes a termination condition: stop after the first iteration, which reduces time cost by a factor of two to four.

MLR-MCL The refinement phase of MLR-MCL starts from the coarsest graph to the original one, i.e. $G_m, \ldots, G_2, G_1$. In each refinement from G_i to G_{i-1}, R-MCL is first run for 4 to 5 iterations. Then the flow from the coarser graph G_i is projected onto the refined graph G_{i-1}. Given the flow distribution of a node in the coarser graph, the flow projection can be done by choosing one of its constituent nodes (in the larger graph) and assigning all the flow into it to the chosen constituent node. After the flow projection, we get a new transition matrix M and can move on to next refinement from G_{i-1} to G_{i-2}. We keep doing this until we reach the original graph.

When we reach the original graph after refinement, R-MCL is performed until convergence. Finally, we interpret the transition matrix M we obtain to figure out the clustering result.

Graclus The refinement of Graclus is quite similar to MLR-MCL. Starting from the coarsest graph G_m, we perform the refinement until we reach the original graph G_0 (namely G). Suppose we are refining the graph from G_i to G_{i-1}. We get the initial clustering for G_{i-1} from G_i by simply following this: nodes in the same cluster on G_i cause their constituent nodes on G_{i-1} to be in the same cluster. We then improve this initial clustering by using weighted kernel k-means. Given the adjacency matrix of the current graph and the objective function for graph clustering, we can set the weights and kernel matrix and run weighted kernel k-means. Note the initial clustering above is usually quite desirable so the k-means can converge very fast. Eventually, we run weighted kernel k-means on the original graph, which generates the final result of communities. Besides, weighted kernel k-means can be greatly sped up by focusing only on the boundary nodes, i.e. nodes that contain an edge to a node in another cluster. This optimization can bring much efficiency with little loss in cluster quality.

Table 2.2 Characteristics of four multilevel community discovery algorithms

	Require # of communities as input?	Produce communities of equal size?	Core partitioning algorithm	Partitioning algorithm usage
METIS	Yes	Yes	Kernighan-Lin algorithm	Only on the most contracted network
MLR-MCL	Yes	No	Markov clustering	On contracted network at each level, during refinement
Graclus	Yes	No	Weighted kernel k-means	On contracted network at each level, during refinement
Louvain	No	No	Modularity optimization	On contracted network at each level, during contraction

Louvain Because partitioning has already been performed at each level during the contraction phase, the Louvain method has a trivial projection phase: just release all the original nodes from the multinode in the smallest contracted graph and assign nodes absorbed into the same multinode the same community label.

2.2.5 Empirical Results and Summary

In this section, we have introduced four community discovery algorithms that share the same pattern of following a three-phase workflow: contraction, partitioning, and refinement. These methods differ in their core partitioning methods, as well as in the stage at which their partitioning subroutine is invoked. Table 2.2 outlines several key characteristics that make each algorithm distinct from others.

In the literature where these methods were originally proposed, it is typically found that the multilevel paradigm significantly speeds up the computation, often leading to implementations that are two to three orders faster than their counterparts without the multilevel approach. However, few studies exist that benchmark these algorithms and directly compare their performances. To provide a more comprehensive picture on the effectiveness and efficiency of these algorithms, we perform a series of experiments on multiple real-world networks. Specifically, we downloaded six distinct networks from the Stanford large network dataset repository,[4] including both social networks and web networks. Network sizes are listed in the first two

---

[4]http://snap.stanford.edu/data/index.html.

Table 2.3 Information on network size, and F-1 scores of communities identified by four multilevel algorithms

	$|V|$	$|E|$	METIS	MLR-MCL	Graclus	Louvain
Facebook	4039	88234	0.2356	0.2701	0.3026	**0.3868**
Twitter	81306	1342303	0.1628	0.1146	**0.2147**	0.1086
Google+	107614	12238285	0.1664	0.0100	**0.1789**	0.0549
Youtube	1134890	2987624	**0.0441**	0.0068	N/A	0.0100
LiveJournal	3997962	34681189	**0.1864**	0.1497	N/A	0.1527
Amazon	334863	925872	0.4465	**0.5001**	N/A	0.2759

The best-performing algorithm on each network is boldfaced. If an algorithm does not finish on a particular network, the corresponding cell is marked "N/A"

columns in Table 2.3, and more detailed description of the datasets can be found on the repository webpage. These networks are then transformed to unweighted and undirected networks. For METIS, MLR-MCL and Graclus, we also provide the number of ground truth communities as input.

Table 2.3 also reports the quality of communities that are identified by each algorithm, using F-1 scores. The formulation of F-1 score follows the one in [53], which assesses both the quality of discovered communities as well as the coverage of ground truth communities. Specifically, given $\hat{C}$, the set of detected communities, and C^*, the set of ground truth communities, the F-1 score reported in the table is calculated by:

$$\frac{1}{2} \cdot \left[\frac{1}{|\hat{C}|} \cdot \sum_{\hat{c} \in \hat{C}} \max_{c^* \in C^*} f(\hat{c}, c^*) + \frac{1}{|C^*|} \cdot \sum_{c^* \in C^*} \max_{\hat{c} \in \hat{C}} f(\hat{c}, c^*) \right]$$

where $f(\hat{c}, c^*)$ is the typical harmonic mean of $\hat{c}$'s precision and recall, with regard to c^*. That is, F-1 scores of best matchings for all detected communities as well as ground truth communities are averaged. Note that, since overlapping communities are present in the ground truth information, F-1 scores are biased against the four algorithms under discussion. The amounts of time (in seconds) for each algorithm to run are listed in Table 2.4.

Table 2.4 Running time (in seconds) by four multilevel algorithms

	METIS	MLR-MCL	Graclus	Louvain
Facebook	0	0	0	0
Twitter	7	14	42	**1**
Google+	31	122	35	**2**
Youtube	68	334	N/A	**7**
LiveJournal	682	2957	N/A	**123**
Amazon	22	10	N/A	**2**

The fastest algorithm on each network is boldfaced. If an algorithm does not finish on a particular network, the corresponding cell is marked "N/A"

As seen from both tables, the scalability of Graclus is limited when compared with others. It fails to finish on the three largest networks (Youtube, LiveJournal, Amazon), and those cells are marked "N/A" accordingly. The Louvain algorithm boasts a pronounced advantage in terms of efficiency, as it is uniformly faster than others. However, in terms of output quality, there is no clear winner across the board. Each algorithm is the best-performer on at least one network, and faster algorithms do not necessarily produce results of a higher quality. For practitioners of community discovery, this leaves an open choice of the underlying algorithm. If the number of communities in the network is specified in advance, or if there is a relatively small range for that value, it is highly suggested to experiment with various algorithms. Otherwise, the Louvain algorithm may be preferred because it does not require the number of communities as input.

2.3 Speeding up Community Discovery by Network Sampling

In the previous section, we have introduced a multilevel paradigm in community detection, based on the rationale that a community detection algorithm runs faster on a graph with fewer nodes and/or edges. Here, we discuss another commonly-used approach to generate small graphs: sampling. By selecting a subset of nodes and/or edges from the original graph, we also obtain a smaller graph to operate on, hence speeding up the computation process. Since network sampling is used for pre-processing, and independent from the subsequent community detection algorithm, it has the potential of providing performance improvement to all community discovery algorithms.

Although the concept of sampling is straightforward and easy to understand, its implementation will have direct implications on the results of community detection, in terms of both effectiveness and efficiency. Specifically, it has been shown that naively sampling nodes or edges by uniform randomness will introduce bias into the resultant graph, which will affect the results negatively. In this section, we will review a series of sampling methods that have been proposed, and describe the intuition, strategy and performance behind each of them.

Sampling methods can be divided into two broad categories: those that only select a subset of nodes and those that preserve all nodes. In the following discussion, we refer to the first type as *node sampling*, and the second type as *edge sampling*.[5] Table 2.5 lists the algorithms to be discussed in each category. For node sampling, a relevant problem is how to obtain community assignments for *all* nodes after a community detection algorithm has been run on the sampled network. We will discuss the solution to this problem as well, in Sect. 2.3.1.

---

[5]Note that node sampling can also be achieved by creating an edge-induced subgraph from a subset of edges, therefore the node selection process is not always explicitly performed. The key distinction here is whether all nodes from the original graph are kept in the resultant sample graph.

Table 2.5 Classification of network sampling algorithms

Node sampling (Sect. 2.3.1)	Random node sampling
	Random walk sampling with restart
	Random walk sampling with jump
	Forest fire sampling
	Expansion-based snowball sampling
Edge sampling (Sect. 2.3.2)	Random edge sampling
	Structural similarity-based sampling
	Structure- and content-based sampling

2.3.1 Node Sampling for Community Discovery

Walk-Based Sampling The first category of node sampling approaches to be discussed here are based on random walk and its variants, and they often mimic the exploratory behavior in real-world activities. Given a network, a node starts by exploring its vicinity according to a probabilistic way. The exploration continues recursively on node(s) that has just been explored, until n ($n < |V|$), a specified number, nodes have been visited. At that point, all nodes and edges that have been accessed during the walk are extracted and constitute the sampled graph. We introduce three walk-based methods: random walk with restart, random walk with random jump, and forest fire model [25].

Random Walk with Restart To perform a random walk with restart, we randomly select a starting node u^0 in the graph. Let u^i be the node that the random walk process is visiting at step i. At the $i+1$st step, with a probability of p, we will select one node $v \in \Gamma_{u^i}$ uniformly and *walk* to v, hence the method's name. Otherwise, we will move to u^0 (referred to as "restart"), even if u^0 is not connected with u^i. Random walk terminates when n nodes are reached, or the number of steps exceeds a threshold.

If the input graph G is not connected, the sampled graph will be confined to the connected component that u^0 belongs to, because by design the random walk will never reach other components. As a result, the number of sampled nodes is upper-bounded by the number of nodes in the connected component, which can be less than n.

A common practice to address this problem is to start another random walk if not enough nodes have been sampled after a number of steps. This can be repeated multiple times, until n distinct nodes have been accessed in total. Then the union of sampled graphs from all walks are returned as the sample.

Random Walk with Jump Random walk with jump also performs walking at each step with a probability p. However, with probability $1 - p$ the walk will randomly select any node in the graph to jump to. This is the key distinction from random walk with restart, which only allows jumping back to u^0, and it helps to let the walk out when it is stuck in a local neighborhood or connected component, alleviating the problem of a disconnected graph.

By definition, p in both types of random walk can be any value between 0 and 1. Typically the value of p is much greater than $1 - p$, so that walks are less likely to be terminated by restarting/jumping and the sampled graph can retain more community structure from the original graph. In practice, p is often set to 0.85.

Forest Fire Model The forest fire model is analogous to the action of fire spreading in woods. Unlike random walk where only one node is selected at a time by either walking, jumping or restarting, forest fire can possibly select multiple nodes and visit all of them simultaneously in the next step. As a result, the sequence of nodes sampled is no longer linear, but rather like a tree.

The forest fire model accepts one parameter $p \in [0, 1)$, which controls the number of neighbors to visit at each step.[6] To start, a seed node u^0 is randomly chosen. Then an integer x is drawn from a geometric distribution with mean $\frac{p}{1-p}$. Such geometric distribution models the number of binary trials it takes before the first success appears, and p is the probability of failure. Naturally, as p increases, the value of x is expected to be greater, too. Existing literature has recommended setting p to 0.7 [24].

After the value x is decided, u^0 will randomly select x of its unvisited neighbors and "burn" them. It is possible that less than x nodes can be found to satisfy the requirement, because the degree of u^0 is less than x or less than x neighbors are still unvisited. In that case, the forest fire model will burn all of them.

The process continues until n nodes have been sampled or no more nodes can be burned, at which time nodes and edges that have been burned are returned as the sampled graph. At each step, one or more nodes are burning neighbors simultaneously, and this distinguishes forest fire from random walk. Also note that a node can be burned at most once, in order to prevent cycling. If the fire dies out before a sufficient number of nodes have been sampled, additional runs of forest fire can be done.

Evaluation and comparison of those walk-based methods are discussed in [24], where the authors compare the distribution of various graph statistics between the original graph and the sampled graph. The statistics include degree, size of connected component, hop-plot and clustering coefficient. Random walk with restart and forest fire generally outperform other approaches, including random node selection and random edge selection. Furthermore, those methods are able to match properties of the original graph with as few as 15 % of nodes.

Expansion-Based Sampling Another type of node sampling is expansion-based methods. Before describing the algorithm, we first define the meaning of "expansion". Given a set of nodes S on graph G, its *expansion factor* is calculated as

$$X(S) \equiv \frac{|\Gamma_S|}{|S|}$$

---

[6]The forest fire model described here is slightly different from that originally proposed in [25], which operates on directed graphs and thus has two parameters to control the "burning" of in- and out-links, respectively.

Correspondingly, the *maximum expander set* of size k, as defined in [31], is a set of k nodes with the maximal expansion factor:

$$\arg \max_{S:|S|=k} X(S)$$

Expansion-based sampling methods hinge on the conjecture that samples with high expansion factors are more representative of the original graph's community structure, compared with samples with low expansion factors. Since nodes with high expansion factors are usually bridges nodes leading to new communities, a sampled graph that includes those nodes is likely to contain most communities in the original network.

Based on this intuition, the problem of identifying a good sample of the network becomes finding the maximal expansion set of a specific size. However, solving the maximal expansion set problem exactly has high complexity due to its combinatorial nature, and two approximate sampling methods are proposed in [31].

Snowball Sampling The first approach, snowball sampling, is a greedy algorithm which adds the node that maximally improves the expansion at each step, given the current set of sampled nodes. Let $S^0 = \emptyset$ be the initial set of sampled nodes, then at the ith step, we update the new sample set as $S^i = S^{i-1} \cup \{u\}$, where $u = \arg \max_{u \in V - S^{i-1}} |\Gamma_u - (\Gamma_{S^{i-1}} \cup S^{i-1})|$. That is, adding u to the current sample set S introduces more new neighbors than any other node outside of S does. Alternatively, one can adopt a stochastic approach and select a node with a probability proportional to its improvement of expansion. This can account for occasional cases where nodes with near-highest expansion improvement actually lead to more communities.

Markov Chain Monte Carlo (MCMC) The second approach for expansion sampling is to use Markov Chain Monte Carlo (MCMC), where each of G's subgraphs of size n (the desired sample size) is considered as one state in the Markov chain. Recall that the definition of expansion factor of a sample set S is $\frac{|\Gamma_S|}{|S|}$. The maximal possible expansion factor for any set S is $\frac{|V-S|}{|S|}$, i.e. S can reach every node in G with one hop. The normalized expansion factor is therefore

$$\frac{|\Gamma_S|}{|V - S|}$$

and this value is used as the quality score for a sample S in the Markov chain.

The Markov chain consists of each subset of n nodes as a state, and it starts by randomly choosing a state S^0 that has n nodes. At the ith step, we find a candidate state S^i_{can} by randomly replacing one node in S^{i-1} with a node not in $V - S^{i-1}$. Depending on the quality scores (that is, the normalized expansion factor defined above) of S^{i-1} and S^i_{can}, there are two outcomes. If the quality score of S^i_{can} is greater than that of S^{i-1}, we accept it as the next state, letting $S^i = S^i_{can}$. Otherwise, we only accept it with a probability of

$$\left[\frac{quality(S^{i-1})}{quality(S^i_{can})} \right]^p$$

where $p = 10\frac{|E|}{|V|}\log_{10}|V|$, a function of both network size and the edge-to-node ratio [17]. If S^i_{can} fails to be accepted, we keep $S^i = S^{i-1}$.

When reaching the stationary distribution, sampling from the Markov chain becomes equivalent to sampling from all subgraphs of size n according to their quality scores. If S is the node set sampled from the Markov chain, we return the node-induced subgraph of S on G as the sampled graph.

Inferring Community Assignments for All Nodes Given a sampled graph from any aforementioned node sampling technique, we can run community detection algorithms on it efficiently because of the much smaller scale. One question unresolved, however, is how community assignments of nodes in the sampled graph can be translated back to other nodes in the original network, since the goal is to perform community detection on *all* nodes in the graph.

To that end, one can resort to relational learning techniques, where community label is the attribute of interest. This is a univariate collective inferencing problem [30], whose input are $G = (V, E)$ and $x_u, \forall u \in S$, i.e. the community labels for nodes in the sampled graph. The goal is to learn the exact community label or the distribution over possible labels for each unsampled node $u \in V - S$. A number of collective inference methods have been proposed and evaluated, and in [30] the authors find that relaxation labeling with a weighted majority relation model yields the best overall performance. In [31], the authors compare the quality of communities identified by several sampling methods. Their observation is that expansion-based sampling combined with the aforementioned inference technique produces community labels that are closest to running the community detection algorithm on the entire graph directly.

2.3.2 Edge Sampling for Community Discovery

Contrary to node sampling, where only a subset of nodes is retained, edge sampling aims at selecting edges with certain criterion while preserving all nodes. One advantage of edge sampling, therefore, is that community assignments can be learned on *all* nodes at once without the need of further inference.

Since the purpose of sampling is to create a representative subnetwork that captures the graph's community structure, naive techniques do not fare well. For example, selecting edges by equal probability is known to be biased towards high-degree nodes. Therefore, the edge selection criterion needs to consider the importance of each edge in the community structure. Here, we introduce two methods which utilize the notion of *similarity* in performing edge sampling.

Sampling Using Structural Similarity Intuition The intuition behind sampling based on structural similarity [46] can be stated as: An edge is likely to (not) connect two distinct clusters if the adjacency lists of its two incident nodes have high (low) overlap. High overlap of adjacency lists indicates a large number of triangles that the edge belongs to, hence a high likelihood of the edge residing in a dense region, i.e. a cluster. We view those edges as having high structural similarity.

By preferentially retaining edges with high structural similarity which are likely to be intra-cluster, we expect to preserve the community structure in the sampled graph. Note that in order to keep the sampled graph significantly smaller than the original graph, it is inevitable that some high-similarity edges will be discarded during the sampling process. However, provided that a great fraction of low-similarity noise edges are removed as well, we will still be able to recover the community assignments of nodes from the sampled graph.

Calculating structural similarity The next question is to identify high-similarity edges efficiently. While edge centrality measures, such as betweenness central-ity [32], have been proposed before to find "bottleneck" edges, i.e. low-similarity edges, they are prohibitively expensive to calculate with a complexity of $O(|V| \cdot |E|)$. To address this issue, one can calculate the Jaccard similarity of two incident nodes' adjacency lists and use it as the edge's structural similarity. For an edge (u, v), we view the neighborhoods of u and v as two sets, and the Jaccard similarity between the two sets is defined as:

$$sim(u, v) = \frac{|\Gamma_u \cap \Gamma_v|}{|\Gamma_u \cup \Gamma_v|}$$

More importantly, established methods like min-wise hashing [4] can be leveraged to estimate the Jaccard similarity of two sets in constant time. To generate one min-wise hash of Γ_u, we apply π, a permutation of V, on it and take the minimal value after the permutation. Formally, the hash value $h_\pi(\Gamma_u)$ (or $h_\pi(u)$ for short) is:

$$h_\pi(u) \equiv h_\pi(\Gamma_u) = \min_{v \in \Gamma_u} (\pi(v))$$

A min-wise hash signature of length k for u is generated by randomly drawing k permutations $\pi_1 \ldots \pi_k$ and concatenating the resultant hash values $h_{\pi_1}(u) \ldots h_{\pi_k}(u)$. The same set of permutations are applied to all adjacency lists to generate the corre-sponding length-k signature for each node in V. The following statistic is an unbiased estimator of the Jaccard similarity between Γ_u and Γ_v:

$$\hat{sim}(u, v) \equiv \frac{1}{k} \sum_{n=1}^{k} I[h_{\pi_n}(u) = h_{\pi_n}(v)]$$
$$E[\hat{sim}(u, v)] = sim(u, v)$$

where $I[\bullet]$ is the identity function, and it only takes $O(k)$ time to compute, a constant to the size of G.

Global and local sampling Given the structural similarity value of each edge in G, sampling can be done in one of two ways. In *global sampling*, all edges are sorted in decreasing order of their structural similarity values, and a number of top-ranked edges are retained. While easy to implement, this scheme suffers from a key drawback that it treats all edges in the graph equally and does not distinguish between clusters of varying densities. In practice, it will be able to preserve the structure of denser communities but not relatively sparse communities, since edges in the latter will have lower structural similarity and be pruned away. Global sampling also risks disconnecting the graph, since it is possible that all edges incident to a node are removed.

An alternative strategy is *local sampling*, where sampling is performed within each node's neighborhood separately. The number of incident edges that each node can keep is a function of the node's degree, for example, a power function d^e where d is degree and e is a user-specified sampling exponent ($e < 1$). This eliminates the need for a global threshold. Operating on each node separately also keeps the graph connected, as each node will be connected to at least one neighbor. Furthermore, the strict concavity of the power function ensures that sampling on high-degree nodes is more aggressive, i.e. a larger proportion of edges are removed from them. This is desirable, since high-degree nodes tend to straddle multiple clusters, and thus contain a higher fraction of inter-cluster edges.

Sampling using structural and content similarities Many real-world graphs are associated with abundant content and/or attribute information,[7] apart from the inherent network topology. The existence of content information can be leveraged to eliminate the impact of noise in the network and strengthen the community signal. This is studied in [44] where the authors investigate edge sampling based on both structural and content similarities.

Calculating content information similarity Given any two nodes of interest, the first step is to calculate their similarity based on the corresponding content information. One approach is to measure the cosine similarity between two nodes' content vectors, since many types of information can be represented as feature vectors, such as TF-IDF values for documents, SIFT features for images, as well as discrete and continuous attributes.

Furthermore, hashing via random projection method [7] can be used to efficiently estimate the cosine similarity. Let $c_u \in \mathbb{R}^d_{\geq 0}$ be the content vector of node u, we can draw a random vector $\mathbf{r} \in \{0, 1\}^d$ and use $h_{\mathbf{r}}(u) \equiv sgn(c_u \cdot \mathbf{r})$ as one hash value for c_u. Similar to the case of min-wise hashing, if we draw k different random projections and apply them to each content vector, the following result provides a way to estimate the cosine similarity of two vectors in constant time:

---

[7]Both content and attribute information are modeled as an auxiliary feature vector associated with each node in the graph, so that the formulation is applicable to text, image, and many other forms of information, all of which will be referred to as "content information" henceforth.

$$E\left[\frac{1}{k}\sum_{n=1}^{k}I[h_{\mathbf{r_n}}(u) = h_{\mathbf{r_n}}(v)]\right] = 1 - \frac{\arccos(\cos(\mathbf{c}_u, \mathbf{c}_v))}{\pi}$$

Combining structural and content similarities Before fusing two types of similarity, it is important to note that edges not currently present in the graph G should also be considered. The intuition is that if a pair of nodes shares common neighbors and contents but are not directly connected in G, they would otherwise be omitted.

To that end, one can independently find K neighbors with most similar content vectors for each node, and denote this set of edges as $E_{content}$.[8] For each node, we then consider its neighborhood under $E \cup E_{content}$ and combine the structural similarity and content similarity of each edge therein. For simplicity, the combination can be done as averaging with equal weight, and in practice no significant difference in the quality of resultant communities is observed when the weight is varied.

Local sampling can then be performed using the combined similarity values of edges, following the same procedure described previously. It is worth noting that the process can possibly introduce new edges that do not exist in G, via the creation of $E_{content}$, therefore the resultant graph is not always a subgraph of G. In the case of such edge "recovery", however, the corresponding edges always have high combined similarity and are very likely to be intra-community.

Sampling using combined similarity is particularly beneficial to graphs that are already sparse, where otherwise little improvement could be obtained by sampling using structural similarity alone. By considering content vectors during the sampling process, information encoded in edges is greatly enriched, leading to communities of higher quality with more meaningful real-world implications. On graphs of modest density, the combined sampling strategy also outperforms other approaches without significant detriment to efficiency.

2.3.3 Empirical Results and Summary

In this section, we have described various approaches in the realm of network sampling. Rather than working as standalone algorithms, those methods aim at preprocessing a network, keeping only a subset of nodes and/or edges in the network. The benefit to any subsequent community discovery algorithm is two-fold: preprocessing reduces the size of the network, and it preserves the community structure, instead of noise, in the network.

Network sampling algorithms can be divided into two general categories: those that keep a selected subset of nodes (i.e. node sampling in Sect. 2.3.1), and those that retain all nodes but fewer edges (i.e. edge sampling in Sect. 2.3.2). Existing work in

---

[8] An empirical guideline to select K is to let the size of $E_{content}$ be similar to that of E.

node sampling has approached it from various angles, and has contributed methods such as walk- and expansion-based sampling. Edge sampling has also shown promising results, as it biases towards edges that are more likely to reside in a community. Furthermore, structural similarity can be integrated with auxiliary information, such as content or attributes, when it is available, so that a more informed sampling decision can be reached.

The effectiveness and efficiency of sampling are evaluated in [46], where real-world networks are processed by various edge-sampling schemes, in order to compare sampled networks with the same set of nodes. The experiments are run on a combination of:

- Three social networks: Orkut ($|V| = 3072626$, $|E| = 117185083$), Twitter ($|V| = 146170$, $|E| = 83271147$),[9] Flickr ($|V| = 31019$, $|E| = 520040$).
- Four sampling methods: random edge sampling, forest fire (Sect. 2.3.1),[10] global and local similarity-based sampling (Sect. 2.3.2).
- Three multilevel community discovery algorithms (Sect. 2.2): METIS, MLR-MCL, Graclus.

Contrary to the benchmark networks used in Sect. 2.2, no ground truth information is associated with the three datasets evaluated here. Therefore, averaged conductance [8, 26] is used to measure the structural quality of communities that are discovered. The conductance of a community is the total number of edges leaving it, divided by the total number of edges with endpoint in the community, or the total number of edges with endpoint in the complement of the community, whichever is smaller. A low conductance value of a community represents a small inter-community edge volume, thus clear separation of it from the rest of the network. The conductance values of all communities are averaged to measure the overall structural quality.

The improvements of network sampling on conductance and running time are shown in Tables 2.6 and 2.7, respectively. The running time of a sampling method includes times for both the sampling process itself and community discovery on the subsequent sampled network. Across the board, local sampling based on structural similarity demonstrates the best balance between quality improvement and speedup. Although simpler sampling methods (random edge sampling, forest fire sampling) are faster, they do not preserve the community structure in the network, resulting in lower structural quality of the output communities. Global similarity-based sampling suffers from similar issues, as it tends to generate an extraordinarily high proportion of singletons, disconnecting them from the rest of the network.

---

[9]This is different from the Twitter network described in Sect. 2.2.5.

[10]Although forest fire is designed for node sampling, one can perform forest fire repeatedly, each time on a randomly-selected unburned node, until most nodes are burned. The collection of all burned edges are considered sampled edges.

Table 2.6 [Reproduced from [46]] Conductance of communities identified on the original networks ("Orig.") and networks preprocessed by random edge sampling ("RE"), forest fire sampling ("FF"), global similarity-based sampling ("GS"), and local similarity-based sampling ("LS")

	METIS					MLR-MCL					Graclus				
	Orig.	RE	FF	GS	LS	Orig.	RE	FF	GS	LS	Orig.	RE	FF	GS	LS
Orkut	0.85	0.82	0.82	0.76	**0.76**	0.78	0.85	0.86	0.91	**0.78**	N/A	N/A	N/A	N/A	N/A
Twitter	0.95	1.00	0.99	0.97	**0.96**	0.90	0.99	0.99	0.89	**0.86**	0.90	1.00	0.99	0.97	**0.91**
Flickr	0.87	0.91	0.91	**0.71**[11]	0.84	0.71	0.83	0.88	0.72	**0.70**	0.66	0.72	0.71	**0.66**	0.72

The lower the conductance, the higher quality the discovered communities have. The best-performing sampling method on each pair of network and community discovery algorithm is boldfaced. If a community discovery algorithm does not finish on a particular network, the corresponding cell is marked "N/A". Although global similarity-based sampling enables low conductance on Flickr, it generates 30 % singletons on this network, whose contributions to the conductance are not included

Table 2.7 [Reproduced from [46]] Running time (in seconds) on the original network and speedup achieved by network sampling, including the time of both sampling *and* community discovery on the resultant sampled network

	METIS					MLR-MCL					Graclus				
	Orig.	RE	FF	GS	LS	Orig.	RE	FF	GS	LS	Orig.	RE	FF	GS	LS
Orkut	14373	13x	12x	30x	36x	21079	6x	6x	39x	22x	N/A	N/A	N/A	N/A	N/A
Twitter	2307	35x	14x	85x	6x	14569	63x	16x	188x	22x	1518	138x	138x	66x	5x
Flickr	5	8x	9x	1x	3x	17	3x	3x	2x	4x	1	2x	2x	1x	2x

If a community discovery algorithm does not finish on a particular network, the corresponding cell is marked "N/A"

2.4 Exploiting Parallelism and Distributed Architectures in Community Discovery

All algorithms described so far in this chapter operate as single-thread processes on a single machine, and that leaves two problems to be addressed. First of all, the parallelism that is inherent to many community discovery algorithms has not been fully exploited. Two forms of parallelism are being considered here: data parallelism that allows accessing multiple segments of data for computation at the same time, and control parallelism that enables the execution of the algorithm on multiple nodes or communities simultaneously. The second problem is rooted in the fact that network data is growing at an unprecedented rate, and more and more frequently exceeds the RAM capacity of a single machine. To be able to handle very large networks, we will need to resort to various distributed computing architectures that have been developed over the years, such as message passing, MapReduce, and others.

In this section, we discuss some promising directions that have the potential of solving these two issues in community discovery. We will first emphasize the critical role that (sparse) matrix/vector operations play in many community discovery algorithms (Sect. 2.4.1). This underpins the possibility of scaling up community discovery by leveraging computation kernels on various frameworks, including OpenMP, Many Integrated Core (MIC), General-Purpose GPU (GPGPU), and Hadoop. While the discussion focuses on selected families of community discovery algorithms, the findings are generalizable to many others, as long as they are composed of matrix/vector operations.

We will also introduce the parallelization of several community discovery algorithms that are based on optimizing certain objective function values. For many algorithms in this category [20, 41, 53], the serial version was proposed first, and subsequent algorithm speedup is accomplished by parallelizing critical subroutines that are otherwise time-consuming, such as the calculation of objective function values. Depending on the problem scale, algorithms have been proposed for both shared-memory systems (Sect. 2.4.2) and distributed-memory systems (Sect. 2.4.2). We will introduce one instance for each type of system.

2.4.1 Speeding up and Scaling up Matrix Operation-Based Algorithms

Many community discovery problems such as Markov clustering, spectral clustering, and matrix factorization can be reduced to matrix operations. Much progress has been made in performing parallel matrix operations efficiently, which directly contributes to faster and more scalable community discovery algorithms. Here, we describe the optimizations for two types of them: Markov clustering (Sect. 2.4.1) and spectral clustering (Sect. 2.4.1).

Fast MLR-MCL with Efficient Sparse Matrix-Matrix Multiplication (SpMM)
As seen in Sect. 2.2, MLR-MCL implements a multilevel version of regularized
Markov clustering (R-MCL). Perhaps not surprisingly, the most time-consuming
block in MLR-MCL is R-MCL, because it involves multiplying two large sparse
matrices, M and M_G. If one can exploit the data sparsity and speed up the multiplication subroutine, the efficiency of MLR-MCL can be significantly improved.
The same reasoning applies to other matrix operation-based community discovery
algorithms as well.

To this end, researchers have recently investigated the effect of applying SpMM
kernels to MLR-MCL on various parallel architectures. In [33], the authors success-
fully improve the performance of MLR-MCL on multi-processor CPUs by designing
a novel SpMM computation kernel. In order to perform SpMM efficiently, memory
footprint analysis is performed so that the workload is well-balanced among processors. Experiments on eleven networks report a speedup of up to 10x. More importantly, the utility of the SpMM kernel implemented in this work has a broader impact
beyond one single algorithm. Given its superior performance against the Intel Math
Kernel Library on both multi-processor CPU and the new multi-core MIC architecture (2x on average), similar speedups can be expected if the kernel is properly
applied to other matrix-based community discovery algorithms.

Another promising direction in accelerating matrix operations is GPGPU programming. The architecture of GPUs is by design highly parallel, and computation
can be performed by on-board chips accessing high-throughput on-board memory,
without incurring latency between GPU and CPU. As a result, GPGPU has become
a powerful and low-cost platform that is suitable for matrix-matrix multiplication
and other similar operations. Such advantages have been leveraged in [6], where a
CUDA-based implementation of MCL (CUDA-MCL) is proposed and has proven
highly efficient. Future research efforts are warranted to extend this work to MLR-
MCL, as well as other community discovery algorithms that can utilize SpMM or
SpMV(ector) kernels.

Hadoop-Based Eigensolver for Scalable Spectral Clustering Spectral graph theory has been extensively studied [8], and researchers have drawn a close link between
the spectral properties of a graph and its community structure. Briefly speaking, the
goal of spectral clustering is to represent nodes by their representations induced from
the top k eigenvectors of matrix $D^{-\frac{1}{2}}(D - A)D^{-\frac{1}{2}}$, equivalent to eigenvectors associated with the k smallest eigenvalues of matrix $D^{-\frac{1}{2}}AD^{-\frac{1}{2}}$. K-means clustering can
be run on those length-k vectors to find community assignments for nodes [50].

While it may be tempting to apply spectral clustering on large networks using
distributed computing, in practice non-trivial efforts are required. Storing network
information is straightforward, as only $|V| * k \ll |E|$ values need to be stored. How-
ever, finding the k eigenvectors requires significant memory, and consequently existing eigensolvers (e.g. PLAPACK, ScaLAPACK) do not scale to billion-by-billion
matrices.

To address this challenge, a Hadoop-based eigensolver called HEigen is proposed [18]. It employs the Lanczos algorithm, and selectively reorthogonalizes vec-

tors to avoid generating spurious eigenvalues. Expensive operations such as matrix-vector and matrix-matrix multiplication are distributed using the MapReduce framework. HEigen also uses blocking to transfer data of multiple nodes at once, so that a significant amount of time is saved in network transfer. Furthermore, data size skewness is also exploited, and small vectors/matrices are sent to mappers as distributed caches in Hadoop.

According to the evaluation on HEigen's scalability and efficiency, it is able to scale to graphs with billions of edges. Several design choices facilitate reducing the running time, and the cached matrix-matrix multiplication kernel contributes most to the speedup (76X compared with a naive implementation of the multiplication kernel). However, the quality of spectral clustering is not measured, presumably due to the lack of ground truth for these very large networks or the difficulty in calculating clustering quality measures (e.g. conductance, normalized cut, normalized mutual information) itself. In the future, one remedy is to evaluate the performance of this Hadoop-based spectral clustering algorithm on synthetic networks generated by benchmark suites such as LFR [22], where the gold standard is readily available.

2.4.2 Parallelizing Objective Function Optimization-Based Algorithms

Here, we introduce two parallel community discovery algorithms that are based on optimizing the value of a certain objective function. SCD (Sect. 2.4.2) maximizes the weighted clustering coefficient, whereas ParMETIS (Sect. 2.4.2) minimizes the edge-cut among communities. They both can be parallelized thanks to repeating local computations. One distinction is that SCD is implemented on shared-memory systems, while ParMETIS is designed for distributed-memory systems, facing the additional challenge of reducing communication cost.

Scalable Community Detection (SCD) SCD [41] is a two-phase algorithm which parallelizes repeating computations. It sits on the Pareto frontier of time complexity and quality coordinates among all state-of-the-art algorithms. It optimizes a modularity-based function: Weighted Clustering Coefficient (WCC) [40], which essentially counts the number of triangles. The objective function and the movement function (discussed later) can be computed locally while requiring global information. As a result, the algorithm can be parallelized on a shared memory framework using techniques such as OpenMP and the like.

WCC is a community metric based on the number of triangles. Intuitively, for a node v and a community C, the more triangles v closes within C, the more likely v belongs to C, and the higher its WCC value with regard to C is. The WCC of a community is the average WCC over all nodes in the community, and the WCC of the community assignments in a network is the weighted average WCC over all communities.

SCD has two partitioning phases plus a preprocessing phase, which removes edges that are far from any triangle. The initial partitioning first computes the local clustering coefficient [47] of each node, and sorts all nodes in descending order of their local clustering coefficients. Then it uses each node in the ranking as the center of a star to partition the graph, which makes each community a star with a high local clustering coefficient node as its center. The local clustering coefficient computation can be parallelized where each thread computes the local clustering coefficients of a subset of nodes.

The refinement partitioning phase moves nodes among communities as follows. For each node in the graph, its movement function is computed. When all movement functions are obtained, the partition and WCC are updated. This process repeats until the WCC value converges. The movement function of a node decides whether and how to move a node based on the WCC gain of the action, and it can be either (1) moving the node to another selected community, or (2) keeping the node in its current community. Both outcomes can lead to the creation or removal of a single-node community. The computation of the movement function can also be parallelized where each thread computes the movement function of a subset of nodes.

ParMETIS ParMETIS [20] is the parallel version of METIS (Sect. 2.2.1). It is designed for tasks like solving linear systems and computing finite element meshes in a distributed manner. Hence the implicit assumption is that the number of partitions/communities is no greater than the number of processors. This framework achieves a significant time reduction compared with the serial version of METIS, while maintaining comparable quality in terms of edge-cut.

Framework and challenges Similar to the serial version, ParMETIS also contains three phases: contraction, partitioning and refinement. The contraction phase is similar to that in the serial version except that multiple processors participate in the computation of maximal matching. While it is straightforward in a shared-memory system, a great number of communications and synchronizations are required to obtain a good matching in a distributed-memory architecture. A *local matching*, where each processor only computes matching of vertices in its own memory, can perform decently only when the graph has already been well-partitioned and each partition component is stored in a processor. This pre-condition is unrealistic since it is exactly the goal of the algorithm: to obtain a good partitioning of the graph. On the other hand, a *global matching*, where each processor considers vertices in other processors while computing matching, requires a high degree of fine-grained inter-processor communication. Moreover, a distributed architecture may encounter circular matching among processors, which makes some local optimum inaccessible.

After the coarsening phase, the graph has already been significantly reduced and one processor can handle the partitioning computation efficiently. Yet, since the graph is stored distributedly, moving data to a single processor still incurs additional cost. ParMETIS computes a p-way partitioning (p is the number of processors) via a recursive bisection algorithm similar to [19], and each processor explores a recursive branch.

During the refinement phase, ParMETIS refines partitioning while uncoarsening the series of graphs. Again, circular movement poses the same challenge as that in the contraction phase. A scheme proposed by [10] suggests that multiple runs of vertex movement between disjoint pairwise partitions can avoid the circular movement problem. The bottleneck, however, is that if each partition i has k_i neighboring partitions, the number of runs is no less than $\max_i k_i$. Another drawback of this scheme is that the local greedy approach lacks a global view and can easily be trapped at a low quality local optimum.

A coloring-based scheme to avoid circular matching and movement To overcome the aforementioned challenges, a method approach based on graph coloring is proposed here. Recall that a coloring of a graph partitions a graph into κ independent sets, where κ is its chromatic number. The constraint that every time only the vertices of the same color are moved avoids circular matching and movement. To color a graph, Luby's algorithm [29], an incremental algorithm which works well on shared-memory architectures, is modified and adopted.

- **Concurrent coloring of graph vertices** On a distributed-memory architecture, a multinode and its neighbors might be stored in different processors. Therefore, the communication cost of inquiry a neighbor's location may be large. Moreover, the original Luby's algorithm has significant synchronization overheads. A variant of Luby's algorithm, which trades quality[11] for concurrency and time efficiency, is proposed here. The variant is simple: prior to the execution of Luby's algorithm, a *communication setup* phase occurs, where each vertex's external relation, i.e. whether a vertex has a neighbor located in another processor, is determined. Not all nodes are colored in each iteration, and the algorithm terminates when a large fraction of nodes are colored.

- **Matching after coloring** Matching after coloring can avoid circular matching and achieve high concurrency. The matching algorithm based on a colored graph is efficient when parallelized, and it works as follows: Initially each vertex has a mark variable called *Match* with a value of -1. At the end of computation, the *Match* variable of a matched vertex is its partner. Iterating on each color, each unmatched vertex selects one of its unmatched neighbors based on the heavy-edge heuristic, and updates both vertices' *Match* variables to be each other. Multiple vertices may attempt matching the same vertex. On a shared-memory architecture, this is solved by a first-come-first-match strategy. On a distributed-memory architecture, upon receiving all matching requests, the to-be-matched vertex determines its partner based on the heavy-edge heuristic and rejects other matching requests. Matching computation terminates after all colors have a chance to match.

- **Refining after coloring** Implemented in a way similar to the matching procedure, moving a vertex color by color from a partition to another also avoids circular movement. There are two optimization techniques to be considered here. The first one stems from the observation that on a distributed-memory architecture, the algorithm does not actually move a vertex from the processor containing one

---

[11]The computed independent set is no longer guaranteed to be maximal.

partition to the processor that contains another partition. Rather, it only need to assign each vertex (multinode) a partition ID. The other optimization deals with the balance constraint in each partition. Since one partition may be stored distributedly, at the end of each color's movement, the weights of the partitions are globally recomputed and each processor updates the related information.

2.4.3 Summary

In this section, we have listed several promising approaches of scaling up community discovery algorithms by exploiting the intrinsic parallelism and existing distributed computing frameworks such as message passing and MapReduce. We first point out that many community discovery algorithms essentially involve matrix-matrix multiplications and other similar operations, and the underlying matrices are often sparse. This enables us to leverage matrix operation kernels that have been proposed on various architectures including multi-processor CPU, many-core CPU, GPGPU, and Hadoop, and to obtain significant speedup of community discovery algorithms such as Markov clustering and spectral clustering. We then discuss how both shared-memory and distributed-memory systems can be adapted to perform community discovery based on optimizing objective function values. The two instances described, SCD and ParMETIS, are able to execute orders of magnitude faster than their serial counterparts, with only minor impact on the output quality.

There exists more work in the literature that aims at parallelizing community discovery algorithms, such as parallel label propagation [34], parallel Louvain method [48], and parallel modularity-based agglomerative clustering [43]. While we do not describe them in details in this section, they also deserve substantial research attention.

2.5 Conclusion

In this chapter, we have presented three categories of simple approaches that aim at performing effective community discovery in an efficient and scalable fashion. We first describe a generic contract-and-conquer multilevel framework, where a network is recursively contracted into a series of increasingly smaller networks, so that a core community discovery algorithm can run efficiently on the miniature networks. We then review the idea of sampling vertices and/or edges in a network via various strategies, and we show that one can indeed reduce the network size, thus accelerating the community discovery process, and retain its community structure at the same time. Finally, we outline existing efforts and future work directions for performing community discovery in a parallel or distributed computing environment, in order to ensure sufficient storage for large-scale networks as well as to speed up the computation. It is important to note that these three groups of methods are not mutually exclusive, and there are great potentials in combining them to design new community discovery algorithms that can process networks of tera-scale (or even larger) in a reasonable amount of time.

We believe that for a community discovery algorithm to be practical for large networks, it needs to follow simple but effective design principles. As a result, we focus on the three aforementioned categories which are well-tested in empirical evaluations and are highly flexible. For more thorough reviews of state-of-the-art methods in the field of community discovery in general, readers can refer to various recent surveys [14, 35, 37, 38].

Specifically, we limit the algorithms discussed in this chapter to those that discover disjoint communities, instead of allowing communities to overlap. Detecting overlapping communities is another focal point in community discovery that is being actively studied [23, 28, 53], and they can benefit from all the three approaches introduced in this chapter. Furthermore, most algorithms covered here also require parameters in some forms to determine the number of communities to discover. In practice, if such information is absent, one can often estimate the value based on some empirical rules of thumb, such as the one in [27].

Apart from overlapping and non-parametric community discovery, there are other outstanding challenges in the realm of user community discovery that are worthy of significant future efforts. In particular they include:

- **Community discovery in graph streams** Graph data in many domains are changing rapidly, such as the addition and removal of user connections in online social networks. In such cases, it becomes inefficient to apply static community discovery algorithms to a collection of network snapshots. Further complicating the problem is the fact that graph data may arrive in a streaming fashion, making it infeasible to store updates and revisit them in the future. The states of communities need to be maintained and updated in an efficient way, in order to avoid backlog in the processing pipeline. To date, only a small number of work [2] has approached this problem directly.
- **Community discovery in signed networks** A signed network is a network whose edges can represent positive or negative relationships. Such relationships can be explicit, e.g. stated friendship or rivalry between two social network users, or implicit, e.g. empirically-measured excitation or inhibition between two proteins. Existing literature on mining communities from signed networks [11, 52] only operates on small networks that have at most thousands of nodes, and has not attained the ability to efficiently handle large-scale user networks.
- **Community discovery combining structure and attribute/content information** Many network datasets are accompanied by a rich collection of auxiliary information, such as social network user attributes and content. Prior work has explored the use of these data in addition to structural information, and managed to identify communities of users that are dense in connection as well as coherent in attributes/content [44, 54, 55]. While improving the quality of communities that are discovered, these approaches are not as efficient as their structural information-

only counterparts. Therefore, it is important to design more efficient methods that can leverage attribute and content information in community discovery.

The three paradigms summarized in this chapter have all demonstrated superior flexibility and the ability to improve algorithmic efficiency and scalability. In the future, we envision wide adoption of these paradigms in well-investigated as well as emerging community discovery problems, in order to create more powerful tools for identifying user communities in large networks. Since these frameworks are not mutually exclusive but rather complementary, it is also viable to leverage multiple of them in conjunction, and the potential improvement of performance and output quality can be profound.

Acknowledgments We are thankful to the Editors and anonymous reviewers for their valuable comments, insightful suggestions and constructive feedback that greatly helped improving this article.

This work is supported by NSF Grants **IIS-1111118**, **CCF-1240651**, and **DMS-1418265**. Any opinions, findings, and conclusions or recommendations expressed in this material are those of the author(s) and do not necessarily reflect the views of the National Science Foundation.

References

1. Adamic LA, Glance N (2005) The political blogosphere and the 2004 US election: divided they blog. In: Proceedings of the 3rd international workshop on link discovery. ACM, pp 36–43
2. Aggarwal CC, Zhao Y, Philip SY (2010) On clustering graph streams. In: SDM. SIAM, pp 478–489
3. Blondel VD, Guillaume JL, Lambiotte R, Lefebvre E (2008) Fast unfolding of communities in large networks. J Stat Mech: Theory Exp 2008(10):P10008
4. Broder AZ, Charikar M, Frieze AM, Mitzenmacher M (1998) Min-wise independent permutations. In: Proceedings of the thirtieth annual ACM symposium on theory of computing. ACM, pp 327–336
5. Bui TN, Jones C (1993) A heuristic for reducing fill-in in sparse matrix factorization. In: PPSC, pp 445–452
6. Bustamam A, Burrage K, Hamilton NA (2012) Fast parallel Markov clustering in bioinformatics using massively parallel computing on GPU with CUDA and ELLPACK-R sparse format. IEEE/ACM Trans Comput Biol Bioinform (TCBB) 9(3):679–692
7. Charikar MS (2002) Similarity estimation techniques from rounding algorithms. In: Proceedings of the thirty-fourth annual ACM symposium on theory of computing. ACM, pp 380–388
8. Chung FR (1997) Spectral graph theory, vol 92. American Mathematical Society, Providence
9. Dhillon I, Guan Y, Kulis B (2007) Weighted graph cuts without eigenvectors a multilevel approach. IEEE Trans Pattern Anal Mach Intell 29(11):1944
10. Diniz PC, Plimpton S, Hendrickson B, Leland RW (1995) Parallel algorithms for dynamically partitioning unstructured grids. In: PPSC, pp 615–620
11. Doreian P, Mrvar A (2009) Partitioning signed social networks. Soc Netw 31(1):1–11
12. Fiduccia CM, Mattheyses RM (1982) A linear-time heuristic for improving network partitions. In: 19th conference on design automation. IEEE, pp 175–181
13. Fiedler M (1973) Algebraic connectivity of graphs. Czechoslov Math J 23(2):298–305
14. Fortunato S (2010) Community detection in graphs. Phys Rep 486(3–5):75–174
15. George A, Liu J (1981) Computer solution of large sparse positive definite systems. Prentice Hall, Englewood Cliffs

16. Heath MT, Ng E, Peyton BW (1991) Parallel algorithms for sparse linear systems. SIAM Rev 33(3):420–460
17. Hubler C, Kriegel HP, Borgwardt K, Ghahramani Z (2008) Metropolis algorithms for representative subgraph sampling. In: Eighth IEEE international conference on data mining, ICDM'08. IEEE, pp 283–292
18. Kang U, Meeder B, Papalexakis EE, Faloutsos C (2014) HEigen: spectral analysis for billion-scale graphs. IEEE Trans Knowl Data Eng 26(2):350–362
19. Karypis G, Kumar V (1998) A fast and high quality multilevel scheme for partitioning irregular graphs. SIAM J Sci Comput 20(1):359–392
20. Karypis G, Kumar V (1999) Parallel multilevel series k-way partitioning scheme for irregular graphs. Siam Rev 41(2):278–300
21. Kernighan BW, Lin S (1970) An efficient heuristic procedure for partitioning graphs. Bell Syst Tech J 49(2):291–307
22. Lancichinetti A, Fortunato S, Radicchi F (2008) Benchmark graphs for testing community detection algorithms. Phys Rev E 78(4):046110
23. Lancichinetti A, Radicchi F, Ramasco JJ, Fortunato S (2011) Finding statistically significant communities in networks. PLOS ONE 6(4):e18961
24. Leskovec J, Faloutsos C (2006) Sampling from large graphs. In: Proceedings of the 12th ACM SIGKDD international conference on knowledge discovery and data mining. ACM, pp 631–636
25. Leskovec J, Kleinberg J, Faloutsos C (2005) Graphs over time: densification laws, shrinking diameters and possible explanations. In: Proceedings of the eleventh ACM SIGKDD international conference on Knowledge discovery in data mining. ACM, pp 177–187
26. Leskovec J, Lang KJ, Dasgupta A, Mahoney MW (2008) Statistical properties of community structure in large social and information networks. In: Proceedings of the 17th international conference on world wide web. ACM, pp 695–704
27. Leskovec J, Lang KJ, Mahoney M (2010) Empirical comparison of algorithms for network community detection. In: Proceedings of the 19th international conference on world wide web. ACM, pp 631–640
28. Leung IX, Hui P, Lio P, Crowcroft J (2009) Towards real-time community detection in large networks. Phys Rev E 79(6):066107
29. Luby M (1986) A simple parallel algorithm for the maximal independent set problem. SIAM J Comput 15(4):1036–1053
30. Macskassy SA, Provost F (2007) Classification in networked data: a toolkit and a univariate case study. J Mach Learn Res 8:935–983
31. Maiya AS, Berger-Wolf TY (2010) Sampling community structure. In: Proceedings of the 19th international conference on world wide web. ACM, pp 701–710
32. Newman ME, Girvan M (2004) Finding and evaluating community structure in networks. Phys Rev E 69(2):026113
33. Niu Q, Lai PW, Faisal SM, Parthasarathy S, Sadayappan P (2014) A fast implementation of mlr-mcl algorithm on multi-core processors. In: 21st annual international conference on high performance computing, HiPC 2014, Goa, India, 17–20 December 2014
34. Ovelgonne M (2013) Distributed community detection in web-scale networks. In: 2013 IEEE/ACM international conference on advances in social networks analysis and mining (ASONAM). IEEE, pp 66–73
35. Papadopoulos S, Kompatsiaris Y, Vakali A, Spyridonos P (2012) Community detection in social media. Data Min Knowl Discov 24(3):515–554
36. Parlett BN (1980) The symmetric eigenvalue problem, vol 7. SIAM, Philadelphia
37. Parthasarathy S, Faisal SM (2013) Network clustering. CRC Press, Boca Raton, pp 415–456
38. Parthasarathy S, Ruan Y, Satuluri V (2011) Community discovery in social networks: applications, methods and emerging trends. Social network data analytics. Springer, Berlin, pp 79–113
39. Pemmaraju S, Skiena S (2003) Computational discrete mathematics: combinatorics and graph theory with mathematica. Cambridge University Press, New York
40. Prat-Pérez A, Dominguez-Sal D, Brunat JM, Larriba-Pey JL (2012) Shaping communities out of triangles. In: Proceedings of the 21st ACM international conference on information and knowledge management. ACM, pp 1677–1681

41. Prat-Pérez A, Dominguez-Sal D, Larriba-Pey JL (2014) High quality, scalable and parallel community detection for large real graphs. In: Proceedings of the 23rd international conference on world wide web, international world wide web conferences steering committee, pp 225–236
42. Richter Y, Yom-Tov E, Slonim N (2010) Predicting customer churn in mobile networks through analysis of social groups. In: SDM. SIAM, vol 2010, pp 732–741
43. Riedy EJ, Meyerhenke H, Ediger D, Bader DA (2012) Parallel community detection for massive graphs. Parallel processing and applied mathematics. Springer, Berlin, pp 286–296
44. Ruan Y, Fuhry D, Parthasarathy S (2013) Efficient community detection in large networks using content and links. In: Proceedings of the 22nd international conference on world wide web, international world wide web conferences steering committee, pp 1089–1098
45. Satuluri V, Parthasarathy S (2009) Scalable graph clustering using stochastic flows: applications to community discovery. In: Proceedings of the 15th ACM SIGKDD international conference on knowledge discovery and data mining. ACM, pp 737–746
46. Satuluri V, Parthasarathy S, Ruan Y (2011) Local graph sparsification for scalable clustering. In: Proceedings of the 2011 international conference on management of data. ACM, pp 721–732
47. Soffer SN, Vázquez A (2005) Network clustering coefficient without degree-correlation biases. Phys Rev E 71(5):057101
48. Staudt CL, Meyerhenke H (2013) Engineering high-performance community detection heuristics for massive graphs. In: Proceedings of the 2013 42nd international conference on parallel processing. IEEE Computer Society, pp 180–189
49. Van Dongen SM (2000) Graph clustering by flow simulation. Ph.D. thesis, University of Utrecht
50. Von Luxburg U (2007) A tutorial on spectral clustering. Stat Comput 17(4):395–416
51. Xie J, Kelley S, Szymanski BK (2013) Overlapping community detection in networks: the state-of-the-art and comparative study. ACM Comput Surv (CSUR) 45(4):43
52. Yang B, Cheung WK, Liu J (2007) Community mining from signed social networks. IEEE Trans Knowl Data Eng 19(10):1333–1348
53. Yang J, Leskovec J (2013) Overlapping community detection at scale: a nonnegative matrix factorization approach. In: Proceedings of the sixth ACM international conference on web search and data mining. ACM, pp 587–596
54. Yang J, McAuley J, Leskovec J (2013) Community detection in networks with node attributes. In: 2013 IEEE 13th international conference on data mining (ICDM). IEEE, pp 1151–1156
55. Yang T, Jin R, Chi Y, Zhu S (2009) Combining link and content for community detection: a discriminative approach. In: Proceedings of the 15th ACM SIGKDD international conference on knowledge discovery and data mining. ACM, pp 927–936
56. Zachary WW (1977) An information flow model for conflict and fission in small groups. J Anthropol Res 33:452–473

Chapter 3
Community Discovery in Multi-Mode Networks

Isaac Jones, Lei Tang and Huan Liu

Abstract As social media becomes more feature-rich and the capability for interactions between users becomes more complex as a result, it may become necessary to expand the models used in data analysis to represent more complex interactions and networks. To that effect, researchers have begun using graphs with different types of vertices or even hyperedges to represent more complex networks. In this chapter, we will explore some of the community detection approaches state-of-the-art research uses to deal with the increasing complexity of social networks, and particularly representing those networks as multi-mode networks (or heterogeneous networks). This chapter will cover the approaches used as well as the graph representations of complex networks. Though the work studied uses social networks as the basis for analysis, the use of multi-mode networks and hyperedges is principled in any analysis task where the complexity of the data calls for multiple types of entities with interactions involving two or more entities in the network.

3.1 Motivation

In November 2010, one of the biggest takedowns of illegal botnets occurred when Dutch authorities systematically dismantled a network of 30 million infected machines.[1] These machines were located across the globe and were responsible for sending out over 30 million spam messages every day. The reason this type of takedown is possible is through community analysis, the detection of community structures. The infected computers in the botnet destroyed by the Dutch authorities forms a community similar, though obviously more nefarious than, the one formed

---

[1] http://www.zdnet.com/article/dutch-police-take-down-bredolab-botnet/.

I. Jones · H. Liu
Arizona State University, Tempe, USA

L. Tang (✉)
Head of Data Science, Clari Inc., 100 W. Evelyn Ave, Suite 210,
Mountain view, CA 94041, USA
e-mail: leitang@acm.org

© Springer International Publishing Switzerland 2015
G. Paliouras et al. (eds.), *User Community Discovery*, Human–Computer
Interaction Series, DOI 10.1007/978-3-319-23835-7_3

55

by a group of high school classmates or members of a tennis club. By performing some of the same analysis on communication networks that we do on social networks, we can uncover covert networks like the botnets the Dutch authorities did. However, since this 2010 takedown, both social media networks and the botnets that operate online have gotten more complex, to enhance user experience in the former case and to evade detection in the latter case. This may seem like a strange parallel to draw, but both social media networks and communication networks have similarities that make their analysis similar. For example, on Twitter and Facebook the following and friend links (respectively) can be seen as communication pathways between computers in a botnet, and tweets or posts can be seen as the messages that go across these communication pathways.

Since 2010, social media networks have continued to add features. In 2012, Twitter acquired and integrated the features from Vine, a popular video-sharing network. Facebook famously acquired Instagram, and subsequently its feature set, in a billion dollar deal. In addition, Twitter launched Twitter Music in 2013, adding even more features for its users. The addition of these feature layers to their host social media networks makes them more appealing to users, but it also makes the representation of these networks more difficult for community detection and other network analysis. Consider the standard network representation that we might use on a Facebook network, how would we represent the action of commenting on a posted Instagram photo? This newfound complexity is not easily handled by traditional network formulations. One possible way to represent this new data is by adding supplementary graphs, linking users and their photos, users and their comments, comments and the photos they are posted on, and so forth, for as many graphs is necessary. However, this could be inconvenient representation and only grows more complex as more features are added and interactions become richer.

One sensible alternative is to use a *multi-mode* graph. These types of graphs, as we will detail throughout this chapter, are capable of representing an arbitrary number of feature layers in a network and scale quickly and easily to represent interactions between those features. To use the previous example; comments, photos, and users can all be easily represented on one graph without the complexity of maintaining supplementary graphs.

Another challenge beyond is the noisiness of interaction data in communications networks. For instance, as of late 2014, users posted 70 million images to Instagram *every day*, and for some analysis tasks a great portion of those images are bound to be irrelevant. However, a great variety of analysis tasks occur on social media networks, so keeping as many data points as possible is important in case that data becomes relevant in future tasks. This shifting relevance of data makes noise a major concern for researchers. The multi-mode networks are an excellent way to deal with this noise since they remain compatible with the network denoising processes that researchers rely on to winnow down data to only its salient features. These denoising processes rely on the availability of outside information to power their ability to filter out unneeded information. Since multimode networks have that information easily available, in fact built right in to the graph, they can be more effective.

The sheer quantity of noise in the system also makes spurious results inevitable. No system provides perfect accuracy with no false positives, and this provides its own set of challenges for researchers. The risks associated with false positives from data analysis are well documented within the financial auditing community. Dealing with some of the impacts is an unfortunate part of the job in this community. *The Forensic Examiner* featured a six-page article[2] outlining the risks associated with fraud detection specifically and some management strategies for fraud detection experts. Though multi-mode networks do not directly combat the false positive problem, the ability of multi-mode networks to effectively and efficiently factor in more information will assist in making the techniques that utilize them more effective, giving the users better tools for their decision making process.

Another challenge that the enormous size, noisiness, and complexity combine to bring the fore is the volatility of social media network. With billions of users of active users every month, Facebooks social network can hardly be expected to remain static for any appreciable length of time. This has been a continuous challenge for analysts of social media networks [16] and has recently been addressed with various methods that take the changing nature of social networks into account, appropriately classed as *evolutionary* methods. Though we deal only with static network snapshots in this chapter, a number of the methods we look at have either the capability or extensions designed to handle time-varying networks [13]. Key to the evolutionary methods is the ability of multi-mode networks to handle additional information in its network representation, which means that evolutionary methods and multi-mode representations are a natural fit for one another. If the time-dependent structure of the network can be encoded into the multi-mode representation, standard analysis techniques can be used on the networks. This would provide significant potential for analyzing these types of networks, since time information can be easily represented as another mode in the representation.

Multi-mode networks clearly have a significant usefulness when it comes to representing complex social media data and other communication data. The new data demands of increasingly complex social and technical interactions online can be elegantly met by this new network representation that enables and even facilitates analysis. It stands to reason that fields outside of social network analysis can even benefit from using this representation in their techniques. In this chapter, we will discuss three techniques that take advantage of multi-mode networks in their analysis and their results help make the case that this avenue of research is valuable for future work. However, many researchers have considered multi-mode networks in their work, so some terminology may be confusing to readers who aren't familiar with these types of networks already. In the next section, the terminology that will be used in this chapter is introduced and alternative terminology is presented.

---

[2]http://www.all-about-forensic-science.com/support-files/fraud-detection.pdf.

3.2 Definitions

The feature rich and increasingly complex nature of social networks has caused many researchers to simultaneously develop both methodology and terminology for dealing with these increasingly complex networks. In order to maintain clarity and consistency throughout the chapter, we will start by defining some of the common terms used by researchers, as well as presenting alternative terms with similar meanings used by the research community.

3.2.1 Multi-Mode Networks

In traditional graph theory, an underlying assumption is that all of the vertices in the network being inspected are of the same type. For example, a graph representing a social network might consist of only vertices representing users of that network. Concomitantly, the edges between vertices in this network would represent relationships between the users represented by vertices. Figure 3.1 demonstrates a simple example of such a network.

Networks like those depicted in Fig. 3.1 have received extensive attention both in the existing scientific literature and in previous chapters. As such, the content of this chapter will focus on the more complex networks alluded to above. In this text, and in portions of the existing literature, these networks are referred to as *mulit-mode networks*. In order to better understand this term, it is useful to break it down into its component parts and consider them independently. Here, *network* is used interchangeably with *graph*, and has the same meaning that "graph" does. The other part of the term, *multi-mode*, refers to the computing definition of "mode," a way of operating or using a system. In this case, the system in question is the vertices specified in the network or graph. These vertices adhere to one of a multiplicity of ways of operation in the network.

By way of example, consider the social network discussed above. In the stated formulation, we already represent users of the network as vertices and their explicit relationships as edges. Suppose that the social network also has a messaging feature and we want to represent messages passed from one user to another on the network. We could change the edges to indicate that a message has been sent between two

Fig. 3.1 An example of a uni-mode network. Image courtesy of Wikipedia

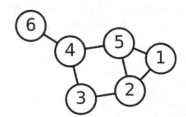

Fig. 3.2 An example social
network with message
vertices

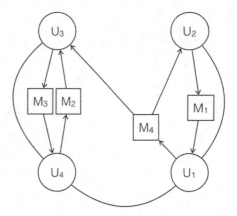

users, but that has two possible problems. Firstly, it is possible that messages can be
sent to more than one person, which would be impossible to capture in the current
formulation. There are other edge types that can capture this relationship, which
we will discuss in Sect. 3.2.2. Secondly, and possibly more importantly, this erases
the information in the network about the relationships between users that may be
important for analysis conducted on the network. In order to represent this more
complex set of relationships, we can instead add a mode to the existing set of vertices
and represent messages sent between users as vertices using this new mode. Then,
directed edges going from these new vertices to the users represent the senders and
receivers of the messages. And example of a possible network using this formulation
is given in Fig. 3.2.

The network in the example above is an example of a graph with two modes, a *bi-
mode network* or *2-mode network*. If, instead of the small toy network, we had a very
complex network like Facebook[3] where users perform a wide variety of actions like
posting images, posting links, posting statuses, commenting on statuses, replying to
comments, commenting on fan pages, and so on, representing each of these actions
as a mode of the network could result in a very high modality. Thus, for simplicity,
any network with more than one mode is simply referred to as a *multi-mode network*.

In addition to the terminology used above, other researchers have other terms
they prefer. For example, networks like the one depicted in Fig. 3.2 are referred to
in [11] as *heterogeneous* networks. This calls attention to the contrast between the
network of Fig. 3.1, which is *homogeneous* because it contains only one type of
vertex. In this way, referring to a network as *heterogeneous* is equivalent to referring
to it as *multi-mode*. In addition, these types of networks are referred to in [8] as
multi-dimensional networks, where "dimensional" refers to the increase in matrix
dimensions necessary to represent the network in its adjacency matrix form. Note
that the same term, *multi-dimensional networks*, is used in [2, 15] to represent a

---

[3] www.facebook.com.

Fig. 3.3 A graph
demonstrating hyperedges.
Image courtesy of Wikipedia

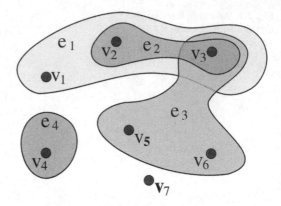

uni-mode network with multiple types of interactions between vertices of the single
mode, which are also referred to as multiplex or multi-relational networks [4].

3.2.2 Hyperedge and Hypergraph

When a network possesses multiple modes, the complexity of interactions between
vertices also increases. A *simple edge* represents the interaction between two vertices.
This definition of edges can be extended to include more than two vertices, resulting in
hyperedges as shown in Fig. 3.3. This expansion of simple edge to hyperedge captures
more information, but also increases complexity, similar to the way that expanding
a network's modality increases complexity. Note that any graph that contains edges
of increased complexity like hyperedges is called a *hypergraph*.

In simple uni-mode networks, edges necessarily occur between two vertices of
the same type. In multi-mode networks, one edge can involve vertices of one or two
modes, or even more than two modes. For example, in [8], the user actions on the
Digg[4] network are modeled as a five-mode network with vertices representing users,
stories, comments, topics, or keywords. *Hyperedges* are used to represent complex
relationships between these objects; for example, a comment action involves vertices
from three modes: user, story, and comment.

Since hypergraphs and, particularly, hyperedges are specifically included to capture relationships between vertices, it may be valuable to re-imagine the network of
Fig. 3.2 as a hypergraph. Figure 3.4 demonstrates this conversion.

While "hyperedge" and "hypergraph" have their roots in mathematics literature,
researchers in computer science often use alternate terminology to refer to these
concepts and types of graphs. For example, *multi-relational* is used in [8] to capture
the idea that not only do the hyperedges used in the representation capture relations
the way that a relational database does, but that there are many different possible
types of relations. In addition, *metagraph* is used in [8] to describe a graph that has

---

[4]www.digg.com.

Fig. 3.4 The two-mode graph of Fig. 3.2 converted to a hypergraph. Note that M_1 and M_2 were removed to reduce clutter

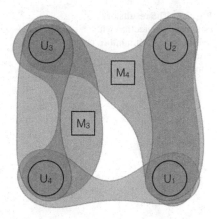

both the properties of a hypergraph and a multi-mode graph. Further adding notational complexity, the term *metagraph* is used in [3] to indicate that a graph consists of both standard vertices and aggregate vertices that represent fine-grained communities. Some researchers, however, choose to avoid the complexity of hypergraphs by changing the network representation. For example, in [11], the authors choose to re-formulate the network as a Star Network in order to avoid using hyperedges, which we will discuss in more detail in Sect. 3.4.2.

In this chapter, we will use the term *multi-mode network* to refer to networks with more than one type of vertex and *hyperedges* to refer to edge representations that are more complex than the traditional edges. Accordingly, any graph that contains hyperedges will be referred to as a *hypergraph*.

3.3 Problem Formulation

Community detection on multi-mode networks or hypergraphs requires careful formulation in order to make the problem tractable. While the basis of the formulation remains the same, individual researchers formulate the problem in different ways in order to apply their unique methods to the problem. However, commonalities exist in the formulations. Here, we will discuss the formulation in terms of those commonalities. In Sect. 3.4 we will discuss the specific modifications to the formulation that are necessary for each approach.

3.3.1 Community Detection

Fundamentally, the problem of community detection can be formulated as follows: Given a set of n actors, represented by vertices, $\mathbf{N} = \{n_1, n_2, \ldots, n_n\}$ the task of

Fig. 3.5 The results of
community detection with
overlapping communities on
a sample network. Image
courtesy of mathworks

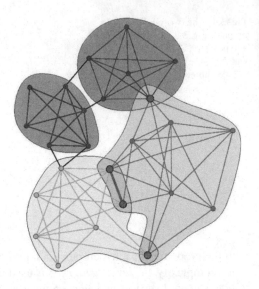

community detection is to partition the vertices into k groups, called communities, such that $\mathbf{C}_i = \{n_{1_i}, n_{2_i}, \ldots, n_{m_i}\}$. In this case, community C_i is of size m_i, but communities need not be of a uniform size, nor are communities necessarily exclusive. Indeed, an argument can be made (and has, frequently) that non-exclusive communities are more representative of real social networks [12]. Figure 3.5 demonstrates an example of detecting communities on a network with only one type of vertex.

However, this formulation obviously falls short when expanded to multi-mode communities. In multi-mode networks, the set of vertices cannot be as simply partitioned. This is because uni-mode community detection algorithms assume that all vertices in the network are of the same type. Obviously, this assumption is not valid on multi-mode networks. For the example discussed in Sect. 3.2, it would be unsatisfactory if we treat all vertices the same and cluster the vertices representing users and the vertices representing messages into the same cluster. Putting them into one cluster would imply that the vertices are "equivalent." This would allow the clustering algorithm to treat messages and users identically, which could lead to clusters of users including messages, even messages that were not sent by any of the users in the cluster. Thus, the problem formulation must be modified to take into account the mode information for multi-mode networks.

3.3.2 Multi-Mode Communities

As discussed, the variations in vertex modality must be represented, and this additional complexity has cascading effects in the formulation. In this section, we will cover changes to the basic community detection formulation that must be made to expand to a multi-mode network. In particular, the set of all vertices is defined by:

$$\mathcal{N} = \{\mathbf{N}_t\}_{t=1}^{T}$$

This means that given T types of vertices, the set of all vertices is divided into smaller sets corresponding to the type of vertex. This ensures that each type of vertex is treated differently, unlike the previous formulation. Of course, it would be possible to do community detection on only one of the N_t terms, but as discussed before, this removes valuable information. Instead, each of the T terms in $\mathcal{N}$ is clustered into one of k_t communities. Note that in this case, the number of communities can vary based on the type of the vertex. Thus, what community membership indicates can vary from mode to mode. For example, continuing the example used in Sect. 3.2, the message mode could have a cluster for messages about sports and one for messages about pet care while the user dimensions contains clusterings based on high school graduating class. Certainly, there are members from every graduating class who are interested in sports, and the same for pet lovers.

In order to capture the cross-mode information, we must also capture the relationships between vertices of different modalities. To do this, we define a relationship matrix between vertices. This matrix

$$R^{i,j} \in \mathbb{R}^{|N_{t_i}| \times |N_{t_j}|}$$

represents both the existence and strength of a relationship between elements of modality i and j. Note that in this formulation, i and j can be equal, and this matrix represents the relationships between vertices of the same modality. Typically, 0 is used to indicate that no relationship exists between two given vertices and 1 is used to indicate that such a relationship does exist. However, [0, 1] normalized values have been used by some researchers to indicate the strength of this relationship as well as the presence.

In addition to representing the vertices and their relationships, it is necessary to represent the object of the community detection problem, the communities themselves. In the generic multi-mode community detection problem formulation, we assume that communities are bounded to only one mode of the graph, and so we define *community indicator* or *community membership* matrix as:

$$C^{i,j} \in \{0, 1\}^{|N_{t_i}| \times k_i}.$$

as before, k_i represents the number of communities into which mode i is partitioned. Note that since communities do not transcend modal boundaries, it is not necessary for the set of all C matrices to contain cross-modal relationships, as was required to properly represent the relationships between vertices in the relationship matrix.

In addition to the interactions between vertices in the graph, we also assume that communities in the graph are not totally independent, even across modalities. It would be inappropriate to assume, for example, that the community of messages about pet care and the community of users interested in pet care artist completely independently. Obviously, these two groups are related, even though they are in different modes of the network. Thus, we define a community interaction matrix

$$A^{i,j} \in R^{k_i \times k_j},$$

Note that this matrix is smaller than the vertex interaction matrix, as the number of communities is much less than the number of vertices. This matrix can also serve as an abstraction of all cross-mode relationships to a smaller feature space.

Note that all the notations above assume that there are no hyperedges in the graph. As we shall see later, these notations can be extended in a consistent way (using tensors, to be discussed later) to handle hyperedges and hypergraphs.

3.4 Methods

In this section, we will discuss three different approaches to performing community detection on multi-mode networks. The methods discussed will be those presented by Tang et al. in [14], Sun et al. in [11], and Lin et al. in [8]. Each of these methods will be referred to by the names the authors gave their systems. These are, respectively: EMMC, NetClus, and Metafac. At the end of this section, we compare all the three methods and discuss their connections.

3.4.1 Evolutionary Multi-Mode Clustering

Presented by Tang et al. in [14], Evolutionary Multi-Mode Clustering (EMMC) is formulated in such a way that it takes community changes over time into account (thus *evolving*). However, this does not affect its ability to detect communities in multi-mode networks. While evolutionary clustering is an emerging field of community detection research and has its own challenges and applications, it is not within scope for this chapter, so the evolutionary portion of this work will be disregarded.

The EMMC method starts out with an assumption that the relationship matrix R captures interactions of the communities of interest in the graph. Mathematically:

$$R^{i,j} \approx C^i A^{i,j} (C^j)'$$

Here, $A^{i,j}$ is the confounding factor that links the community memberships in mode i and j, which is the community interaction matrix discussed in the previous section. Consequently, it is reasonable to attempt to estimate the community membership of two modes of the network as:

$$\min \ ||R^{i,j} - C^i A^{i,j} (C^j)'||_F^2 \tag{3.1}$$

$$s.t. \ C^i \in \{0, 1\}^{|N_{t_i}| \times k_i} \quad \sum_{k=1}^{k_i} C_k^i = 1 \tag{3.2}$$

$$C^j \in \{0, 1\}^{|N_{t_j}| \times k_j} \quad \sum_{k=1}^{k_j} C_k^j = 1 \tag{3.3}$$

The objective function in Eq. (3.1) attempts to minimize the Frobenius Norm of two matrices. Combining this objective for all cross-mode interactions, it follows that:

$$\min \sum_i \sum_j \ w_{i,j} ||R^{i,j} - C^i A^{i,j} (C^j)'||_F^2 \tag{3.4}$$

$$s.t. \ C^i \in \{0, 1\}^{|N_{t_i}| \times k_i}, \quad \sum_{k=1}^{k_i} C_k^i = 1 \ \text{ for all } i = 1, 2, \ldots, T \tag{3.5}$$

where $w_{i,j}$ is the weight assigned to the interaction between modes i and j. Summing up the results over all pairs of dimensions ensures that the relationships between all pairs of modes are taken into account. Since there is no constraint that $i \neq j$, communities within the same mode are also taken into account.

However, due to the discrete nature of constraints in Eq. (3.5), the minimization problem is NP-Hard. In order to alleviate this issue, the authors use a well-studied technique in the spectral clustering literature [17]. This technique is to relax the discrete constraints into continuous constraints. By using continuous constraints, we can think of the community indication matrix as indicating a "level of membership" for each community. This also has the effect of transforming the single-community solution proposed initially to an overlapping community solution. Since the community indication matrix can now have more than one non-zero value, we can say that a vertex belongs primarily to the community with which it has the highest value, but partially to all of the other communities with which it has a non-zero value. This relaxation transforms the constraints in Eq. (3.5) into:

$$(C^i)'C^i = I_{k_i}. \tag{3.6}$$

In English, this mean that the community indicator matrix is column orthogonal, which yields the following final problem formulation:

$$\min \sum_i \sum_j \ w^{i,j} ||R^{i,j} - C^i A^{i,j} (C^j)'||_F^2 \tag{3.7}$$

$$s.t. \ (C^i)'C^i = I_{k_i} \tag{3.8}$$

There is no analytical solution to the problem above because of the simultaneous unknowns C^i, C^j, and $A^{i,j}$. However, alternating optimization can be adapted to solve it. That is, we can compute one variable while fixing all other variables. When fixing C^i and C^j, the optimal $A^{i,j}$ is as follows:

$$A^{i,j} = (C^i)^T R^{i,j} C^j \tag{3.9}$$

It can be shown that the optimal C^i, given all other variables, is the left singular vector of a matrix P that consists of several sub-matrices concated column-wise:

$$P^i = \left[\left\{ \sqrt{w^{i,j}} R^{i,j} C^j \right\} \right] \tag{3.10}$$

Hence, EMMC can be solved iteratively. In each iteration, we cycle through all modes and then update C^i as the left singular vectors of the matrix P^i.

3.4.2 Net-Clustering

Sun et al. describe in [11] a method for performing multi-mode community detection based on transforming a traditional multi-mode network into a type of network called a *star network*. This modification to the network results in some changes to the problem formulation we presented in Sect. 3.3, as well as requiring discussion of the Star Network modification for clarity.

In order to understand the NetClus formulation, it is important to first discuss the network representation the authors use for the multi-mode network. Consider the original formulation of the network:

$$G = \langle \mathcal{N}, E \rangle$$
$$\text{where } \mathcal{N} = \{\mathbf{N}_t\}_{t=1}^T$$

In the formulation used in [11], an additional element is added to the graph definition, a set of weights on the set of edges E, these weights (denoted W for the set and W_{n_i, n_j} for the weight of an individual edge) correspond to the real-values entries of the adjacency matrix R previously mentioned. In addition, the authors of NetClus add another constraint to the network, the *star network* constraint.

The star network constraint imposes a limitation on the connectivity of edges in the network. Normally, an edge in the network is represented by $e = \langle n_i, n_j \rangle$ where the vertices n_i and n_j can be from any modality in T. However, the star network constraint designates a particular member of T ($t = 1$ for simplicity) as the *target type* and forces all edges to have exactly one endpoint in the target type. That is, the set of all edges E has an additional constraint that:

$$\forall e \in E, e = \langle n_i, n_j \rangle, n_i \in N_1, n_j \in N_t (t \neq 1) \tag{3.11}$$

Note that this also imposes the constraint that vertices in the target type may not be connected to one another. For notational purposes, modes of the network other than the first mode are referred to as *attribute types*. Because the star network scheme places such a high emphasis on the target type, using this scheme facilitates the clustering in the mode of the target type, thus the term "target." However, forcing edges to have one end in the target type reduces the ability of a star network formulation to represent real-world graphs. The advantage of using a star network formulation in this context is that the removal of edges between vertices of the target types forces a communities detected in the target type to have attribute vertices linking the vertices of the target type. Based on the attribute vertices used as linkages, this forces a community to have some meaning to human interpreters, serving as both a explanation for the community's existence and a sanity check on that community's existence. These modification to the formulation of the problem power the strengths of the NetClus algorithm.

In particular, the authors define a *net cluster* as a cluster that consists of a target vertex and its highly relevant attribute vertices. Though the authors model the domain they study as a multi-mode star network, it is perhaps more intuitive to interpret the cluster definition and algorithm by thinking of target vertices as objects and attribute vertices as the object's different attributes. Consequently, a cluster is mainly composed of target vertices and their most frequently considered attributes.

Unlike EMMC, NetClus does not minimize an matrix approximation error function to obtain its results. Instead, the algorithm adopts a k-means-like method to compute the most likely assignments of target type vertices to clusters. The NetClus algorithm can be described by the following steps, according to the authors in [11]:

1. Generate initial partitions for target objects and induce initial net-clusters from the original networks according to these partitions, i.e., $\{C_i^0\}_{i=1}^k$;
2. For each cluster, compute out the conditional probability that one attribute vertex is associated with the cluster. i.e., $\{P(x|C_i^t)\}_{i=1}^k$;
3. Calculate the posterior probabilities for each target object $(p(C_i^t|x))$ and then adjust their cluster assignment according to the new measure defined by the posterior probabilities to each cluster.
4. Repeat Steps 2 and 3 until the cluster does not change significantly, i.e., $\{C_i^*\}_{i=1}^k = \{C_i^t\}_{i=1}^k = \{C_i^{t-1}\}_{i=1}^k$.
5. Calculate the posterior probabilities for each attribute object $(p(C_k^*|x))$ in each net-cluster.

Step 2 can be thought of as finding a ranking on the target vertices to best describe the interactions observed in the cluster. This distribution is similar to using "sufficient statistics" to describe the cluster, which is comparable to the cluster centroid in classical k-means clustering algorithm. Step 3 then updates the cluster assignment for each attribute vertex.

As a general approach to the problem, NetClus is an exemplar of methods based on iterative improvement of a model that mathematically describes the data. In this case, the authors of NetClus chose to use a probabilistic model that iteratively improves clusters based on the probability that a particular instance of the target type with its linked attribute type objects is generated by the clusters the algorithm identifies as being strongly related.

3.4.3 MetaGraph Factorization

Presented by Lin et al. in [8], the final method, MetaFac extends conventional multi-mode networks to include hyperedges as discussed in Sect. 3.2. Unlike EMMC, where all edges are interactions between exactly two vertices and possibly of different modes, MetaFac tackles the cases when multiple modes interact simultaneously. In order to handle community discovery in these hypergraphs, we must extend the traditional matrix representation to *tensors*, a form of higher-order matrices, to represent hyperedges. Tensors are a useful mathematical construct for representing hypergraphs due to their flexibility and the properties of the construction. A brief overview of tensor mathematics is given in [8] and further information can be found in [1]. Though tensor mathematics is not within scope here, some coverage will be necessary in the course of discussing the problem formulation.

We start with simple case of conventional edges representing two-way interactions. Let x_{ij} represent the interaction of two entities (possibly from different modes), k denote a community, $p_{k \to i}$ indicate how likely an interaction in the kth community involves entity i, and p_k be the probability of any interaction in the kth community. Given these things, the probability of interaction can be approximated by:

$$x_{ij} \approx \sum_k p_k \cdot p_{k \to i} \cdot p_{k \to j} \tag{3.12}$$

A 3-way interaction is a simple extension:

$$x_{i_1 i_2 i_3} \approx \sum_k p_k \cdot p_{k \to i_1} \cdot p_{k \to i_2} \cdot p_{k \to i_3} \tag{3.13}$$

Hence, a set of interactions among three modes can be rewritten as

$$\mathcal{X} \approx \sum_k p_k \cdot u_k^{(1)} \circ u_k^{(2)} \circ u_k^{(3)} = [\mathbf{z}] \prod_{m=1}^{3} \times_m \mathbf{U}^{(m)} \tag{3.14}$$

Here $\mathcal{X}$ is the data tensor representing all interaction involving three modes and $\mathbf{Z}$ is the core tensor.

Using tensors, as mentioned above, the authors of [8] formulate MetaFac as an optimization problem. The known inputs to the problem solution are the metagraph[5] $G = \langle V, E \rangle$. Unlike the original definition of a graph, E is represented by a tensor

---

[5]Recall from Sect. 3.2, that a metagraph is a multi-mode graph by another name.

that involves multiple modes for each hyperedge in the original multi-mode graph. These edges are represented as $\mathscr{X}^{(i)}$, where i is a unique value for each hyperedge. The authors of MetaFac chose KL-divergence [7] (denoted $D(\cdot||\cdot)$) to determine the quality of their estimation. Since the KL-divergence is only defined on a single relation (one instance of $\mathscr{X}^i$), the contribution to the total divergence from each relation must be summed up as follows:

$$\min \sum_{r \in E} D(\mathscr{X}^{(r)}||[\mathbf{z}] \cdot \prod_{m:v^{(m)} \in e^{(r)}} \mathbf{U}^{(m)} \qquad (3.15)$$

$$s.t. \mathbf{U}^{(q)}_{ik} = 1 \ \forall q \forall k \qquad (3.16)$$

Note that in Eq. (3.15), $v^{(m)} \in e^{(r)}$ is used to indicate that $v^{(m)}$ is one of the vertices involved in hyperedge r. By minimizing this cost over the two free variables, $[\mathbf{z}]$ and $\mathbf{U}^*$, we can find community interaction core tensor, represented by $[\mathbf{z}]$, and a set of community memberships, represented by $\mathbf{U}^*$, that reconstruct the observed data as accurately as possible. This is subject to some regularizing constraints as specified in Eq. (3.16). to ensure that $\mathbf{U}^{(q)}$ is a representation of interaction probabilities.

Optimizing the MetaFac objective function is non-trivial and we encourage reader to refer to the source paper for algorithm details. Generally speaking, the authors propose to perform an iterative process. At each iteration, the author compute the optimal $[\mathbf{z}]$ and $\mathbf{U}^*$ alternatively.

3.4.4 Discussions

In the previous subsections, we have briefly reviewed three different approaches to find communities for multi-mode networks. Below we summarize the data sets studied for each method.

Data and Comparison For EMMC, two network data sets are selected; the Enron email corpus, made public in the wake of the October 2001 scandal, and Digital Bibliography & Library Project (DBLP) data. For the Enron data, the authors constructed a three-mode network. The three modes used are users, messages (e-mails), and words. Users are linked to both the messages that they send and those that they receive. Messages and words are in turn linked together by usage in a particular message. Figure 3.6 show a visual representation of the cross-mode linkages in the data set. The DBLP data is modeled as a network with four modes: papers, authors, terms (words in the title), and venues (conferences or journals). The cross-modal links used for this dataset are the obvious ones, and are depicted in Fig. 3.7.

The authors of NetClus use a similar, but not identical, DBLP data set, setting paper as the target mode and venue, author, and term the other attribute modes.

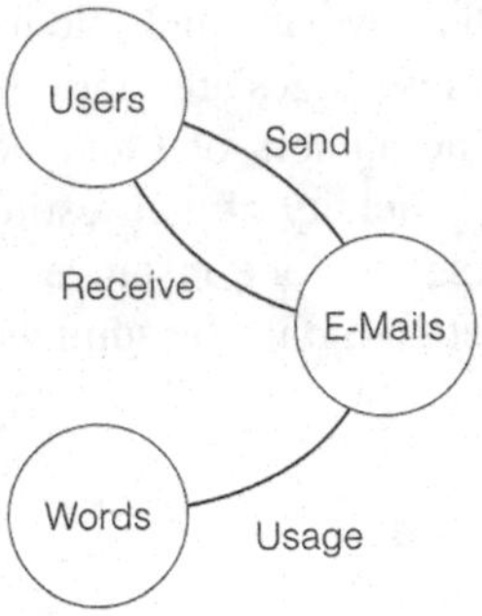

Fig. 3.6 A visual representation of the cross-mode links in the Enron E-mail corpus

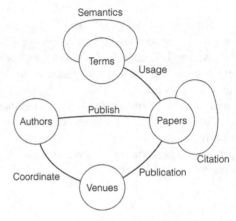

Fig. 3.7 A visual representation of the cross-mode links in the DBLP corpus

Relation	Modes
Content	Story, Keyword, Topic
Contact	User, User
Submit	User, Story
Digg	User, Story
Comment	User, Story, Comment
Reply	User, Comment

Table 3.1 Relations used in MetaFac performed on the Digg datasets and the modes they connect

The authors of MetaFac model the activities on Digg[6] using hyperedges. The data set contains five modes: users, stories, comments, keywords, and topics. In addition, it contains hyperedges connecting these modes. Table 3.1 describes the different hyperedges and the modes they connect. Note that in this dataset, Submit and Digg connect the same modes.

At first glance, the three methods look very different, because each method proposes to handle different types of multi-mode networks. In particular, EMMC aims to handle general multi-mode networks with only two-way interactions. MetaFac

---

[6]www.digg.com.

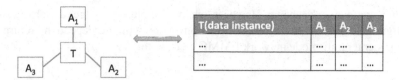

Fig. 3.8 Conversion between star network and data-attribute table

can be thought of as an extension of EMMC with a modification to handle care of multi-way interactions represented by hyperedges, though different loss functions are used for approximation. NetClus, on the contrary, transforms a multi-mode network into a star network. Note that not all networks can be represented by this star network schema. Taking advantage of this schema, a k-means like algorithm can be adopted to compute the communities of target mode vertices. In terms of algorithms, all three methods are iterative, with the clustering results of one mode updated based on the clustering or Interaction probability of other modes.

Connections A multi-mode network representation blurs the conventional definition of *attributes*, *vertices*, and *relations*. For example, NetClus studies multi-mode networks with one target mode and others being attribute modes. Since vertices in attribute modes interact only with those of the target mode, we can think of them as attributes of the target mode vertices to which they are connected. Equivalently, each attribute mode represents one feature, and vertices in that mode become different attribute values, as shown in Fig. 3.8. This makes the NetClus algorithm looks very much like a k-means clustering algorithm handling data associated with different attributes.

On the other hand, hyperedges complicate the community detection problem in multi-mode networks. However, hyperedges can be "flattened," and thus reduced to normal edges, by adding more modes to the network. We can create one additional mode for each hyperedge relation, then each hyperedge becomes one vertex in that mode. Obviously, all the modes involved in the original hyperedge will be connected to this new mode. Figure 3.9 demonstrates such a change. Essentially, a hyperedge relation involving m modes is converted into m two-way interactions between the m modes and one newly created hyperedge mode. Interestingly, such a change is

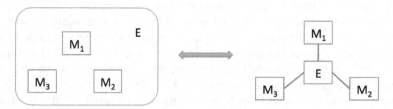

Fig. 3.9 Conversion between hyperedge and flattened multi-mode network

exactly a *star network* schema. However, when multiple hyperedges are observed in the original network, then the modes after conversion will interdependent, returning to the general multi-mode network EMMC deals with.

3.5 Extensions

As alluded to in Sect. 3.4, community detection efforts have multiple extensions above and beyond simply detecting communities. In both [11] and [14], the basic community detection problem is extended into an evolving communities problem. In this section, the community detection extensions of Community Evolution, Link Prediction, and Ranking will be introduced and briefly discussed.

3.5.1 Community Evolution

The first extension, *community evolution*, deals with the time-varying nature of social networks. Part of the nature of social networks is that they are fundamentally dynamic constructs. Links between users are constantly formed and removed, and with these links community structures change; sometimes growing, sometimes shrinking. In some cases, communities merge together and become one larger community. The work described in [14] and [11] contains a discussion of evolving communities as well as simple modifications to the models already presented that enable analysis of community evolution. As demonstrated by [5], evolutionary clustering continues to be a popular extension of community detection as social networks become more mature and more time-varying data is available.

3.5.2 Link Prediction

Communities detected by community detection algorithms inherently represent areas of denser connectivity in the underlying graph. In standard community detection, *modularity*, a measure of the density of connections inside the community compared with those outside, is commonly used as an indicator of community quality [9]. It is reasonable, then, to assume that areas of the graph that have high density of connections will also have a high number of new connections. Thus, it is reasonable to assume that detected communities will indicate locations where new links are likely to form. MetaFac, the method discussed in Sect. 3.4.3 was used by the authors of [8] to make predictions on new links between entities. The results of this prediction demonstrate the potential of community detection algorithms to supplement link prediction algorithms.

3.5.3 Ranking

Lastly, in the real world, each community tends to have a single individual or small group that are highly influential. The problem of finding influential users or vertices in network data is a longstanding problem. This has lead to the development of algorithms like PageRank [10] and its precursor, HITS [6]. Finding influential users given the network is a well-studied problem, but like the work in Link Prediction, ranking problems can benefit from exploiting community structure. The NetClus work described in Sect. 3.4.2 also contains a ranking component to find highly ranked conferences in the Data Mining area [11]. The rankings they find from the DBLP data set match their evaluation of the conferences present in the data set.

3.6 Summary

Community detection [13], and by extension multi-mode community detection, is a highly dynamic, fast-moving field. Multi-mode community detection, in particular, has great potential to provide insight into networks that are becoming increasingly complex with the evolution of social media. As social networks become increasingly expressive and allow their users to conduct more and more of their daily business online, the modality of the network and size of the possible relationship set will have to increase to compensate for this. Current trends in social media support the idea that social networks will become increasingly complex. Facebook[7] continues to add more and more ways for users to interact with one another. Twitter[8] recently debuted the Vine[9] video-sharing service as a way to integrate another form of media, in this case video, into the Twitter social network. Google has made great (albeit controversial) steps by integrating their services together and thus increasingly the number of ways that users of Google's services can interact with one another. Recently, Google opted to integrate Google Plus services with their widely popular YouTube service, requiring users to use their Google Plus identity to comment on YouTube videos. While this was unpopular with YouTube's users,[10] it is easy to see from a community detection perspective how this change massively increased the amount of available data, both in size and complexity.

As the data sets for detecting communities in multi-mode communities become larger and larger, increasingly sophisticated algorithms are needed to draw meaningful conclusions from that data. The various motivational reasons discussed in Sect. 3.1 drive both commercial interests and more academically inclined researchers to strive for better and better community results. The various cross-disciplinary applications

---

[7]www.facebook.com.

[8]www.twitter.com.

[9]https://vine.co/.

[10]www.forbes.com/sites/insertcoin/2013/11/09/google-plus-creates-uproar-over-forced-youtube-integration/.

discussed briefly in Sect. 3.5 make community detection a widely followed research area, as researchers from a wide variety of disciplines incorporate the latest results from community detection into their work to improve performance.

Acknowledgments We would like the thank Dr. Papadopoulos and the other editors and reviewers for their helpful comments about the content of this chapter, as well as the members of the DMML lab at ASU for the same.

References

1. Bader BW, Kolda TG (2006) Algorithm 862: Matlab tensor classes for fast algorithm prototyping. ACM Trans Math Softw (TOMS) 32(4):635–653
2. Berlingerio M, Coscia M, Giannotti F, Monreale A, Pedreschi D (2013) Multidimensional networks: foundations of structural analysis. World wide Web 16(5–6):567–593
3. Blondel VD, Guillaume JL, Lambiotte R, Lefebvre E (2008) Fast unfolding of communities in large networks. J Stat Mech: theory Exp 2008(10): P10008
4. Cai D, Shao Z, He X, Yan X, Han J (2005) Community mining from multi-relational networks. In: Knowledge discovery in databases: PKDD 2005. Springer, pp 445–452
5. Gupta M, Aggarwal C, Han J, Sun Y (2010) Evolutionary clustering and analysis of heterogeneous information networks. Technical report, IBM research report
6. Kleinberg JM (1999) Hubs, authorities, and communities. ACM Comput Surv (CSUR) 31(4es):5
7. Kullback S, Leibler RA (1951) On information and sufficiency. Ann Math Stat 22(1):79–86
8. Lin YR, Sun J, Castro P, Konuru R, Sundaram H, Kelliher A (2009) MetaFac: community discovery via relational hypergraph factorization. In: Proceedings of the 15th ACM SIGKDD international conference on knowledge discovery and data mining. ACM, pp 527–536
9. Newman ME (2006) Modularity and community structure in networks. Proc Natl Acad Sci 103(23):8577–8582
10. Page L, Brin S, Motwani R, Winograd T (1999) The PageRank citation ranking: bringing order to the web
11. Sun Y, Yu Y, Han J (2009) Ranking-based clustering of heterogeneous information networks with star network schema. In: Proceedings of the 15th ACM SIGKDD international conference on knowledge discovery and data mining. ACM, pp 797–806
12. Tang L, Liu H (2009) Relational learning via latent social dimensions. In: Proceedings of the 15th ACM SIGKDD international conference on knowledge discovery and data mining. ACM, pp 817–826
13. Tang L, Liu H (2010) Community detection and mining in social media. Synth Lect Data Min Knowl Discov 2(1):1–137
14. Tang L, Liu H, Zhang J, Nazeri Z (2008) Community evolution in dynamic multi-mode networks. In: Proceedings of the 14th ACM SIGKDD international conference on knowledge discovery and data mining. ACM, pp 677–685
15. Tang L, Wang X, Liu H (2009) Uncovering groups via heterogeneous interaction analysis. In: ninth IEEE international conference on data mining, ICDM'09. IEEE, pp 503–512
16. Zafarani R, Abbasi MA, Liu H (2014) Social media mining: an introduction. Cambridge University Press, Cambridge
17. Zha H, He X, Ding C, Gu M, Simon HD (2001) Spectral relaxation for k-means clustering. NIPS 1:1057–1064

Chapter 4
Discovering Communities in Multi-relational Networks

Zhiang Wu, Zhan Bu, Jie Cao and Yi Zhuang

Abstract Multi-relational networks (in short as MRNs) refer to such networks including one-typed nodes but associated with each other in poly-relations. MRNs are prevalent in the real world. For example, interactions in social networks include various kinds of information diffusion: email exchange, instant messaging services and so on. Community detection is a long-standing yet very difficult task in social network analysis, especially when meeting MRNs. This chapter gradually explores the research into discovering communities from MRNs. It begins by introducing the generalized modularity of the MRN, which paves the way for applying modularity optimization-based community detection methods on MRNs. However, the main-stream methods for discovering communities on MRNs are to integrate information from multiple dimensions. The existing integration methods fall into four categories: network integration, utility integration, feature integration, and partition integration. Learning or ranking the weight for each relation in MRN constitutes building blocks of network, utility and feature integrations. Thus, we turn our attention into several co-ranking frameworks on MRNs. We then discuss two different kinds of partition integration strategies, including the frequent pattern mining based method and the consensus clustering based method. Finally, for the purpose of conducting performance validation, we present several techniques for constructing the MRN based on both multivariate data and forum data.

Z. Wu (✉) · Z. Bu · J. Cao
National Center for International Joint Research on E-Business Information
Processing (NECC), School of Information Engineering, Nanjing University
of Finance and Economics, Nanjing, China
e-mail: zawuster@gmail.com

Y. Zhuang
College of Computer and Information Engineering, Zhejiang Gongshang University,
Hangzhou, China

© Springer International Publishing Switzerland 2015   75
G. Paliouras et al. (eds.), *User Community Discovery*, Human–Computer
Interaction Series, DOI 10.1007/978-3-319-23835-7_4

4.1 Introduction

Multi-relational networks (MRNs), being composed of one-typed nodes but multi-typed relations, have been found ubiquitous in the real world. For example, in Twitter, the multi-relations among users contain followers or followees, retweeting tweets, publishing relevant tweets with others, and so on. There are also various types of relations among users in social networks, including friendship, contact, co-subscription or co-tagging to the same resource, co-contact with the third one, and so on. Another important reason attracting a great deal of focus to MRNs is that the MRN is closely related to the time-dependent network [18]. That is, if taking every snapshot as a network in one relation, the time-dependent network becomes a MRN. Relations in MRNs can be either explicit or implicit [3]. Explicit relations directly reflect the various interactions in reality, but implicit relations are inferred from the available data to reflect different interesting qualities of the interactions.

Some studies target at establishing theoretical basis for multi-relational network analysis, such as algebra operations [22] and analytical measures extensions [2, 3]. Community discovery in MRNs has become one of the prevailing topic among studies on multi-relational network analysis. Similar to community detection methods with global models in single-relational networks, Mucha et al. [18] proposed the generalized modularity (Q function), and aimed to optimize this criterion defined over the network partition. However, most of studies [26, 32, 34] attempted to integrate information from multiple dimensions to discover the shared community structure across multiple network dimensions. According to the four components involved in a network, the existing integration methods can be summarized as four categories: *network integration*, *utility integration*, *feature integration*, and *partition integration* [26]. After any integration strategy applied on a MRN, various community detection methods (such as spectral clustering, block models, latent space approach, and modularity optimization) will be applicable on the MRN. An unified view for integration and then community detection has been given in [26, 28].

The goal of three integration strategies, i.e., network integration, utility integration, and feature integration, is very similar. That is, they target at transforming a MRN to a SRN, by integrating topological, utility matrices, and structural features from multiple relations with average or biased weights, respectively. So, how to learn/rank the weight for every relation becomes an important problem during the integration process. In this chapter, we discuss several co-ranking frameworks on the multi-relational data/network, which differentiates with the unified view introduced in [26, 28]. As for partition integration, we review two different methods including the frequent pattern mining based method and the consensus clustering based method.

The remainder of this chapter is organized as follows. In Sect. 4.2, we formulate the problem of community discovery on multi-relational networks. In Sect. 4.3, we introduce the concept of generalized modularity, which lays the foundation for modularity optimization based community detection. In Sect. 4.4, we first overview network/utility/feature integration strategies, and thus highlight co-ranking techniques that serve as building blocks for these integration strategies. In Sect. 4.5, we present two kinds of partition integration methods. We discuss some issues for conducting performance validation on MRNs in Sect. 4.6, and finally conclude this chapter in Sect. 4.7.

4.2 Problem Formulation

This section provides preliminary knowledge of the MRN and community discovery on it, which serves as a consolidated reference for the following sections. A single-relational network is usually represented as an adjacency matrix that is also known as a two-way tensor because it has two dimensions. Stated in this way, an MRN can be represented as a three-way tensor consisting of a series of matrix "slice". We formally define the MRN as follows:

Definition 4.1 (*Multi-relational Network*) A m-relational network is defined as a set of graphs $M = (V, \mathbb{E} = \{E_1, \ldots, E_m \subseteq (V \times V)\})$, where V denotes the node set with n elements, and $\mathbb{E}$ is the m-relational edge set. Let $\mathcal{A} \in \{0, 1\}^{n \times n \times m}$ be a three-way tensor, then

$$\mathcal{A}^d_{i,j} = \begin{cases} 1 & if (i, j) \in E_d : 1 \le d \le m \\ 0 & otherwise \end{cases} \tag{4.1}$$

In this formulation, $\mathcal{A}$ represents the primary structure by which every adjacency matrix "slice" $\mathcal{A}^d \in \{0, 1\}^{n \times n}$ is indexed. An MRN actually contains *homogeneous* nodes but *heterogeneous* relations, which is different with the multi-mode network or the heterogeneous network [28]. Figure 4.1 illustrates the difference between the MRN and the multi-mode network. Although much research has been done on discovering communities from static or dynamic multi-mode networks [24, 27, 28], the scope of this chapter is limited to community detection from MRNs.

Since nodes in an MRN are homogeneous, the problem of discovering communities on MRNs is similar to that on SRNs. That is, community detection aims to find a good K-way partition $\mathcal{P} = \{C_1, \ldots, C_K\}$, where C_k is the kth community, and $C_1 \bigcup \cdots \bigcup C_K \subseteq V$. K can either be given in advance or determined by the community detection algorithm itself. For a crisp partition, we have an additional requirement: $C_k \bigcap C_{k'} = \emptyset \ \forall \ k \ne k'$. However, for a overlapping or fuzzy partition, overlapping communities can be represented as a membership matrix $\mathbf{U} = [u_{i,k}], i = 1, \ldots, n, k = 1, \ldots, K$, where $0 \le u_{i,k} \le 1$ denotes the membership that node i belongs to C_k. If node i belongs to only one community, $u_{i,k} = 1$, and it clearly follows that $\sum_{k=1}^{K} u_{i,k} = 1$ for all $1 \le i \le n$.

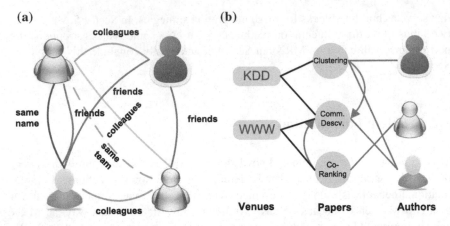

Fig. 4.1 Illustration of the difference between MRN and MMN. **a** The multi-relational network. **b** The multi-mode network

4.3 Generalized Modularity Optimization

The choice of null model is a crucial consideration for modularity definition and thus for community detection. In the early literature, many null models have been proposed for modularity definition in the SRNs, among which, Newman-Girvan's [19] is the most used and best known one. The basic idea behind Newman-Girvan's null model is that a random graph is not expected to have a community structure, so the possible existence of communities is revealed by the comparison between the intra-community edge weight and that expected at random. Other null models for the SRNs along this line can be found in [1, 11, 16]. However, such null models have not been available for MRNs.

Figure 4.2 shows such an example with a typical MRN defined by coupling multiple adjacency matrices, where the connections encoded by the network "slices" are flexible; they can represent variations across time, variations across different types of connections, or even community detection of the same network at different scales. Let $\mathcal{A}_{i,j}^d$ represent the intra-slice coupling that connect node i and node j in slice d, and $\mathcal{C}_i^{d,r}$ indicate the inter-slice coupling that connect node i in slice r to itself in slice d. As these inter-slice couplings are either present or absent by definition, when they do fall inside communities, their contribution in count of intra-community edges exactly cancels that expected at random. Therefore, the usual null models fails to provide any contribution from these inter-slice couplings. In contrast, by formulating a null model in terms of stability of communities under Laplacian dynamics, one can derive a principled generalization of community detection to MRNs [18].

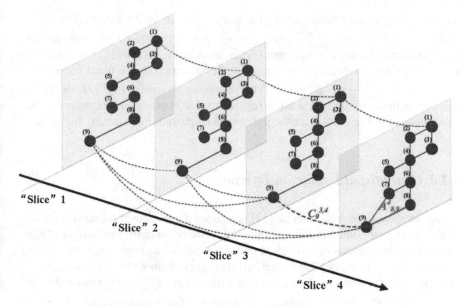

Fig. 4.2 An example of MRN defined by coupling four network "slices"

4.3.1 Laplacian Dynamics Formalism

The Laplacian dynamics formalism, which has been recently developed by Lambiotte et al. [13], is to rederive network modularity from the continuous-time normalized Laplacian dynamics $\dot{p}_i = \sum_j \frac{1}{k_j} \mathcal{A}_{i,j} p_j - p_i$ on a unipartite, undirected network defined by the adjacency matrix components $\mathcal{A}_{i,j}$ with node strengths $k_i = \sum_j \mathcal{A}_{i,j}$. Note that there is a steady state given by $p_j^* = k_j/(2m)$, where $2m = \sum_i k_i = \sum_{i,j} \mathcal{A}_{i,j}$, describes the total strength in the network. So the stability of communities under such dynamics can be measured by directly comparing the joint probability at stationarity of independent appearances at nodes i and j with the linear approximate map from node j to node i. Under the guidance of this direction, Lambiotte et al. quantified a measure of the stability $R(t)$ of a specified partition of the network into communities using the probability that a random walker remains within the same community after time t, in statistically steady conditions, relative to that expected under independence. Given the operator $L_{i,j} = \mathcal{A}_{i,j}/k_j - \delta_{i,j}$ of the dynamics, where $\delta_{i,j}$ is the Kronecker delta, the stability $R(t)$ is defined as following:

$$R(t) = \sum_{i,j} \left[(e^{t\mathbf{L}})_{i,j} p_j^* - p_i^* p_j^* \right] \delta(g_i, g_j), \tag{4.2}$$

where $p_i^* p_j^*$ denotes the contribution from an independence assumption. Expanding the matrix exponential in Eq. (4.2) to first-order in t, we have $(e^{t\mathbf{L}})_{i,j} \simeq \delta_{i,j} + t L_{i,j}$.

As $\delta_{i,j}$ factors always contribute to the sum, $R(t)$ can be directly yielded to the quality function $Q(t) = \frac{1}{2m} \sum_{i,j} [t\mathcal{A}_{i,j} - \frac{k_i k_j}{2m}]\delta(g_i, g_j)$. When $t = 1$, the resulting quality function reduces to Newman-Girvan modularity. Moreover, if both sides of the equation are divided by t, the quality can be written in the usual form: $Q = \frac{1}{2m} \sum_{i,j} [\mathcal{A}_{i,j} - \gamma \frac{k_i k_j}{2m}]\delta(g_i, g_j)$, with the resolution parameter $\gamma = 1/t$. Hence, the stability of the community partition relative to that expected under independence provides a natural definition for the null model employed in the quality function.

4.3.2 Generalized Laplacian Dynamics

Along the above line, Mucha et al. [18] developed a generalized framework of network quality functions that allowed us to study the community structure of MRNs, which are combinations of individual networks coupled through links that connect each node in one network slice to itself in other slices. Without loss of generality, we restricted our attention to undirected network slices (i.e., $\mathcal{A}_{i,j}^d = \mathcal{A}_{j,i}^d$) and undirected couplings (i.e., $C_i^{d,r} = C_i^{r,d}$). Notating the strengths of each node individually in each slice by $k_{i,d} = \sum_i \mathcal{A}_{i,j}^d$, and across slices by $c_{i,d} = \sum_r C_i^{d,r}$. Thus, the multi-slice strength of the node is given by $\kappa_{i,d} = k_{i,d} + c_{i,d}$, and the continuous-time Laplacian dynamics is defined as

$$\dot{p}_{i,d} = \sum_{jr} \frac{\left(\mathcal{A}_{i,j}^d \delta_{d,r} + \delta_{i,j} C_j^{d,r}\right) p_{j,r}}{\kappa_{j,r}} - p_{i,d}, \tag{4.3}$$

which respects the intra-slice nature of $\mathcal{A}_{i,j}^d$ and the inter-slice couplings of $C_j^{d,r}$. The steady state in such case is $p_{j,r}^* = \kappa_{j,r}/(\sum_{j,r} \kappa_{j,r})$. Thus, the associated multi-slice null model can be specified by the probability $\rho_{i,d|j,r}$ of sampling node-slice (i, d) conditional on whether the multi-slice structure allows one to step from node-slice (j, r) to node-slice (i, d).

$$\rho_{i,d|j,r} p_{j,r}^* = \left[\frac{k_{i,d}}{2m_d} \frac{k_{j,r}}{\kappa_{j,r}} \delta_{d,r} + \frac{C_j^{d,r}}{c_{jr}} \frac{c_{j,r}}{\kappa_{j,r}} \delta_{i,j}\right] \frac{\kappa_{j,r}}{\sum_{j,r} \kappa_{j,r}}, \tag{4.4}$$

where $m_d = \sum_i k_{i,d}$. That is, the conditional probability of stepping from (j, r) to (i, d) along an inter-slice coupling is nonzero if $i = j$, and it is proportional to the probability $C_j^{d,r}/k_{j,r}$ of selecting the precise inter-slice link that connects to slice d. Subtracting this conditional joint probability from the linear approximation of the exponential describing the Laplacian dynamics on MRNs, a multi-slice generalization of modularity can be obtained as follows.

$$Q_{MRN} = \frac{1}{\sum_{j,r} \kappa_{j,r}} \sum_{i,j,d,r} \left[\left(A_{i,j,d} - \gamma_d \frac{k_{i,d}k_{j,d}}{2m_d} \right) \delta_{d,r} + \delta_{i,j} C_j^{d,r} \right] \delta(g_{i,d}, g_{j,r}).$$

(4.5)

Some notable remarks for Eq. (4.5) should be highlighted. First, the corresponding resolution parameter for the inter-slice couplings is absorbed into the magnitude of the elements of $C_j^{d,r}$, which is a binary value in $\{0, w\}$. $w = 0$ indicates there is no benefit from extending communities across slices, and therefore the optimal partition is obtained from independent optimization of the corresponding quality function in each slice. Otherwise, when w becomes sufficiently large, the quality-optimizing partitions force the community assignment of a node to remain the same across all slices in which that node appears, and the multi-slice quality reduces to a difference between the adjacency matrix summed over the contributions from the individual slices and the sum over the separate single-slice null models.

Second, a re-weighting technique was used in conditional probabilities, which allows for different resolutions γ_d in each slice. In the absence of such a re-weighting in the interpretation of the stability of the partition, with $\gamma_d = \gamma$ for all d, the corresponding prefactor on $C_j^{d,r}$ absorbed above is $(1 - \gamma)$. Imposing the choice $\gamma = 1$ then recovered the usual interpretation of modularity as a count of the total weight of intra-slice edges minus the weight expected at random, and the specified deterministic $C_j^{d,r}$ contribution was dropped out entirely.

Community discovery in MRNs can then proceed using many of the same computational heuristics that are currently available for single-relational networks. During this process, one may exert special caution about the resolution of communities and the likelihood of complex quality landscapes that necessitate caution in interpreting results on real-world networks.

4.4 Co-Ranking Frameworks

With multi-typed interactions, the community structures hidden in MRNs can be complicated. Integrating information from multiple dimensions for community discovery has become the dominant method [6, 7, 32, 34]. In this section, we first overview three integration strategies, i.e., network integration, utility integration, and feature integration, and thus point out that the key issue in these integration strategies is how to rank the weight for every relation. We then introduce two kinds of co-ranking frameworks (i.e., MultiRank and MutuRank) as a complemental technique to integration methods.

4.4.1 Integration Methods: An Overview

Without loss of generality, let a three-way tensor $S = [s_{i,j,d}]$, $1 \leq i, j \leq n$, $1 \leq d \leq m$ denote the information/object to be integrated. For network integration, $S = A$ is the m-relational edge set. For utility integration, S consists of m utility matrices, which is equivalent to optimizing the objective function over all types of interactions simultaneously [26]. For feature integration, S denotes structural features associated with nodes, commonly extracted by overlapping community detection methods from each relation. If we further let $\vec{p} = [p_1, p_2, \ldots, p_n]$ and $\vec{q} = [q_1, q_2, \ldots, q_m]$ denote vectors representing the importance weights of nodes and relations on an MRN, respectively. The synthesized weight matrix $W = [w_{i,j}]$ can be calculated as follows.

$$w_{i,j} = \sum_{d=1}^{m} q_d \cdot s_{i,j,d}. \tag{4.6}$$

The key task in the integration is to determine the weight vector of relations $\vec{q}$. The simplest way used in [6, 7, 26] modeled $\vec{q}$ as an uniform distribution, i.e., $q_d = \frac{1}{m}$, which obviously failed to distinguish different roles played by various relations. If the network is single-relational, several well-known algorithms such as HITS [12] and PageRank [21] can be applied to rank the importance of nodes, i.e., to compute $\vec{p}$. As the network become multi-relational, nodes and relations exert mutual influences to each other, and people need to co-rank both nodes and relations simultaneously. To address this challenge, two kinds of co-ranking algorithms MultiRank [20] and MutuRank [32, 34] have been presented. Before diving into the algorithmic details, we have to introduce some basic operations and definitions. Let $\mathbb{R}$ be the real field. We define two vectors $A\vec{p}\vec{q} \in \mathbb{R}^n$ and $A\vec{p}\vec{p'} \in \mathbb{R}^m$ as

$$(A\vec{p}\vec{q})_i = \sum_{j=1}^{n} \sum_{d=1}^{m} a_{i,j,d} \cdot p_j \cdot q_d, \quad i = 1, 2, \ldots, n, \tag{4.7}$$

$$(A\vec{p}\vec{p'})_d = \sum_{i=1}^{n} \sum_{j=1}^{n} a_{i,j,d} \cdot p_i \cdot p'_j, \quad d = 1, 2, \ldots, m. \tag{4.8}$$

As we imagine a random walk applied on an MRN, we can construct two transition probability tensors $O = [o_{i,j,d}]$ and $R = [r_{i,j,d}]$ with respect to objects and relations by normalizing the entries of A as follows [20]:

$$o_{i,j,d} = \frac{a_{i,j,d}}{\sum_{l=1}^{n} a_{l,j,d}}, \quad r_{i,j,d} = \frac{a_{i,j,d}}{\sum_{e=1}^{m} a_{i,j,e}}. \tag{4.9}$$

Figure 4.3a illustrates the construction of O and R based upon A. To be specific, tensors O and R have same orders with A, where $o_{i,j,d}$ is normalized by the ith row in dth relation and $r_{i,j,d}$ is normalized by the vertical line fixed by i and j. Let X_t

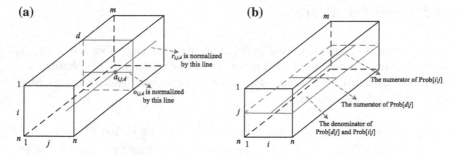

Fig. 4.3 Illustration of some variables in MutiRank and MutuRank. **a** Tensors $\mathcal{O}$ and $\mathcal{R}$. **b** Conditional probabilities

and Y_t be random variables referring to visit at any particular node and to use any particular relation respectively at the time t. We have:

$$o_{i,j,d} = \text{Prob}[X_t = i | X_{t-1} = j, Y_t = d], \qquad (4.10)$$

$$r_{i,j,d} = \text{Prob}[Y_t = d | X_t = i, X_{t-1} = j]. \qquad (4.11)$$

Clearly, the sequence of random variables $(X_t, Y_t : t = 0, 1, \ldots)$ is a Markov chain. The co-ranking algorithms try to compute the following probabilities with respect to two transition probability tensors $\mathcal{O}$ and $\mathcal{R}$.

$$\text{Prob}[X_t = i] = \sum_{j=1}^{n} \sum_{d=1}^{m} o_{i,j,d} \cdot \text{Prob}[X_{t-1} = j, Y_t = d], \qquad (4.12)$$

$$\text{Prob}[Y_t = d] = \sum_{i=1}^{n} \sum_{j=1}^{n} r_{i,j,d} \cdot \text{Prob}[X_t = i, X_{t-1} = j]. \qquad (4.13)$$

Therefore, $\vec{p}$ and $\vec{q}$ are equilibrium/stationary distributions of nodes and relations. The most important property of the stationary distributions is that if the network M is non-bipartite, then the distributions of X_t and Y_t tend to stationary distributions, as $t \to \infty$. Formally, we have:

$$p_i = \lim_{t \to \infty} \text{Prob}(X_t = i), \quad q_d = \lim_{t \to \infty} \text{Prob}(Y_t = d).$$

From above analysis, we can summarize that to compute two joint probability distributions $\text{Prob}[X_{t-1} = j, Y_t = d]$ and $\text{Prob}[X_t = i, X_{t-1} = j]$ becomes the key operation for determining the stationary distributions $\vec{p}$ and $\vec{q}$. For this, MultiRank and MutuRank have presented different solutions, which will be introduced in the following sub-sections.

4.4.2 MultiRank Algorithm

The important assumption in MultiRank [20] is that two random variables (i.e., X_t and Y_t) are independent from each other. Two joint probability distributions can therefore be modeled as a product form of individual probability distributions. More precisely, MultiRank assumed that

$$\text{Prob}[X_{t-1} = j, Y_t = d] = \text{Prob}[X_{t-1} = j] \cdot \text{Prob}[Y_t = d], \qquad (4.14)$$
$$\text{Prob}[X_t = i, X_{t-1} = j] = \text{Prob}[X_{t-1} = j] \cdot \text{Prob}[X_t = i]. \qquad (4.15)$$

Under this assumption, Eqs. (4.12) and (4.13) can be written as the iteration form with respect to t.

$$p_i^{(t+1)} = \sum_{j=1}^{n} \sum_{d=1}^{m} o_{i,j,d} \cdot p_j^{(t)} \cdot q_d^{(t)}, \qquad (4.16)$$

$$q_d^{(t+1)} = \sum_{i=1}^{n} \sum_{j=1}^{n} r_{i,j,d} \cdot p_i^{(t)} \cdot p_j^{(t)}. \qquad (4.17)$$

We can see from Eqs. (4.16) and (4.17) that the MultiRank makes full use of the mutual influence between relations and nodes. Specifically, the mutual feedback here means that: (i) the importance of a relation depends on the probability distribution of nodes and the importance of other relations, i.e., a relation, selected by high-weight nodes with high probabilities, deserves high weight itself; (ii) the importance of a node depends on the probability distribution of relations and its neighbors' importance, i.e., a node, linked by high-weight nodes with strong and high-weight relations, deserves high-weight. By using the tensor operation shown in Eqs. (4.7) and (4.8), we can represent Eqs. (4.16) and (4.17) in a concise manner, i.e., matrix notations.

$$\overrightarrow{p^{(t+1)}} = \mathcal{O}\overrightarrow{p^{(t)}}\overrightarrow{q^{(t)}}, \quad \overrightarrow{q^{(t+1)}} = \mathcal{R}\overrightarrow{p^{(t)}}\overrightarrow{p^{(t)}}. \qquad (4.18)$$

According to Eq. (4.18), an iterative algorithm can naturally be designed to compute $\overrightarrow{p}$ and $\overrightarrow{q}$ for the MultiRank. It starts by assigning random values as $\overrightarrow{p^{(0)}}$ and $\overrightarrow{q^{(0)}}$, and then applies iterative computation based on Eq. (4.18) until the Frobenius norm converges to a tolerance value.

4.4.3 MutuRank Algorithm

The assumption that X_t and Y_t are independent from each other in MultiRank might be too strong. However, the distributions of nodes and relations are actually coupled together. We therefore propose to use the conditional probability for modeling two joint probability distributions [32, 34].

$$\text{Prob}[X_{t-1} = j, Y_t = d] = \text{Prob}[X_{t-1} = j] \cdot \text{Prob}[Y_t = d|X_{t-1} = j], \quad (4.19)$$

$$\text{Prob}[X_t = i, X_{t-1} = j] = \text{Prob}[X_{t-1} = j] \cdot \text{Prob}[X_t = i|X_{t-1} = j]. \quad (4.20)$$

Given a node j, the probabilities for selecting the dth relation, and for transiting from j to its neighbor i are as follows. Figure 4.3b shows the computations of two conditional probabilities in three-way tensor.

$$\text{Prob}[Y_t = d|X_{t-1} = j] = \text{Prob}[d|j] = \frac{q_d \cdot \sum_{l=1}^{n} a_{j,l,d}}{\sum_{l=1}^{n} \sum_{d=1}^{m} q_d \cdot a_{j,l,d}}, \quad (4.21)$$

$$\text{Prob}[X_t = i|X_{t-1} = j] = \text{Prob}[i|j] = \frac{\sum_{d=1}^{m} q_d \cdot a_{j,i,d}}{\sum_{l=1}^{n} \sum_{d=1}^{m} q_d \cdot a_{j,l,d}}. \quad (4.22)$$

Therefore, by using conditional probabilities, Eqs. (4.12) and (4.13) become:

$$p_i^{(t+1)} = \sum_{j=1}^{n} \sum_{d=1}^{m} p_j^{(t)} \cdot o_{i,j,d} \cdot \frac{q_d^{(t)} \cdot \sum_{l=1}^{n} a_{j,l,d}}{\sum_{l=1}^{n} \sum_{d=1}^{m} q_d^{(t)} \cdot a_{j,l,d}}, \quad (4.23)$$

$$q_d^{(t+1)} = \sum_{i=1}^{n} \sum_{j=1}^{n} p_j^{(t)} \cdot r_{i,j,d} \cdot \frac{\sum_{d=1}^{m} q_d^{(t)} \cdot a_{j,i,d}}{\sum_{l=1}^{n} \sum_{d=1}^{m} q_d^{(t)} \cdot a_{j,l,d}}. \quad (4.24)$$

The iterative form of MutuRank shown in Eqs. (4.23) and (4.24) seemed somewhat complicated. However, similar to any random walk model, we also can represent MutuRank using concise matrix notations. To this end, we have to define two auxiliary matrixes $\mathbf{V} = [\vec{V}_j]_{m \times 1}$ and $\mathbf{U} = [\vec{U}_j]_{n \times 1}$, $j = 1, \ldots, n$. $\mathbf{V}$ and $\mathbf{U}$ are $n \times m$ and $n \times m$ dimensional, and they are represented by $nm \times 1$ dimensional vectors $\vec{V}_j$ and $n \times 1$ dimensional vectors $\vec{U}_j$, respectively. $\vec{V}_j = [v_{j,d}]$ and $\vec{U}_j = [u_{j,i}]$ are defined as:

$$v_{j,d} = q_d \cdot \sum_{l=1}^{n} s_{j,l,d}, \quad u_{j,i} = \sum_{d=1}^{m} q_d \cdot s_{j,i,d}.$$

If we let $\mathbf{V}$ and $\mathbf{U}$ be row-normalized, we have:

$$\text{Prob}(Y_t = d|X_{t-1} = j) = v_{j,d}, \quad \text{Prob}(X_t = i|X_{t-1} = j) = u_{j,i}.$$

Under the tensor operations, Eqs. (4.23) and (4.24) can be simplified as:

$$\overrightarrow{p^{(t+1)}} = \mathcal{O}\overrightarrow{p^{(t)}}\mathbf{V}, \quad \overrightarrow{q^{(t+1)}} = \mathcal{R}\overrightarrow{p^{(t)}}\mathbf{U}. \quad (4.25)$$

Obviously, $\overrightarrow{p}$ and $\overrightarrow{q}$ of the MutuRank also can be computed by an iterative algorithm being similar to MultiRank.

4.5 Partition Integration

If we consider a MRN as m independent single-relational network, we can utilize any community detection method on every slice. As the community partition of each slice is ready, partition integration takes effect, and it targets at assembling multiple community partitions as a consensus single community partition. In this section, we introduce two different kinds of method for partition integration.

4.5.1 Frequent Itemsets Mining Based Method

Berlingerio et al. [4] devised a novel algorithm named frequent pAttern mining-BAsed Community discoverer in mUltidimensional networkS (ABACUS for short) for partition integration. ABACUS is able to extract communities from MRNs based on frequent closed itemsets mining from single-relational community memberships.

The key to understand ABACUS is how to use *transaction model* to represent the results of community partition on each slice. The transaction model builds the bridge from partition integration to frequent itemsets mining. In ABACUS, each transaction, i.e., a record in the transaction database, corresponds to a node, where an item is a pair *(dimension, community)*, expressing the membership of the node in the various dimensions. In the field of association analysis, frequent closed itemsets provide a minimal representation of itemsets without losing their support information. An itemset X is closed if none of its immediate supersets has exactly the same support count as X [25]. Therefore, under the transaction model adopted by ABACUS, a frequent closed itemset consists of a set of nodes, and it represents nodes in this itemset are frequently grouped together in different slices. As the support count of an itemset exceeds a pre-defined threshold, nodes in this itemset are extracted as a community.

Consider a simple MRN with six nodes and three relations. After the community partition of each slice is ready, the lattice view of pattern mining in ABACUS is shown in Fig. 4.4. "TID" corresponds to the node ID, and each item corresponds to a community. For instance, "A=VLDB-1" represents the #1 community in "VLDB" relation. The mined frequent closed itemsets shown in dotted-lined rectangles are communities extracted by ABACUS. For example, nodes 1, 2 and 3 share their memberships to the communities "VLDB-2" and "KDD-1", which implies they are closely interrelated.

Although the pattern mining method is novel and enlightening, it leaves us too many research issues. On the one hand, a large number of studies pointed out that the frequent patterns [8, 25, 33], i.e., itemsets, are not always interesting, such as the

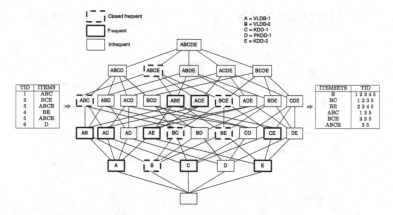

Fig. 4.4 An illustration example for ABACUS

famous "coffee–tea" example. Also, interesting patterns might always infrequent. A set of well-accepted criteria were established for evaluating the interestingness of patterns, such as lift, cosine, All-confidence, etc., but as a pattern describes a set of nodes in social networks, how to measure the interestingness from the community perspective, and thus how to mine them in an efficient manner deserve the deep research. On the other hand, patterns are always nested and most of them may be very small. So, how to exploit patterns to discover communities with rationale size, or even to reveal hierarchical community structures also deserved the future research.

4.5.2 Consensus Clustering Based Method

Consensus clustering, also known as cluster ensemble or clustering aggregation, aims to find a single partitioning of data from multiple existing basic partitionings [10, 14, 31]. In the literature, lots of consensus clustering algorithms have been proposed, such as the graph-based methods [23], the co-association matrix-based methods [10], the K-means-based methods [31], and other heuristic approaches [9]. However, most research on consensus clustering focused on text data, and few attentions have been paid to exploiting consensus clustering for community discovery on graph data.

Recently, Lancichinetti and Fortunato [15] proposed the Algorithm which Integrates Consensus Clustering in a given community detection Method (AICCM for short) on *single-relational networks*. Consensus clustering is used by AICCM to enhance the quality and robustness of any given community detection method. We introduce the main idea of AICCM by an example as shown in Fig. 4.5. First, it employed a given community detection method for several times to obtain several basic partitionings, e.g., (1)–(4) in the left part of Fig. 4.5. Second, it assembled all

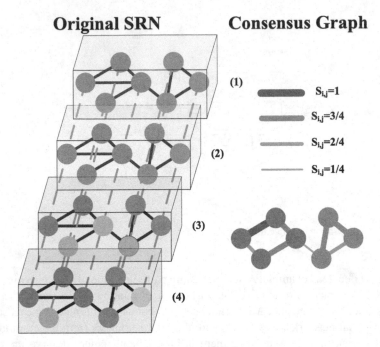

Fig. 4.5 An illustration example for the consensus graph

basic partitionings to get an overall similarity matrix S. Let $H^d \in \{0, 1\}^{n \times k^d}$, $1 \leq d \leq m$ denote a binary membership indicator matrix of a basic partitioning. S is computed as

$$S = \frac{1}{m}HH^T = \frac{1}{m}\sum_{d=1}^{m} H^d (H^d)^T. \qquad (4.26)$$

The similarity matrix S can be regraded as an adjacent matrix of a weighted consensus graph illustrated on the right part of Fig. 4.5, where the thickness of each edge is proportional to its weight. In the consensus graph the cluster structure of the original network is more visible: the two communities have become "weak" cliques, with "heavy" edges, whereas the connections between them are quite weak. Interestingly, this improvement has been achieved despite the absence of two inaccurate partitions H^3 and H^4. After that, AICCM again applies the same algorithm on this consensus graph four times to acquire four partitions. If the partitions are all equal, stop; otherwise, repeat the above steps.

Applying consensus clustering for partition integration on MRNs is straightforward, when we take the basic partition H^d as the results of community detection on dth relation. In [26], three graph-based methods [23], including Cluster-based Similarity Partitioning Algorithm (CSPA), HyperGraph-Partitioning Algorithm (HGPA), and Meta-CLustering Algorithm (MCLA), have been used for partition integration.

CSPA first assemble basic partitionings as a consensus graph being same as AICCM, and then apply any community detection method on that graph. HGPA is to repartition the data using the given clusters as indications of strong bonds, and to formulate consensus clustering as the hypergraph partitioning problem. Analogously, MCLA is to group and collapse related hyperedges, and thus to assign each object to the collapsed hyperedge in which it participates most strongly. The hyperedges that are considered related for the purpose of collapsing are determined by a graph-based clustering of hyperedges.

Despite of much above-mentioned research efforts, some research issues still exist. The computed similarity matrix by CSPA is usually much denser, which would make the application of any clustering algorithm computationally expensive. HGPA may be not appropriate if the natural MRN data clusters are highly imbalanced. Moreover, MCLA is more data-dependent, i.e., performing poorly on some benchmark datasets [29]. Meanwhile, the efficiency is always a major concern of consensus clustering, since it is a combinatorial optimization problem in essence. Therefore, when facing graph data especially big graph data, how to design both effective and efficient consensus clustering algorithms for partition integration remains a great challenge.

4.6 Experimental Networks

Over the past few decades, a large amount of real-world single-relational networks have been published, containing from hundreds of nodes to millions of nodes. A typical network repository is Stanford large network dataset collection (http://snap. stanford.edu/data/). However, the public real-world datasets for MRNs are absolutely rare. To the best of our knowledge, only one dataset named 3T [17] containing multiple social relationships was collected directly from people's daily life, but unfortunately, it is now not public to researchers due to privacy concerns. There are commonly two ways for researchers to construct MRNs to validate their new methods or algorithms: using the synthetic data, and constructing MRNs based on attribute values collected from the real-world websites [4, 6, 7, 20, 28, 32].

The synthetic data is usually simple and relatively smaller, but the ground-truth is known, which enables researchers to utilize it for basic performance comparison. Otherwise, MRNs constructed on real-world attributes are often complex and large, but the ground-truth is unknown. Thus, the internal measures and semantic information are often used for performance validation. The DBLP is the most used dataset for constructing the MRN. Some MRNs can be directly crawled from websites, such as YouTube used in [28]. In this section, we introduce the technique for constructing the MRN on DBLP data, which can also be applied to other similar data. Then, we discuss how to construct MRNs based on forum data.

4.6.1 Constructing MRN on DBLP Data

The DBLP becomes the most popular data for performance validation in MRN research field due to the following reasons. First, the semantic of authors is clear. For example, Jiawei Han is a well-accepted authority in data mining. Second, the categories associated with conferences and papers are easier to be obtained. One typical source for rankings and categories of authoritative conferences in computer science is the website (http://webdocs.cs.ualberta.ca/~zaiane/htmldocs/ConfRanking.html).

Publication information on DBLP includes title, authors, reference list (i.e., citations), conference/journal name, abstract, and classification categories. Based upon these attributes, many kinds of different MRNs can be constructed. In community discovery, nodes often correspond to authors, and multiple relations often correspond to categories such as data mining, databases, multimedia, and so on. Thus, the attributes can be used usually include the publication number of every author on every category, or citations of an author through a category. So, the key task of constructing a MRN is how to compute the weight between author in each category, i.e., relation. Let $p_{i,d}$ and $p_{j,d}$ denote the attribute values of two researchers i and j on dth category. Tensor $\mathcal{A}$ is computed as [6, 7]

$$\mathcal{A}^d_{i,j} = e^{-(p_{i,d}-p_{j,d})^2}. \tag{4.27}$$

A variant of Eq. (4.27) is presented in [32].

$$\mathcal{A}^d_{i,j} = e^{-\left(\frac{2(p_{i,d}-p_{j,d})}{p_{i,d}+p_{j,d}}\right)^2}. \tag{4.28}$$

Although using the difference value to measure the relation strength in MRN is widely-used, it may not reflect the truth in some cases. For instance, node i is an famous expert who has published a great many papers in a category, and node j is i's student who published few papers. Thus, according to Eq. (4.27) or (4.28), the relation strength between i and j is weak, but they are strongly connected in the real world. So, how to define the relation strength (or similarity) based on attributes remains an important issue to be solved. Despite of this, it is interesting to use this technique to transform multivariate UCI datasets with ground-truth to MRNs. For example, the Iris dataset has 4 attributes and 150 instances, and it is used to construct a MRN with 150 nodes and 4 relations by computing the relation strength between instances on every relations.

4.6.2 Constructing MRN on Forum Data

Online forums (e.g., Google Groups, HardForum, and Tianya) are appealing places for members of which to communicate due to their openness and freedom.

Generally, forum data include two categories: the initial article and the reply article. The initial article is the initiator/organizer of a topic, while a reply article comments on an initial article or another reply article so as to continue the discussion. Therefore, given an initial article (i.e., a topic), lots of forum users will be involved into discussion (i.e., interactions) under that topic. These interactions are indicated by the replier ID, recipient ID, reply time, and the content contained in each reply article. Mining text data about discussion articles can reveal multiple hidden interactions between users, which implicitly forms a MRN.

We have conducted some initial research on forum data processing (e.g., Tianya). In particular, we presented several kinds of measurement models for various interactions between users, including undirected dense/sparse (UDN/USN), interest(IN), emotion(EN) and similar view networks(SVN) [5, 35], which can be used to constructed a MRN on forum data. According to community discovery and evaluation on each dimension, we obtained some interesting findings. First, though community structures are not very clear on interest and similar view dimensions, users in the same group tend to have similar interests or consistent perspectives. Second, the emotional dimension played the most important role among multiple relations, on which the identified communities are strongly segregated with each other. This implies the emotional information on forum can better guide the community discovery.

Here, we introduce a possible way for constructing MRNs using the data from Tianya, a popular bulletin-board service in China. Let each node in the MRN $i \subseteq V$ corresponds to a registered user ID on Tianya forum, and each edge $(i, j) \subseteq \mathbb{E}$ represents a specific interaction mined from users' comment activities. Also, Let $n_{i,j}$ be the number of times that user i writes a comment to user j.

We construct a five-relational network using the data from Tianya, a popular bulletin-board service in China. Every registered user identification (ID) in Tianya forum corresponds to a node $i \subseteq V$ in a MRN. Edges $(i, j) \subseteq \mathbb{E}$ represent some social relations between two users that results Tensor $\mathcal{A}$ is computed as

$$
\mathcal{A}_{i,j}^d = \begin{cases}
n_{i,j} + n_{j,i} & if (i, j) \in E_{UDN} \\
\min(n_{i,j}, n_{j,i}) & if (i, j) \in E_{USN} \\
\sum_{p \subseteq P_{i,j}} \min(n_{i,p}, n_{j,p}) & if (i, j) \in E_{IN} \\
trust_{i,j} & if (i, j) \in E_{EN} \\
AC_{i,j} & if (i, j) \in E_{SVN}
\end{cases}
\tag{4.29}
$$

where $P_{i,j}$ is the set of users to whom user i and j together comment. The sign of a given comment can be defined as positive or negative based on the average semantic orientation of seed emotional words in the review [30]. If we use $E_{i,j,k}$ to represent the emotion value of kth reply from user i to j, the "trust" between user i and user j, $trust_{i,j}$, can be defined as

$$
trust_{i,j} = \frac{\sum_{k=1}^{n_{i,j}} E_{i,j,k} + \sum_{k=1}^{n_{j,i}} E_{j,i,k}}{n_{i,j} + n_{j,i}},
\tag{4.30}
$$

Bu et al. [5] further indicated that the similar user pair should have similar interests and consistent perspectives to most topics they participate together. So, the attitude consistency of user i and j, $AC_{i,j}$ is defined as:

$$AC_{i,j} = \frac{\sum_{t \subseteq T_{i,j}} \sum_{p \subseteq P_{i,j}^t} \sigma(\xi_{i,p}^t, \xi_{j,p}^t)}{\sum_{t \subseteq T_{i,j}} card(P_{i,j}^t)}, \tag{4.31}$$

where $\xi_{i,p}^t$ is the perspective from user i to user p under the topic t. $P_{i,j}^t$ is a user set, it includes the users to whom user i and j together comment in the discussion of topic t. $T_{i,j}$ is a topic set, it includes the topics which are together discussed by user i and j. $card(\cdot)$ returns the total number of users in the user set. And $\sigma(x, y)$ is a judgment function determined by x and y, which obeys:

$$\sigma(x, y) = \begin{cases} 1 & \text{if } x > 0.5, \ y > 0.5 \text{ or } x < 0.5, \ y < 0.5 \\ 0 & \text{otherwise} \end{cases} \tag{4.32}$$

The range of $AC_{i,j}$ is between 0 and 1, and a higher value corresponds to a greater degree of attitude consistency of the given user pair to their together-reply topics/users.

Figure 4.6a shows a tree structure corresponding to a small thread of depth 4. Labels denote the user who writes the contribution and valid comments are shown within the gray region. The post triggers three responses from users A, C and D.

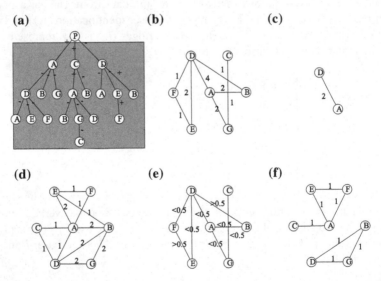

Fig. 4.6 An illustration example for the Tianya MRN. **a** An example of discussion list. **b** Undirected dense network. **c** Undirected sparse network. **d** Interest network. **e** Emotion network. **f** Similar view network

At the second nesting level, eight comments appear. At the third level, there are still seven comments and finally, there is one last comment from C. The attitude of every comment can be represented using $+$ or $-$, with $+$ denoting a user is supportive to the viewpoint and $-$ otherwise. The corresponding undirected dense/sparse, interest, emotion and similar view networks excavated from original thread of comments are shown in Fig. 4.6b–f respectively. The weight attached to each edge represents the strength of connections between the corresponding members.

4.7 Summary

This chapter defined the community discovery problem on multi-relational networks and reviewed representative research on this problem. We start by introducing the generalized modularity of the MRN, which paves the way for applying modularity optimization-based community detection methods on MRNs. According to the classification of the mainstream method—integration methods, including network integration, utility integration, feature integration, and partition integration. We introduced several co-ranking frameworks on MRNs, which could learn the biased weights of every relations for more precise integrations. We then discussed two typical methods for the partition integration, including frequent itemsets mining based method and consensus clustering based method. Last but not the least, due to the lack of real-world MRNs, we presented several techniques for constructing the MRN based on both multivariate data and forum data. This provides operational and practical experimental techniques to MRN-related research.

Acknowledgments This research was partially supported by the National Natural Science Foundation of China (NSFC) under Grants 71571093, 71372188 and 61502222, National Center for International Joint Research on E-Business Information Processing under Grant 2013B01035, National Key Technologies R&D Program of China under Grant 2013BAH16F01, National Soft Science Research Program under Grant 2013GXS4B081, the Program of Natural Science Foundation of Zhejiang Province under Grant LY13F020008, the Ministry of Education of Humanities and Social Sciences Project under Grant 14YJCZH235, Industry Projects in Jiangsu S&T Pillar Program under Grants BE2014141 and BE2012185, and Key/Surface Project of Natural Science Research in Jiangsu Provincial Colleges and Universities under Grants 12KJA520001, 14KJA520001, 15KJB520012 and 14KJB520015.

References

1. Barber MJ (2007) Modularity and community detection in bipartite networks. Phys Rev E 76(6):066102
2. Berlingerio M, Coscia M, Giannotti F (2011) Finding and characterizing communities in multidimensional networks. In: ASONAM. IEEE Computer Society, pp 490–494
3. Berlingerio M, Coscia M, Giannotti F, Monreale A, Pedreschi D (2013) Multidimensional networks: foundations of structural analysis. World Wide Web 16(5–6):567–593

4. Berlingerio M, Pinelli F, Calabrese F (2013) Abacus: frequent pattern mining-based community discovery in multidimensional networks. Data Min Knowl Discov 27(3):294–320
5. Bu Z, Zhang C, Xia Z, Wang J (2013) A fast parallel modularity optimization algorithm (FPMQA) for community detection in online social network. Knowl-Based Syst 50:246–259
6. Cai D, Shao Z, He X, Yan X, Han J (2005) Community mining from multi-relational networks. In: Knowledge discovery in databases: PKDD 2005. Springer, pp 445–452
7. Cai D, Shao Z, He X, Yan X, Han J (2005) Mining hidden community in heterogeneous social networks. In: Proceedings of the 3rd international workshop on link discovery. ACM, pp 58–65
8. Cao J, Wu Z, Wu J (2014) Scaling up cosine interesting pattern discovery: a depth-first method. Inf Sci 57(5):1–12
9. Fischer B, Buhmann JM (2003) Path-based clustering for grouping of smooth curves and texture segmentation. IEEE Trans Pattern Anal Mach Intell 25(4):513–518
10. Fred AL, Jain AK (2005) Combining multiple clusterings using evidence accumulation. IEEE Trans Pattern Anal Mach Intell 27(6):835–850
11. Gómez S, Jensen P, Arenas A (2009) Analysis of community structure in networks of correlated data. Phys Rev E 80(1):016114
12. Kleinberg JM (1999) Authoritative sources in a hyperlinked environment. J ACM (JACM) 46(5):604–632
13. Lambiotte R, Delvenne JC, Barahona M (20078) Laplacian dynamics and multiscale modular structure in networks. arXiv preprint arXiv:0812.1770
14. Lancichinetti A, Fortunato S (2012) Consensus clustering in complex networks CoRR abs/1203.6093
15. Lancichinetti A, Fortunato S (2012) Consensus clustering in complex networks. Sci Rep 2:336–342
16. Leicht EA, Newman ME (2008) Community structure in directed networks. Phys Rev Lett 100(11):118703
17. Lewis K, Kaufman J, Gonzalez M, Wimmer A, Christakis N (2008) Tastes, ties, and time: a new social network dataset using Facebook.com. Soc Netw 30(4):330–342
18. Mucha PJ, Richardson T, Macon K, Porter MA, Onnela JP (2010) Community structure in time-dependent, multiscale, and multiplex networks. Science 328(5980):876–878
19. Newman ME, Girvan M (2004) Finding and evaluating community structure in networks. Phys Rev E 69(2):026113
20. Ng MKP, Li X, Ye Y (2011) Multirank: co-ranking for objects and relations in multi-relational data. In: Proceedings of the 17th ACM SIGKDD international conference on knowledge discovery and data mining. ACM, pp 1217–1225
21. Page L, Brin S, Motwani R, Winograd T (1999) The PageRank citation ranking: bringing order to the web. Technical report. SIDL-WP-1999-0120, Stanford InfoLab
22. Rodriguez MA, Shinavier J (2010) Exposing multi-relational networks to single-relational network analysis algorithms. J Informetr 4(1):29–41
23. Strehl A, Ghosh J (2003) Cluster ensembles—a knowledge reuse framework for combining multiple partitions. J Mach Learn Res 3:583–617
24. Sun Y, Han J (2012) Mining heterogeneous information networks: principles and methodologies. Synth Lect Data Min Knowl Discov 3(2):1–159
25. Tan PN, Steinbach M, Kumar V (2005) Introduction to data mining. Addison-Wesley, Boston
26. Tang L, Liu H (2010) Community detection and mining in social media. Morgan & Claypool Publishers, California
27. Tang L, Liu H, Zhang J (2012) Identifying evolving groups in dynamic multimode networks. IEEE Trans Knowl Data Eng 24(1):72–85
28. Tang L, Wang X, Liu H (2012) Community detection via heterogeneous interaction analysis. Data Min Knowl Discov 25:1–33
29. Topchy A, Jain AK, Punch W (2005) Clustering ensembles: models of consensus and weak partitions. IEEE Trans Pattern Anal Mach Intell 27(12):1866–1881
30. Turney PD, Littman ML (2003) Measuring praise and criticism: inference of semantic orientation from association. ACM Trans Inf Syst (TOIS) 21(4):315–346

31. Wu J, Liu H, Xiong H, Cao J (2013) A theoretic framework of K-means-based consensus clustering. In: Proceedings of the twenty-third international joint conference on artificial intelligence. AAAI Press, pp 1799–1805
32. Wu Z, Yin W, Cao J, Xu G, Cuzzocrea A (2013) Community detection in multi-relational social networks. In: Web information systems engineering–WISE 2013. Springer, pp 43–56
33. Wu Z, Cao J, Wu J, Wang Y, Liu C (2014) Detecting genuine communities from large-scale social networks: a pattern-based method. Comput J 57(9):1343–1357
34. Wu Z, Cao J, Zhu G, Yin W, Cuzzocrea A, Shi J (2015) Detecting overlapping communities in poly-relational networks. World Wide Web 16:1–18
35. Xia Z, Bu Z (2012) Community detection based on a semantic network. Knowl-Based Syst 26:30–39

Chapter 5
Group Types in Social Media

Luca Maria Aiello

Abstract Dynamics of social systems are the result of the complex superposition of interactions taking place at different scales, ranging from the pairwise communications between individuals to the macroscopic evolutionary patterns of the full interaction graph. Social communities, namely groups of people originated by any spontaneous aggregation process, constitute the mid-ground between such two extremes. Groups are important constituents of social environments as they form the basis for people's participation and engagement beyond their minute dyadic interactions. Communities in online social media have been studied widely in their static and evolutionary aspects, but only recently some attention has been devoted to the exploration of their *nature*. Besides the characterization of online communities along their spatio-temporal and activity features, the recent advancements in the emerging field of computational sociology have provided a new lens to study social aggregations along their social and topical dimensions. Using the online photo sharing community Flickr as a main running example, we survey some techniques that have been used to get a multi-faceted description of group types and we show that different types of groups impact on orthogonal interaction processes on the social graph, such as the diffusion of information along social ties. Our overview supports the intuition that a more nuanced description of groups could not only improve the understanding of the activity of the user base but can also foster a better interpretation of other phenomena occurring on social graphs.

5.1 Bridging Gaps in the Study of Communities

> Most human pleasures have their roots in social life. [...] Much of human suffering as well as much of human happiness has its source in the actions of other human beings. One follows from the other, given the facts of **group** life, where pairs do not exist in complete isolation from other social relations.

L.M. Aiello (✉)
Yahoo Labs, 125 Shaftesbury Avenue, London, UK
e-mail: alucca@yahoo-inc.com

© Springer International Publishing Switzerland 2015   97
G. Paliouras et al. (eds.), *User Community Discovery*, Human–Computer
Interaction Series, DOI 10.1007/978-3-319-23835-7_5

    This is how sociologist Peter Blau introduces the discussion about the structure
of social associations in his famous book "Exchange and Power in Social Life" [11],
acknowledging the pivotal role of groups in providing motivations and rewards for
people in a social ecosystem. Together with dyadic social interactions, groups form
the basis for the social instantiation of any individual.

    Given the centrality and pervasiveness of such social structures in our everyday
life, it is no surprise that their transposition in online social media has gained an
explosive and apparently ever-growing success. Besides providing the possibility to
establish pairwise social connections online, social media allow for the creation of
groups (or communities[1]) that are characterized, depending on the online system
considered, by different properties [30, 40, 44]. As a result, groups in social media
have flourished and they nowadays form a strong basis for user participation and
engagement in online services.

    Groups, either online or offline, have been the object of studies in social sciences
for decades and yet, because the notion of group itself hides an enormous variety of
concepts representing as many group types in real life, it is very difficult to provide
a general definition of what a group really is. In fact, a group can be characterized
simply by a social aggregation involving more than a certain number of actors,
as well as by more abstract concepts such as similarity or interdependence of the
members. One of the most well-established interpretation of the meaning of groups
is based on the notion of *social identity*, an elusive idea that is hard to frame and has
been object of debate and investigation. Social identity is understood by the social
psychologist Henri Tajfel, one of the pioneers of the social identity theory, as the
part of an individual's self-concept deriving from the membership of a social group,
together with the emotional valuation that the membership may imply [56]. Tajfel has
himself acknowledged that the discussion on what identity is can be often "endless
and sterile" [57] because of the complexity of social interactions that surround an
individual.

    On a parallel track, computer science research has partly confirmed some of the
key notions illustrated above through data-driven studies. By intensively investigat-
ing online groups, evidence has been found about the tendency of actors to flock
in communities pushed by a number of reasons including affiliation by similarity,
common interest, conflict with other groups, local proximity, or even just by the need
of defining a distinctive identity with respect to the rest of the population [1–3, 31,
38, 40].

    Despite all the efforts spent in the study of online groups, there are still some major
gaps that just recently have begun to be filled to reach a more coherent, complete
and nuanced description of the nature of groups. First, the research community has
mainly considered groups as homogeneous entities, overlooking the fact that groups
are not all created equal, as they emerge by different collective processes and by the

---

[1]The distinction between "group" and "community" is very subtle and varies in different research fields. If not specified
differently, we will use the two terms interchangeably in this chapter.

different motivations of their founders or members. Such lapse has been exasperated by the tendency of studying different characterizing dimensions of online groups—temporal, structural, spatial, etc.—in separation. Last, although computer science research on online groups has corroborated the theories developed in social sciences, more systematic approaches to the verification of sociological findings with computational methods have been emerging only very recently [18]. As a consequence, a thorough exploration of the *nature* of online groups is still a work in progress, with still very few systematic approaches to characterize groups along multiple quantitative dimensions.

This chapter aims to present recent work that has been directed to address the limitations mentioned above. We will describe work that has contributed to compose the fractiousness within the computer science literature by attempting multifaceted characterizations of groups. The work we describe also attempts to bridge the gap with social science studies by operationalizing theories about communities that have been previously developed in sociology.

Specifically, we will describe a categorization of online groups that considers *spatial*, *temporal* (Sect. 5.4) and *socio-topical* (Sect. 5.5) dimensions for the first time in combination (Sect. 5.6) and that captures in a computational framework an instantiation of the notion of common identity (as opposed to common bond) that has been for long time discussed in social sciences. We explore also the implications of the group size on its activity—in relation with the so-called Dunbar number theory (Sect. 5.8)—and discuss the relationship between communities that are spontaneously created by the user base and those that are algorithmically found by community detection algorithms, based on the density of interactions between actors (Sect. 5.7). Also, to further support the belief that a nuanced characterization of groups matters, especially if informed by notions coming from the social sciences, we speculate about the impact that different group types may have in another important social process occurring in social networks: information diffusion. We follow the intuition that the shape information cascades is partly determined by the type of community in which the piece of information is propagating (Sect. 5.9). Finally, we conclude by briefly discussing the role of social groups in addressing the micro-macro problem in sociology (Sect. 5.10).

Along the remainder of the chapter, our main case-study will be Flickr, the world-famous photo-sharing social platform. The experiments we report have ben run on a large scale Flickr dataset described in Sect. 5.3. Flickr has a rich set of features accessible via public API[2] including a direct social network, explicit declaration of groups, annotated content, dyadic conversations, etc. thus being an ideal dataset to explore different facets of social aggregations.

---

[2]https://www.flickr.com/services/api/.

5.2 Group Characterization in the Literature

Next, to provide a general context of the state of the art on the study of online and offline groups, we review some of the most notable work in the fields of computer science and social sciences that have been published around the topic. That will set the background upon which the following discussion will build on.

5.2.1 Groups in Computer Science

Social online communities have been investigated since the beginning of the social web. Besides spending efforts in finding empirical evidences to support different notions of communities [48], researchers have explored groups in relation to several applications including recommendation and profiling [19, 65]. The static structure, as well as the evolutionary dynamics of communities have been investigated extensively over a variety of large-scale and heterogeneous datasets. Extensive evidence has been produced about the broad distribution of the structural and temporal features of online social groups [16, 38]. Those characteristics are largely determined by the intrinsic group fitness [25] and by the density of social ties connecting their members [6].

Groups are extremely varied in terms of their emerging features, from their size [9] to their purpose [27]. Such variety has triggered a line of research work that attempted to capture the nature of social groups along several axes, but most often with a lack of any quantitative framework for their classification. Consequently, the results achieved in this area are mostly scattered and lack of consistence.

Due to its open nature, Flickr has been the most studied platform in this respect. Early work identified differences in the usage of Flickr groups through user studies and interviews [62], concluding that memory, narrative, relationships maintenance, self-representation, and self-expression are the five main motivations to join a group. Similarly, later work has come up with several alternative and partially overlapping classifications [37, 43].

Negoescu and colleagues have been among the main contributors in the study of Flickr groups. Initially, they manually categorized communities in *geographical*, *topical*, *visual*, and *catch-all* [40]. Following this initial categorization, they propose to detect hypergroups (i.e., groups of groups) based on the similarity of their topical focus, as determined by LDA [45]; on the opposite, Negi et al. have worked on splitting large Flickr communities in smaller subgroups using MoM-LDA on photo tags [39]. Negoescu et al. also analyzed groups in relation to their membership, with special attention to topicality and to peer-to-peer communication [41]. More recently they have discussed about how to represent Flickr groups according to the topics and tags defined by their members [42]. Supported by earlier studies on the same matter [62], they identify "real" groups as those motivated by self-expression and relationship maintenance, in contrast with those built around a specific topic (similarly to the socio-topical split we discuss later).

Motivated by a conceptual framework defined in earlier work [12], Cox et al. intro-duced the measure of "groupness" whose formulation takes into account the size of the group membership, the volume of photos, and the length of group description [16]. They propose to classify groups into *topical* (focused on a theme), *highlighting* (to promote photos to a wider public) and *geographical* (rooted into a specific geolo-cation); however their classification is ultimately arbitrary and not supported by any quantitative result. In partial contrast with previous work [42], their study suggests that small groups are more important than the big ones to improve social interaction dynamics because they operate at "human scale." The work was later extended [28] and the categorization was manually refined into four categories: *location-based*, *award*, *learning*, and *topical* groups.

Prieur et al. discuss the interplay between sociality and topicality in Flickr groups. By using PCA on a set of group features they detect the main components that characterize the group type. They find three main dimensions underlying as many types of groups: *social media-use*, *MySpace-like*, and *photo stockpiling* [47, 50, 51].

Social groups have also been described in terms the engagement of their mem-bers. From a quantitative perspective, the degree of involvement of the members in activities related to the group is varied and strongly dependent on group size [8]. Intra-group activity has been characterized in terms of item sharing practices [40], propensity of people to address other members' questions [66], or coherence of discussion topics [22]. Modeling inner activity of groups has helped in finding effec-tive strategies to predict future group growth [31], recommend group affiliation, or improve the search experience on social platforms [45].

Groups have been studied also in other online platforms. User interaction patterns in groups extracted from YouTube, LiveJournal, DBLP, Orkut, and Yahoo Groups have been investigated in the past [7, 8, 38, 55]. In particular, the tendency to both topicality and sociality and the small-world nature of group interactions has been found in YouTube groups by Laine et al., who also envision in future work an analysis of the interplay between groups and the process of social influence [33].

Besides user-defined groups, the study of automatically detected groups through community detection algorithms has attracted much interest lately [54]. Detected communities are meant to represent meaningful aggregations of people where dense or intense social exchanges take place among their members [26]. Nevertheless, even if there is a variety of synthetic methods to verify the quality of detected communi-ties [34], it is unclear whether such artificial groups capture any notion of community, as perceived by the users. If on the one hand the computation of cluster-goodness metrics over user-created groups can give useful hints about their structural cohe-sion [64], on the other hand a direct comparison between user-created groups and detected communities is still missing, particularly in terms of the amount of social-ity or topical coherence they embed. Only recently researchers have been trying to address this question in a more systematic way [27, 29].

5.2.2 Groups in Social Sciences

Recent work in the field of computational social science tried to characterize communities according to the principles defined by well-known theories from social sciences. Activity and connectivity are heavily correlated with group size in several online social platforms [23, 26, 31], with a consistent patterns that recalls Dunbar's theory on the upper bound of around 150 stable social relationships for an average human [21]. Similarity between group members has been identified also as a factor driving the creation of social communities [59], also because of the tendency of social agents to aggregate according to the homophily principle [2]. However, similarity is not necessarily the strongest indicator for group stability or longevity, as diversity of content shared between group members is a major factor to keep the interest of members alive [36].

Social and thematic components of communities have been widely studied in social science, most of all within the common identity and common bond theory that will be discussed later in this chapter [49, 52, 53]. The principles behind the theory have never been translated into practical metrics to categorize groups, nor tested on large datasets, until recently. On the other hand, data-driven studies have investigated social and thematic components separately when characterizing groups [16]. Preliminary insights on the interplay between such dimensions have been given in exploratory work on Flickr, where signals of correlation between social density and tag dispersion in groups has been found [51] and where two different clusters emerge naturally when plotting the groups size against the number of internal links [9].

5.3 The Flickr Case-Study

As mentioned earlier, all the dimensions that we shall investigate in the following sections are quantitatively measured on a dataset extracted from Flickr. Its wide variety of user groups, the richness of interaction types, and the openness of the data make Flickr an ideal platform for this kind of study. Next, we shortly describe the main features of the dataset.

Users of Flickr can create, moderate and administer their own groups. Most groups allow users to join without an invite, whereas others are by invitation only and joining requires the administrator's permission. We consider a random sample of 500 K public groups created until the end of year 2008. For each of these groups, we extracted all the public information related to them (retrievable via the Flickr public API). All the data have been anonymized and processed in aggregate.

First, we collect the public information of group members about their social interactions:

- *Comments*. User u comments on a photo of user v. This interaction is *mediated* through the photo. We filter out the comments of users on their own photos, obtaining a total of 238M comments.

- *Favorites*. User u marks one of user v's photos as a *favorite*. The interaction is mediated through the favorited photo. We extract 112M favorite interactions.
- *Contacts*. User u adds user v among his contacts. Social contacts in Flickr are directed and may be reciprocated. One person can choose another person as his contact only once and the relation remains in the same state until the contact is removed. There are 71M contacts in our dataset.

Additionally, we also rely on the information related to specific actions that users make to interact with the group itself:

- *Uploads*. User u uploads a photo p to the group *photo pool*. Flickr groups provide pools to store pictures related to the group. Pictures can be stored in multiple pools, but only members of the group can upload a photo to its pool.
- *Subscriptions*. User u joins the group at a certain time.

Last, we collect photo *tags*. The primary set of photos from which we extract tags is the photo pool. In addition, the interactions between members of the group that are mediated through photos (i.e., comments, favorites) result in two additional photo sets from which tags are extracted. In the following, we will consider the three tag sets separately (pool, comments, favorites).

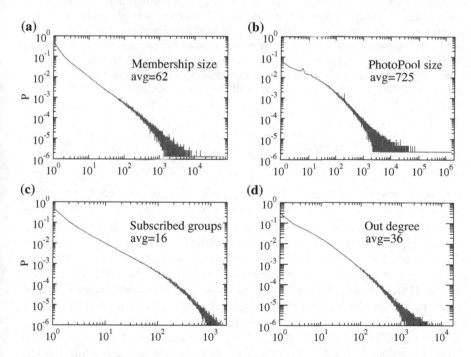

Fig. 5.1 Distributions (PDFs) of the characteristic dimensions of the dataset. Average values are reported in the plots. **a** Number of users in a group; **b** number of photos in a group pool; **c** number of groups a user is subscribed to; **d** out degree of the follower network induced by the users in our sample

The distributions of some of the main dimensions we consider in this study are reported in Fig. 5.1.

5.4 Space and Time Patterns of Groups

Actions within a group take place in a spatial and temporal context. Especially in online groups, where members can communicate even from long distance and maintain connections with relatively low cost, the spatial and temporal patterns can vary quite much. Next, we identify some metrics that can be used effectively to characterize communities along space (Sect. 5.4.1) and time (Sect. 5.4.2) [18], and we use them to classify groups in our Flickr dataset (Sect. 5.4.3).

5.4.1 Spatial Features

The first aspect we take into account is the location, namely the geographical position of the members or of the photos that are uploaded in the group pool. Geographical distribution of group members can indeed be correlated with the purpose of the group, being sometimes very localized (e.g., members of a photography club in the same city) and sometimes very broad (e.g., the club of Nikon camera owners). In his study on the geographical distribution of viewers of a given photo, Van Zwol [63] proposed three metrics to account for geographic sparsity. The first is the average over the geodesic distance geo_d between all the pairs of locations (Fig. 5.2a):

$$geo_d(lat_1, lon_2, lat_2, lon_2)$$
$$= 2r \arcsin\left(\sqrt{\sin^2\left(\frac{lat_1 - lat_2}{2}\right) + \cos(lat_1) \cdot \cos(lat_2) \cdot \sin^2\left(\frac{lon_1, lon2}{2}\right)}\right),$$

This metric scales quadratically with the number of points and it could be computationally prohibitive for large sets of locations. A way to overcome this issue is to estimate the dispersion by computing the standard deviation for the longitudes and latitudes separately and use them to build a bounding box around the centroid of the Cartesian coordinates (Fig. 5.2c). Then the Euclidean distance between the angles of the bounding box is considered as a measure of geographical dispersion. This solution however does not consider the rounded surface of the Earth, thus biasing the results by the latitude: same values at different latitudes could map to very different distances. A direct solution to solve this problem is to use the geodesic distance instead (Fig. 5.2c). Still, even if the geodesic distance accounts for the curvature, it does not consider the Earth as a sphere, as longitude is interpreted as a linear metric (e.g., two points at the two ends of the Bering strait will be considered very far from each other).

Fig. 5.2 Methods to measure dispersion of geolocated points (*red dots*) on a map. **a** Average of pairwise geodesic distances between points. **b** Diagonal of the bounding box defined by the standard deviations of latitude and longitude around the center of gravity (*blue cross*). **c** Same as (**b**) but considering the geodesic distance of the diagonal

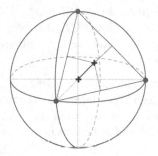

Fig. 5.3 Center-of-Earth distance method to measure dispersion of geolocated points (*red dots*) on the Globe. Points are translated into spatial Cartesian coordinates. The distance from their centroid to the center of the Earth (*blue segment*) is calculated as a measure of dispersion

To address these problems, we use the *Center-of-Earth distance* (coe_d) to directly measure geographical dispersion (Fig. 5.3). We consider each latitude-longitude pair as a polar-azimuth angle in the spherical coordinate system centered on the center of the Earth. We convert all the points into the three-dimensional Cartesian system. As all the points all lie on the spherical surface, their centroid always lies under the Earth's surface. The sparsity is then estimated by the distance of the centroid to the center of the Earth, normalized by the Earth's radius so that its range is in [0, 1]. When just one point is available (or when multiple points overlap), the spread is maximally narrow ($coe_d = 1$), whereas points at the antipodes have a centroid residing exactly at the center of the Earth ($coe_d = 0$), yielding to maximum sparsity. Last, we apply the arc-cosine to the final value to get an angle that more intuitively relates to the spreading of points on the spherical surface. This solution addresses all the limitations of previous approaches because it has linear complexity, it takes into account the Earth's curvature and it considers the World as spherical.

5.4.2 Temporal Features

The temporal footprint of a group is represented by the sequence of events that happen within its boundaries. In the case of Flickr, for example, a photo upload or a new member joining the group could be events that compose the group's temporal trace.

Groups exhibit quite broad temporal patterns and the distributions of events in time are likely unique for each group instance. For this reason, high-level descriptors of the event timeline are needed to compare and cluster different groups according to their temporal profile. To do that, we rely on the statistical properties of the distribution of the events in time, specifically using four different properties: *central tendency*, *dispersion*, *skewness* and *burstiness*. In the following, we consider that all the events take place in a fixed, large time window $[0, T]$ that goes from the beginning of the system under study until the present time. Next, we define their meaning and propose metrics to capture each of them.

Central Tendency. In statistics, the central tendency or centrality of a distribution captures the tendency of the data to cluster around a central value. Given a sequence of timestamps in which group events occurred $(t_0 \cdots t_n) \in [0, T]$, with t_0 and t_n being the timestamps of the first and last events in the group, respectively, we define the central tendency as:

$$\mu_g = \frac{1}{n} \sum_{i=0}^{n} t_i. \tag{5.1}$$

This value expresses the central tendency of the event distribution in time and it is represented in the range $[0, 1]$. Values close to 0 indicate a high concentration of events at the beginning of the group lifetime, as opposed to a prevalence of events close to the present time for values approaching to 1.

Dispersion. A distinctive property of a distribution is its dispersion, namely how stretched or narrow a distribution is. To quantify this notion, we use a corrected version of the standard deviation that considers events on a normalized timeline:

$$\sigma_g = \sqrt{\frac{1}{n-1} \sum_{i=0}^{n} (t_i - \mu_g^t)^2 \frac{1}{n(1 - \mu_g^t)\mu_g^t}}. \tag{5.2}$$

The range of values is $[0, 1]$. Groups with high central tendency have low dispersion, but groups with low dispersion could have also low central tendency. However, a non-corrected standard deviation would correlate heavily with the central tendency: a series of events with $\mu_g = 0.1$ can not have a dispersion higher than 0.5. To disentangle the two metrics, a correction value is required. For the sake of brevity, we do not report the mathematical details here, but a mathematical justification of the correction is reported in the Appendix.

Skewness. Skewness measures the asymmetry of the distribution with respect to its mean. It is calculated with the normalized difference between the median and the mean as follows:

$$\gamma_g = \frac{\mu_g - \text{median}_g}{\min(\mu_g, 1 - \mu_g)}. \tag{5.3}$$

Also in this case, the output values are in the $[0, 1]$ interval. A divergence between the mean and the median implies a skewed distribution as more elements will have values that are either smaller or larger than the median. The correction factor introduced in the denominator ensures the independence between the skewness and the central tendency, as we detail in the Appendix.

Burstiness. Last, we use a burstiness metric to measure the extent to which the group events happen simultaneously in big bursts. To capture this notion, we recur to the inter-event time ($\Delta_g^{t_{ij}} = t_j - t_i, i < j$). We refer to Δ_g^t as the overall series of inter-event times for a group g. The burstiness is defined as follows:

$$\Delta = \log_{10}(\mu(\Delta_g^t)) - \log_{10}(median(\Delta_g^t)). \tag{5.4}$$

The mean of all the inter-event times $\mu(\Delta_g^t)$ is equivalent to the total time between t_0 and t_n, divided by the number of events. The median of the inter-event times has values in the range $[0, \mu(\Delta_g^t)]$. Series with uniformly separated events have equal values of $\mu(\Delta_g^t)$ and median(Δ_g^t), whereas groups with a bursty behavior will have a median(Δ_g^t) that approaches 0.

5.4.3 Spatial and Temporal Groups in Flickr

Next, we apply the metrics of spatial and temporal characterization to the set of Flickr groups described in Sect. 5.3.

From the geographical perspective, we characterize groups using the single coe_d dispersion metric. However, the metric could be computed on different types of geolocated data: declared user location (in the user profile or in their IP address) and photo geotags. We do not consider the user geolocations for two reasons. First, some users do not provide their position in their own profile; additionally, the IP-based geolocation could be quite unreliable [63]. Last, our goal is to characterize groups with the information that is directly related to that group rather than to the users participating to them. For this reason, we consider the geotags attached to the photos uploaded to the group instead. As an example, consider a group that gathers tourists from all over the World who take pictures in Paris. In this case, we rather characterize the group as geographical narrow, as its focus is a single city, rather than describing the geographical dispersion of the member's locations.

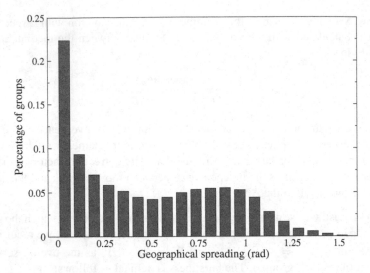

Fig. 5.4 Histogram of the ceo_d dispersion values of Flickr groups (values transformed in radians)

The application of the geographic dispersion metric with photo geotags yields the distribution over groups shown in Fig. 5.4. The histogram has a bi-modal distribution with local maximum around zero that includes the groups containing photos geographically near, and another local maximum around the 0.85 radians ($\approx$50°), that is approximately the angle between Europe and US, which are the two continents with highest data density. A random sample of photos in the dataset produces a peak at the same point (not shown), therefore suggesting that groups with those higher dispersion values are groups where the geographical aspect is not functional to the purpose of the community.

To transition from a continuous value of coe_d to a discrete clustering of groups we apply the X-Means algorithm [46] over the monodimensional space of dispersion values, to avoid manual thresholding. X-Means is a variant of K-Means that allows for an automatic discovery of the optimal number of clusters K in a much faster way than optimizing the parameter K with brute force approaches. Not surprisingly, two clusters are found. The *geo-narrow* cluster, contains the 56 % of groups, and the remaining 44 % belongs to the *geo-wide* cluster.

The temporal metrics can be instantiated on two types of events, namely users joining the group and photos being uploaded in the group pool. Combining those two types of events with the four metrics we use to characterize the event distribution, we obtain eight distinct features. Similarly to the spatial clustering, we apply X-Means to this 8-dimensional feature space, obtaining three different clusters.

The average and standard deviation of every feature are shown in Table 5.1. The three features that are most discriminative are the dispersion and burstiness over users

Table 5.1 Average and standard deviation of every temporal feature for each of the clusters

Clusters	Photos				Users			
	Cent.	Disp.	Skew.	Burst.	Cent.	Disp.	Skew.	Burst.
Evergreen	0.42 ± 0.16	0.56 ± 0.14	0.49 ± 0.16	0.61 ± 0.21	0.47 ± 0.15	0.58 ± 0.13	0.48 ± 0.15	0.81 ± 0.15
Short-lived	0.03 ± 0.07	0.12 ± 0.16	0.60 ± 0.23	0.66 ± 0.21	0.05 ± 0.09	0.16 ± 0.16	0.58 ± 0.27	0.82 ± 0.13
Bursty	0.23 ± 0.16	0.56 ± 0.19	0.71 ± 0.21	0.57 ± 0.22	0.15 ± 0.11	0.60 ± 0.19	0.86 ± 0.15	0.62 ± 0.23

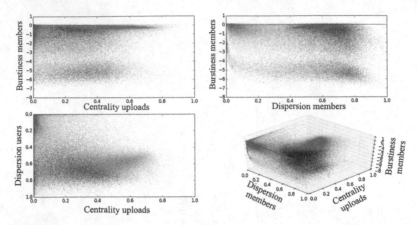

Fig. 5.5 Scatter plot of the groups with respect to the three most discriminative features for the clustering on the temporal dimensions. Bursty groups are depicted in *green*, evergreen in *blue*, and short lived in *red*

joining the group, and the centrality of the uploaded photos. A scatter plot of these three features for each cluster is reported in Fig. 5.5. After inspecting the clusters, we name them *evergreen*, *short-lived* and *bursty*. Next, we report their peculiar features.

Short-lived. The short-lived groups represent 13 % of our sample and are characterized by low centrality and small dispersion. This category includes groups that experienced a low level of activity after they were created and that became inactive shortly after. Examples include limited-scope photo sharing groups whose activity ceases shortly after the photos are uploaded and consumed by small social circles.

Evergreen. The evergreen cluster is the biggest one, containing 52 % of the groups. Groups in this cluster are characterized by high centrality and by dispersion values around 0.5. They were created at a certain point in the past and they have been growing in number of users and photos uniformly until the end of the time period we consider. Examples include groups dedicated to general topics, such as communities of amateur and professional photographers interested in artistic portraits.

Bursty. The remaining 34 % of the groups belong to the Bursty cluster, containing groups with lowest skewness and big burstiness, especially in the number of users joining. Those groups have usually the highest activity at the beginning of their life and from time to time they experience photo uploads or user subscriptions in big batches. Some of these groups are related to recurring (e.g., yearly) events that regularly attract the attention of users.

The evolution of the number of users and photo uploads for the three most representative groups in each class is shown in Fig. 5.6.

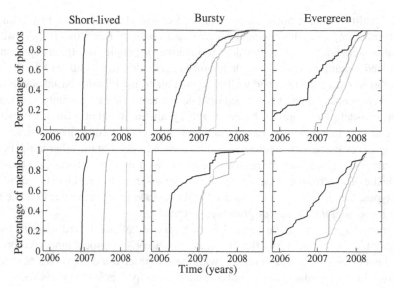

Fig. 5.6 Evolution of each of the three most representative groups in each temporal cluster. Values on the y-axis are normalized by the maximum values reached at the end of the time window of our dataset

5.5 Social and Topical Groups

5.5.1 Common Identity and Common Bond Theory

As mentioned in the introduction, well-established sociological studies have defined a connection between social groups and the process of formation of a social identity of the individual members [56]. The feeling of identity, or in other words the sense of belonging to a community, can be indeed very strong even in groups whose members do not know each other, as group identity can originate merely by defining a collection of people belonging to the same abstract category [60]. In extreme cases, the sense of identity can even emerge when members are randomly assigned to arbitrarily-defined communities [58]. Supporters of a political party, people who suffered from the same illness, members of a fan club, and people interested in the same hobby are all examples of groups that are defined by a common identity.

Groups that convey a strong identity are usually resistant to membership turnover, as individual members are interchangeable as long as the same sense of identity is preserved. However, this is clearly not the case for all the groups we can think of. For example, a person can join a group mainly because he has a direct friendship connection with a member, even without feeling a common identity with the group as a whole. As a result, if the latter leaves the group, the first is likely to quit as well [32, 52]. In this case, individual social links, more than an abstract notion of identity, constitute the backbone that allows the group to survive.

This duality of the groups' nature has been captured and discussed by Prentice in its formalization of the *common identity and common bond* theory [49] which states that, depending on the prevalent motivation of people to join, groups can be categorized as either *bond-based* or *identity-based*. Prentice assumes that the two types of groups have distinct and well-recognizable traits. Identity-based attachment holds when people join a group based on their interest in the community as a whole or in a well-defined common theme shared by all the members. Members whose participation is due to identity-based attachment may not directly engage with anyone and might even participate without revealing their identity. On the other hand, bond-based attachment is driven by personal relations with other members, and thus the main theme of the group may be disregarded. The two processes result in two different group types; for simplicity of exposition, in the following we will refer to those two categories as *social* and *topical* groups respectively.

In practice, groups can be formed from a mixture of bond- and identity-based attachment, even though very often they tend to lean on one aspect more. According to the theory, the group type is related with the *reciprocity* and the *topics* of discussion. Members of social groups tend to establish reciprocal interactions with other members, whereas interactions in topical groups are generally not directly reciprocated. Furthermore, topics of discussion in social groups tend to cover multiple subjects, while in topical groups discussions tend to be related to the group scope, covering specific topics only. According to the theory, social groups are founded on individual relationships between their members, therefore it is harder for newcomers to join and integrate with members that already have strong relationships between each other. As we discussed, this makes social groups more vulnerable to turnover, since the departure of a person's friends may influence her own departure. On the opposite, topical groups are more open to newcomers and more robust to departures.

In recent years, the theory has been widely commented and elaborated by social scientists from a theoretical perspective and through small-scale experiments [52, 53, 61], but no rigorous methodology to distinguish the two types has been developed nor tested on large-scale datasets, until recently [27]. Next, we describe a technique to detect the group type based on the common identity and common bond theory. The method contributes to validate the theory itself but provides also a general framework for automatic classification of user groups in online social media.

5.5.2 From Theory to Metrics

It is possible to construct metrics to differentiate between the two types of groups by quantifying their reciprocity of interactions, and the topical width of the information exchanged between group members. Next, we describe: (i) *reciprocity* metrics, used to quantifying group sociality, (ii) *entropy* of terms, to determine how much the topics of discussion vary within a group, and (iii) *activity* metrics, to measure the liveliness of the group. We discuss how these metrics are combined in Sect. 5.5.4, with specific examples on our Flickr case-study.

Reciprocity. Reciprocity of interaction happens when a user sends any type of message to another user and, subsequently, the recipient responds with a new message. We define *intra-reciprocity* of a group g as:

$$r_g^{\text{int}} = \frac{E_g^{\text{int,rec}}/2}{E_g^{\text{int,rec}}/2 + E_g^{\text{int,nrec}}}, \tag{5.5}$$

where $E_g^{\text{int,rec}}$ and $E_g^{\text{int,nrec}}$ are, respectively, the number of reciprocated and non-reciprocated links internal to the group g. Correspondingly, the *inter-reciprocity* at the border of the group is defined by r_g^{ext}, accounting for the reciprocity between members and non-members.

We normalize the intra-reciprocity score using the average reciprocity value $\left\langle r_g^{\text{int}} \right\rangle$ over all groups:

$$t_g = \frac{r_g^{\text{int}}}{\left\langle r_g^{\text{int}} \right\rangle}. \tag{5.6}$$

The larger the intra-reciprocity, the higher the probability that the group is social. To compensate for the effect of the correlation between reciprocity and the number of internal interactions, and to account for local effects, the intra-reciprocity can be normalized by the inter-reciprocity:

$$u_g = \frac{r_g^{\text{int}} + 1}{r_g^{\text{ext}} + 1}. \tag{5.7}$$

We add 1 to both numerator and denominator to reduce the fluctuations of u_g at low values of r_g^{ext}. This relative reciprocity compares the reciprocity between the members with their reciprocity towards people not belonging to the group.

Topicality. The set of terms $T(g)$ associated with a group indicates the topical diversity of the group. Thus we measure the entropy of the group as:

$$H(g) = - \sum_{t \in T(g)} p(t) \cdot \log_2 p(t), \tag{5.8}$$

where $p(t)$ is the probability of occurrence of the term t in the set $T(g)$. The higher the entropy, the greater is the variety of terms and, according to the theory, the more social the group is. Conversely, the lower the entropy, the more topical the group is. In addition, since not all groups have the same number of terms and the entropy value grows with the total number of terms, we introduce the *normalized entropy* h_g, which is normalized by the average value of entropy for the groups with the same number of terms:

$$h_g = \frac{H(g)}{\langle H(f) \rangle_{|T(g)|=|T(f)|}}.$$ (5.9)

Activity. Even if, according to the common identity and common bond theory, activity is not a discriminative factor to discern social from topical groups, it is useful to characterize the liveliness of a community. Activity is quantified in terms of the number of internal interactions normalized by the expected number of internal interactions for a set of nodes with the same degree sequence:

$$a_g = \frac{E_g^{\mathrm{int}}}{(D_g^{\mathrm{in}} D_g^{\mathrm{out}})/E}.$$ (5.10)

D_g^{in} and D_g^{out} are the total numbers of interactions originated by or targeted to members of the group g. E is the total number of interactions in the network. Values higher than 1 are obtained when the number of interactions internal to the group is higher than the number of interactions expected in a random scenario with the same group activity volume.

Another way of measuring activity of a community is to compare density of its internal interactions with the density of interactions with the external world:

$$b_g = \frac{E_g^{\mathrm{int}}/(s_g(s_g - 1))}{E_g^{\mathrm{ext}}/(2(N - s_g)s_g)},$$ (5.11)

where s_g is the cardinality of group g and N is total number of nodes in the network. Values of b_g greater than 1 indicate a density of internal interactions higher than the density interactions between the group and the rest of the network.

5.5.3 Ground Truth of Social and Topical Flickr Groups

The socio-topical dimension we consider is a rather abstract concept; for this reason, a validation step is needed to check whether our metrics are able to correctly capture it. We resort to human editors to build a reliable ground truth of topical an social groups, under the assumption that the human capability of processing the semantics, aesthetics, and sentiment behind text and photos of a group allows for an easy discernment of social and topical groups. For the labeling, we randomly sampled groups that have (i) more than 5 members, (ii) more than 100 internal comments, (iii) relative activities a_g^{com} and b_g^{com} higher than 10^2. The third requirement ensures that the selected groups are active above the expected values in a random case. After this selection we obtained over 34 K groups. The editors were asked to label groups after being presented with the following information:

Group profile. The Flickr group profile consists of the group name, description by the creator of the group, discussion board, photo pool, and map of places where photos uploaded to the group pool were taken.

Comments. We provide the text of all the comments that are made between the group members. Comments are shown in chronological order and are grouped by thread, if they appear under the same photo. A link to the photo is also provided.

Tags. An alphabetically-sorted list of the 5 most frequent tags attached to the photos that group members commented on.

Editors were shown the information described above and asked to categorize groups as either *social, topical* or *unknown.* The last case is reserved for groups for which text is written in a language unknown to the labeler, making the task impossible to accomplish. Intentionally, no *unsure* category was allowed to keep the categorization strictly binary, as the theory does. Some groups can be both topical and social, and therefore difficult to categorize, but for the sake of clarity and conformity with the theory we kept the categorization binary. Editors were asked to label groups based on well-defined guidelines extracted directly from the common identity and common bond theory [52]. The guidelines involve the inspection of two aspects. First, editors look at photos and comments based on the intuition that knowing each other's real names, spending time together, co-appearing in photos, sharing common past experiences, referencing mutually known places, and disclosing personal information are all signals of the presence of a social relationship [15], as opposed to topical groups, where the atmosphere is supposed to be more formal and impersonal [53]. Last, the editors inspect the photo tags and the group textual description to assess the semantic coherence that is typical of identity-based groups. Geo-referenced photos taken in a narrow geographical space can be an indication of high sociality, instead.

If both tags and comments are highly social or topical, then the label choice is straightforward. If the tags are highly topical and the comments are not social then the group is labeled as topical, and vice versa. If the tags are a bit topical and comments highly social then the group is labeled as social. The labelers were asked to read as many comments they needed to get to a fairly clear decision.

Clarifying examples have been provided to the labelers to facilitate their task. For instance the "Airlines Austrian" group, tagged with "aircraft", "airport" and "spotting", that contains photos of airplanes from different countries in Europe is a clear example of a topical group. The "Camp Baby 2008" group, containing photos depicting people attending an event and interacting with each other with a friendly attitude is a social one; although the group has a specific topic and, as such, it contributes to the creation of the identity of its members, its social component is greatly predominant.

Multiple independent editors are asked to assess the quality of the extracted ground truth. A total of 101 groups were labeled by 3 people. The inter-labeler agreement, measured as Fleiss' Kappa, is 0.60, meaning that there exists good agreement between labelers. Once high agreement was assessed, we continued with individual labeling for a total of 565 distinct groups. We find the two types of groups being quite balanced in number, with around 48 % of social groups. One of the expectations is that bond-based groups should not be very large, as the human capacity for stable relationships is limited (as later discussed in Sect. 5.8). In line with this expectation, we find that declared groups labeled as social have on average 35 members, whereas groups labeled as topical have on average 172 members.

5.5.4 Group Type Prediction in Flickr

Before assessing experimentally the predictive power of the metrics, we inspect their properties to check how much their values differ between groups labeled as social or topical. In Fig. 5.7, we plot them as a function of the group size, to compare groups of similar sizes to draw unbiased conclusions.

We spot almost no differences in the number of photos (not shown), favorites, and contacts (as in Fig. 5.7b, c) between social and topical groups. The number of comments is, however, around 2 times higher in social groups than in topical groups of similar size (Fig. 5.7a). More differences are found when looking at relative activity (Fig. 5.7d–i), which compares the interaction internal to the group with the overall activity level of users belonging to groups. In all three types of interaction, the relative activity metrics for social groups yield values from 2 up to over 10 times higher than for topical groups.

More importantly, we observe large differences in values of reciprocity and relative reciprocity of comments and favorites. Social groups exhibit significantly higher reciprocity than topical groups (Fig. 5.7j–o), in line with the theory. There is no difference in reciprocity of contacts, plausibly because contacts do not strongly reflect personal relations between connected users. Possibly, since contacts do not need to be reciprocal, users often "follow" people they do not know and do not actively interact with. Finally, we observe much higher values of entropy and normalized entropy in social groups than in topical ones (Fig. 5.7p, q, s, t). This holds for the tags extracted

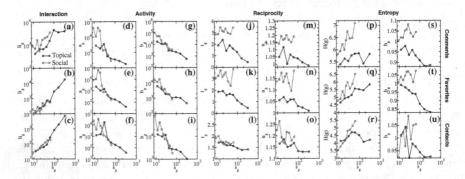

Fig. 5.7 Average (**a–c**) number of interactions, (**d–i**) activity (a_g, b_g), (**j–o**) reciprocity (t_g, u_g), and (**p–u**) entropy ($H(g)$, h_g) of topical (*black circles*) and social (*blue squares*) groups as a function of their size. Each point corresponds to 30 groups. Commenting, favoriting and social linking (contacts) are the three interaction types considered

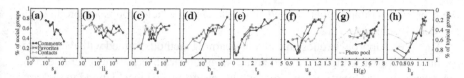

Fig. 5.8 Dependence of fraction f of groups labeled as social on various metrics: computed considering comments, favorites, contacts and photo pools. Each point corresponds to 50 groups

from photos commented, and favorited between members. Assuming that tags of photos represent topics of interaction, the result is consistent with bond attachment. It is expected for members of bond-based groups to engage in interactions covering many different topics, whereas members of identity-based groups focus their interactions on specific topics. Apparently though, this does not hold for the tags extracted from photo pool of the group (Fig. 5.7r, u). This might be explained by the fact that the content of the photo pool does not always reflect well the interactions and relations between members of the group.

We also look at the fraction of groups labeled as social with respect to their size, activity, reciprocity, and entropy (Fig. 5.8). The group size correlates negatively, as expected (Fig. 5.8a). The correlations with the number of interactions and relative activity a_g are quite weak (Fig. 5.8b, c), whereas surprisingly there is a strong correlation on relative activity b_g (Fig. 5.8d). For the lowest values of b_g^{com}, 95 % of the groups are topical, while for the highest, 80 % of the groups are social. High values of b_g can mean stronger group-focus, or even an isolation of the group members from the rest of people they interact with. That might relate to the difficulty of joining bond-based groups due to strong relations existing between their members and to the high investment that is required to create such relations with them [52]. Direct reciprocity of interactions, with the exception of contacts, correlates strongly with social groups (Fig. 5.8e, f). Furthermore, we find that the entropy of tags correlates with group sociality, but entropy based on other sources does not (Fig. 5.8g). However, the normalized entropy performs better and correlates strongly when computed on tags extracted from both comments and favorites (Fig. 5.8h).

The properties of labeled social and topical groups tend to confirm the validity of the principles identified by the common identity and common bond theory. A stronger confirmation would directly come from the ability of the defined metrics to predict the tendency of a group towards sociality or topicality. To this end, we propose and compare two methods to predict the group type and we test their accuracy over our ground truth. The easiest approach to use is a linear combination. To do that, we select the features that directly implement the sociological theory: t_g, u_g, and h_g. Each of them is computed for the 3 different interaction types and bags of tags, yielding a total of 9 values. We transform the values into their t-statistics by subtracting the average and dividing them by the standard deviation. We weight the normalized scores evenly and we sum them up to obtain a single *sociality score* S_g. All of the components are supposed to score high for social groups, therefore the higher the value of the final score the higher the chance that the group is social rather than topical. To convert the score into a binary label, a fixed threshold above which groups are predicted to be social is selected.

The second approach relies on machine-learning methods trained with the features we have identified, using the labeled groups in ground truth as training examples. The classifier outputs a binary prediction for any new group instance defined in the same feature space. Due to the limited size of our corpus of labeled groups, we estimate the classifier performance using 10-fold cross validation. We report results on a Rotation Forest classifier, which performed best in comparison to other popular classification approaches. For this supervised approach we use a wider set of features than the one we used in the linear combination, namely: s_g, E_g^{int}, a_g, b_g, t_g, u_g, $H(g)$, h_g, each applied to the 3 different interaction types and bags of tags. This results in a total of 22 features. We selected such a wide set of features to test if indeed the metrics proposed to distinguish between the social and topical groups are the best ones for the task. The relative predictive power of the features is measured through a feature selection algorithm.

The ratio of social groups increases quickly with the score S_g, as illustrated in Fig. 5.9a, suggesting that the features embedded in the score are able to capture the nature of the groups to some extent. When the score is around zero, groups can be characterized by a mix of social or topical aspects, and a decision on the predominant nature of the group is more difficult. If we fix the threshold for the S_g value to perform a binary group classification, it is clear that several misclassifications will occur, especially around the threshold value. An example for threshold at 0 is shown in Fig. 5.9a. Conversely, the classifier performs much better and achieves the ratio that adheres much more to the actual ratio of social and topical groups.

Both methods, however, fail more frequently for groups with mixed social and topical features. The prediction accuracies of the classifier and of the score-based predictions have an evident drop of performance around 0 (Fig. 5.9b). The accuracy at the extreme values of the score is close to 0.95, while it falls below 0.6 for groups with a score close to 0. Consistently, this drop occurs also in the pairwise agreement between human labelers, measured as a ratio of groups that have been given the same label. Apparently, this is a shortcoming of the binary classification coming from the common identity and common bond theory itself, rather than of the features or the prediction framework.

We compare the performance of the two approaches through ROC curves (Fig. 5.9c), which astray from the selection of a fixed threshold. The curve for the classifier (computed for the 10-fold cross validation) always performs better, and this is reflected in the considerably higher AUC value and accuracy, as shown in Table 5.2.

Finally, to shed light on which are the most predictive features, we rank them using Chi-square feature selection. The top 5 are, in decreasing order of importance: h_g^{com}, t_g^{com}, u_g^{com}, h_g^{fav}, and b_g^{com}. The selected set is the optimal for the prediction performance: retraining the classifier on such restricted set of features results in stable performance, as shown in Table 5.2. The top 4 most predictive features correspond directly to the expectations of the theory. Reciprocity-based metrics and normalized

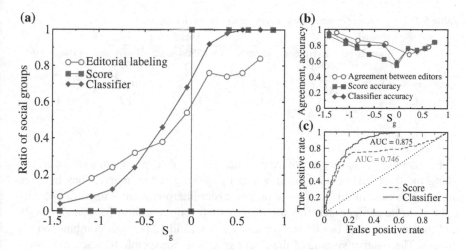

Fig. 5.9 Prediction of group type (social vs. topical). **a** Ratio of groups classified as social (by the labelers, by the linear combination methos with threshold at 0, and by the classifier) versus the sociality score S_g. **b** Accuracy of the two prediction techniques and agreement between labelers against the S_g values. **c** ROC curves for the prediction with the two different techniques

Table 5.2 Group type prediction performance using (i) the score with threshold at 0, (ii) 10-fold cross validation on a Rotation Forest classifier trained on all the features, or (iii) the same classifier trained on the set of top-5 predictive features, according to the Chi Squared feature selection

Method	Accuracy	AUC
Score	0.763	0.749
Classifier	0.801	0.879
Classifierχ^2_{top5}	0.803	0.872

entropy are significantly more predictive than other features. The high position of relative activity b_g^{com} is instead more unexpected.

5.6 Towards a Comprehensive View on Group Types

We have laid down the foundations for a group characterization along the spatial, temporal, and socio-topical aspects separately. A natural question that arises is whether there are some cross-dimension relationships between group types, or in other words, if different clusters of groups in one dimension correspond predominantly to some other type of group in the other dimension. Blending all the metrics in a single model could be a way to answer the question. However, such unifying approach would be quite unpractical because of the different nature of the group characterization problem in different dimensions (clustering for geo-temporal, classification for socio-topical) and because of the difficult interpretation of a model that blends together such diverse types of measures.

Table 5.3 Percentage of groups in each intersection between clusters

	Topical			Social		
	Short-lived (%)	Evergreen (%)	Bursty (%)	Short-lived (%)	Evergreen (%)	Bursty (%)
Geo-narrow	4.8	15.8	5.7	5.3	10.9	12.7
Geo-wide	1.4	15.5	4.2	1.5	9.7	11.4

For these reasons, we use a more modular and simple approach to analyze groups along the three dimensions together just by looking at the intersections between different classes. In this way we obtain an easier interpretation of results. Two spatial (geo-wide and geo-narrow), three temporal (evergreen, short-lived, and bursty), and two socio-topical (social and topical) classes yield 12 possible combinations of classes. The relative volume of the Flickr groups in our sample for each of them is reported in Table 5.3. Interesting patterns emerge. First, social groups have a much higher ratio of bursty to evergreen groups than the topical ones. This is likely caused by the type of social behavior: a group of individuals who know each other would more likely join all the group right after its creation and the group would probably experience a activity bursts in correspondence to the real-life events of the social group. Symmetrically, topical groups tend to belong more to the "evergreen" category as some topics are indeed not tied to the churn of social groups or to temporal trends. Last, we can see a relation between short-lived and geo-narrow groups: groups that live for a short time have way less probability to spread on a big geographical scale; in other words, geo-width is an indicator of a better chance of the group to survive longer.

5.7 Declared Versus Detected Groups

Community detection techniques have been largely employed in recent years to describe the structure of complex social systems [54]. The need for a clearer assessment of the *meaning* of the detected clusters has been often expressed from different angles [34, 64], but never completely satisfied by empirical analysis. Here we contribute to shed light on this matter by comparing user-generated groups (*declared* groups) with groups detected algorithmically (*detected* groups).

To automatically find communities, we apply the OSLOM community detection algorithm [35] over the entire network of social contacts in our dataset. We choose OSLOM because it detects overlapping communities, which is a natural feature of real groups. Moreover, OSLOM has performed well in recent community detection benchmarks [34] and it outperformed other algorithms we tested. OSLOM detected 646 K groups, overall.

First, we check the tendency of detected communities towards sociality or topicality with another round of manual annotation. Three independent annotators labeled

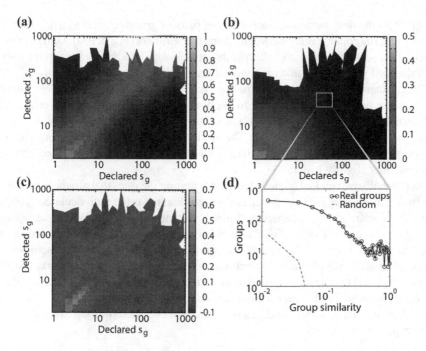

Fig. 5.10 Overlap between declared and detected groups. Jaccard similarity between the member sets of declared and detected groups as a function of their sizes in **a** the actual data, **b** in a null model with randomized groups, and **c** difference between the two. **d** Histogram of the similarity values for a sample of groups in the diagonal

126 distinct detected groups obtaining a Kappa value for detected groups around 0.44. The lower agreement than the one reached for the declared groups is partially determined by the lack of information about the group's profile, not available for detected groups. Among detected groups almost 69 % are labeled as social (vs. 48 % in declared groups).

We then compare the size of declared and detected groups. The size distribution is heavy-tailed and close to power-laws in both cases (not shown) but declared groups tend to be much bigger, having on average 61 members versus 7 members in detected groups. To test if the groups from the two sets overlap, and to what extent, we measure the Jaccard similarity between their sets of members. Similarity is computed for all declared-detected group pairs and for each detected group we select the declared one with the highest similarity value as the best match. We plot the average similarity of the best matches as a function of the size of groups in Fig. 5.10a. For the purpose of comparison with a null model, in Fig. 5.10b we draw the same plot after randomly reshuffling the members of detected groups, while preserving their sizes. We observe that the two plots differ in values significantly along the diagonal, and that the difference between them is substantial, as shown in Fig. 5.10c, meaning that indeed detected groups are, to some extent, similar to the declared ones. Further insights are given by the distribution of similarities of pairs of groups extracted from a small sector of the diagonal, having between 32 and 64 members (Fig. 5.10d). Unlike in the randomized scenario, there are multiple detected groups which overlap significantly with declared groups, and that randomized groups do not show this pattern.

We can therefore conclude that, in some cases the community detection algorithm finds groups which are very similar to the ones defined by the users. Nevertheless, substantial overlap is found for just a small percentage of groups and most of the group pairs have similarity close to 0. The average similarity of detected groups to the best-matching declared groups is 0.082, while for the randomized detected groups is 0.058, only slightly lower.

Additionally, we picked 50 detected groups among the ones that are the most similar to declared groups. These groups have significant overlap with declared groups and should share similar properties. Indeed, the ratio of groups labeled as social among them is closer to that of declared groups and equal to 53 %. We conclude that detected groups are more likely to be social than declared ones. It is a somewhat expected result, since clustering algorithms detect dense parts of a network, and so they are inclined to detect areas with more reciprocal connections. Note that the theory envisions more reciprocal relations in social groups. Thus, community detection algorithms are more likely to find social groups, however, determining to what extent that happens is not trivial.

5.8 The Barrier of Membership Size

The membership size is another important feature of groups, as group size necessarily affects the dynamics of interaction between members.

This intuitive concept has been discussed in depth by the anthropologist Robin Dunbar. In a study he performed in 1992, he measured the correlation between the neocortical volume of primates and the typical size of their social communities [20]. The limits in the size of social groups of primates has been explained primarily by the limited amount of time that an individual could dedicate to social grooming in addition to the organizational issues that arise when communities grow in size and that can be tackled only by enforcing norms that help to maintain them stable.

By extrapolating from the result obtained on primates, Dunbar theorized that the limit of community size for human beings should lie roughly in a ballpark of 100–250, being larger groups too demanding to manage in terms of cognitive efforts for an average person. The anecdotal figure, often presented as the *Dunbar number* is that the maximum size of groups that an individual can manage with reasonable cognitive effort is 150.

The advent of online social media has provided large dataset to verify this theory at scale. One of the most notable attempts has been done by Goncalves et al. [23] on the Twitter by measuring the average social strength ω_i^{out} of each individual i on the mention network:

Fig. 5.11 Out-weight ω_{out} as a function of the out-degree in a Twitter mention network. The *red line* corresponds to the average out-weight, while the *gray shaded area* illustrates the 50% confidence interval. Figure and caption taken from the original publication, courtesy of the authors [23]

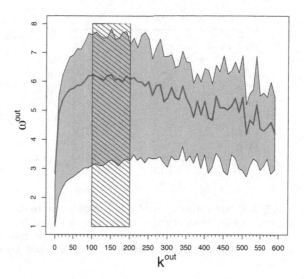

$$\omega_i^{out}(T) = \frac{\sum_i w_{ij}(T)}{k_i^{out}}, \tag{5.12}$$

where w_{ij} is the weight of the edge between users i and j, the weight representing the number of messages exchanged within a time window T, and k_i^{out} is the outdegree of user i, namely the overall number of people he has mentioned durint that time window. In short, ω^{out} represents the amount of attention that the individual pays to her social partners in a certain time frame. Averaging the value of ω^{out} for all the users with the same value of k_{out} and plotting the resulting values against k_{out} results in the trend displayed in Fig. 5.11. The average strength gradually increases until it reaches its maximum between 100 and 200 contacts, signaling that a maximum level of social activity has been reached. Beyond that point, an increase in the number of contacts can no longer be sustained with the same amount of dedication, as Dunbar theorized.

The strong evidence that supports Dunbar's theory in the Twitter scenario by looking at egocentric networks, can be also corroborated with a group-centered perspective. If Dunbar's hypothesis holds, groups that are larger than a certain size will have much lower interaction density between their members than smaller groups. To capture that, we use the activity measure a_g that we have presented in Sect. 5.5.2 and that we report again for the reader's convenience:

$$a_g = \frac{E_g^{int}}{(D_g^{in} D_g^{out})/E},$$

where D_g^{in} and D_g^{out} are total numbers of interactions originated by members of the group g or being targeted to members of this group, and E is the total number of

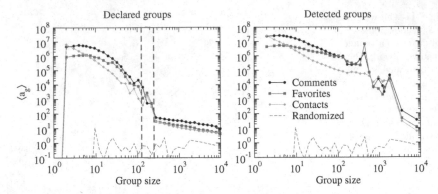

Fig. 5.12 Group activity a_g as a function of the group size for Flickr groups. Activity is measured considering three types of dyadic interactions that might happen inside the group: commenting, favoriting, and creation of following contacts. For the purpose of comparison, we also recompute a_g in randomized null model where the members of groups are reshuffled but their size preserved

interactions in the network. The overall value is higher than 1 when the number of intra-group interactions is higher than the same number expected in a random scenario. When averaging a_g among Flickr groups with the same size, similarly to the analysis that has been conducted on Twitter, we obtain the curve shown in Fig. 5.12.

We observe that the activity decays almost monotonically by construction of the metric: the larger the group, the higher the likelihood of the density of its internal interactions to drop closer to values expected in a random case. However, when measuring a_g for declared groups, a sharp drop of activity occurs for groups with size between 100 and 250. This clearly means that after a certain size, the density of activity within the group cannot be sustained given the high number of participants. When running the same experiment on detected groups, the activity drop is steady and much more moderate. That happens because community detection algorithms tend by design to output node clusters with high numbers of connections between them.

Individuals with thousands of online social contacts are frequent in online social networks; likewise, groups with a membership size beyond the Dunbar number exist as well and indeed there is a large number of groups with thousands of members in Flickr. Those groups however tend either to be pure manifestations of social identity, representing more "social labels" than actual social aggregations (e.g., the group of Canon camera owners), or they are necessarily fragmented in smaller, more active communities. For this reason, when characterizing a group, size is yet another important feature to take into account to reach an unbiased understanding of the group's nature.

5.9 The Role of Groups in Other Social Phenomena

Similarly to social links, groups are structural constituent of the social fabric that mediates most of the interaction dynamics between people. For this reason, the structure of the social network and the phenomena that occur over it are deeply intertwined. Nevertheless, studies in the areas of graph mining and social network analysis are too often conducted in separate sub-branches. One example is the relationship between the study of communities and research on information diffusion. As cleverly noted by Easley and Kleinberg [17], the phenomenon of information diffusion, namely the flow of information along social links generating *information cascades* on a social network, is likely strongly coupled with the concept of community.

In fact, communities usually aggregate people that share some common trait and therefore are more similar to each other than to the rest of the network. The more a community is dissimilar to the external world, the higher the probability of a piece of information that generates inside it to never cross the group borders. In other words: *"cascades and clusters truly are natural opposites clusters block the spread of cascades, and whenever a cascade comes to a stop, there's a cluster that can be used to explain why"* [17].

Recently, this idea inspired the work of Barbieri ct al. [10] who leveraged data on information cascades to detect hidden communities. Given a directed social graph and a set of information cascades observed over it, they propose a stochastic mixture membership generative model to detect communities of nodes that can *explain* such cascades.

We argue that the process of spreading could be determined also by the *type* of communities involved in the process. Intuitively, when a piece of information about a certain topic reaches a community that is interested in the same topic then the information will probably spread easily. But what if a social (instead of topical) community is reached by the information cascade? To shed light on this matter we have run an experiment to check information cascades in relation to the types of groups we identified earlier [18]. To do that, we rely on a well-established work by Cha et al. [13, 14] that uses Flickr to analyze information propagation. They define the process of information diffusion using the favorite information. A piece of information propagates from user u_1 to user u_2 when all the following conditions hold in a strict temporal order:

1. u_2 starts following u_1;
2. u_1 favorites a photo p;
3. u_2 favorites the same photo p.

This experimental framework is motivated by the fact that, in Flickr, users are notified about the photos that their followees favorite. The information diffusion links can be used to reconstruct potentially several information diffusion cascades (also called "diffusion trees"), where the *root* is a user who favorited a photo without having any followees who favorited it before.

To explore the relation between cascades and group types, we have to extend the aforementioned framework by embedding the notion of group. Specifically, we want to check whether a photo that is uploaded to a group pool has a diffusion that is predominantly restricted to that group or spreads beyond the group boundaries. We consider roots of our diffusion trees all the users that comply with the following strict temporal sequence:

1. user u joins group g;
2. photo p is uploaded to g;
3. u favorites p.

For each $(g, p)|g \in G \wedge p \in P$ pair there could be multiple root users, namely multiple members of the group who are not following each other and who all favorite the same photo according to the temporal sequence specified above. We connect all these root users to a common super-root identified by the (g, p) pair. Once the root nodes are identified, we apply the framework by Cha et al., thus obtaining information cascades, each labeled by a unique (g, p) pair. Note that a photo could be uploaded in multiple group pools, thus originating more than one cascade. We consider each of these possible cascades separately.

The method we propose is limited by the fact that the root user might favorite a photo not because it has been published in a group but for any other reason (e.g., it was discovered by random browsing). However, we argue that if the photo has been uploaded to the pool we can assume it to be relevant to the group and the nature of the actual action that triggered the first favorite can be safely disregarded in this type of study.

Given this experimental setup, we compute a pair of values for each cascade. Consider $A_{g,p}$ to be the set of adopters, namely the users who take part in the diffusion tree for the (g, p) pair, and M_g the set of members of group g. We define:

$$c_{g,p} = \frac{|A_{g,p} \cap M_g|}{|M_g|} \tag{5.13}$$

$$s_{g,p} = 1 - \frac{|A_{g,p} \cap M_g|}{|A_{g,p}|} \tag{5.14}$$

The *coverage* $c_{g,p}$ measures how much the group is covered by the information cascade, the portion of group membership that is affected by the spreading process. The *external spreading* $s_{g,p}$ measure, instead, is designed to capture how much more the information spreads outside the group. An example of a cascade is given in Fig. 5.13.

To characterize each group, all the values $c_{g,p}$ and $s_{g,p}$ are averaged for all their photos, leading to the aggregate values c_g and s_g. To study how the information spreads in different group types, we consider the values for each of the group types separately and we compute the average values at fixed group size, to account for any effect possibly given by group dimensionality. The results are shown in Fig. 5.14.

On the socio-topical axis, the difference between different types of group is slight but noticeable, with the topical groups having more coverage and less external spreading (except for a small range of group sizes). This supports the intuition reported in

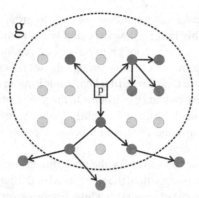

Fig. 5.13 Example of diffusion tree for a photo p uploaded into the photo pool of group g. *Circles* represent users and the *dashed line* marks the boundaries of the group. *Red circles* are the root users. In this example 8 users out of 20 members are nodes of the diffusion tree, leading to $coverage_{g,p} = 0.4$. Also, 3 users outside the group are nodes of the tree, for a total tree size of 11 nodes (except the meta-root), thus leading to $externalCoverage_{g,p} = 0.27$

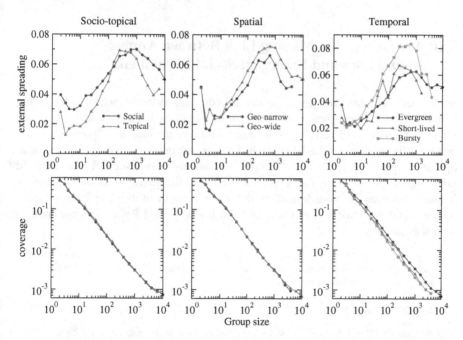

Fig. 5.14 Information diffusion in different group types. Average values of coverage and external spreading for all groups with same number of members. Groups are analyzed according to the three dimensions separately (socio-topical on the *left*, spatial in the *middle*, and temporal on the *right*)

previous work that identifies the boundaries of topical groups as harder to cross by information cascades. This is somehow expected when members of topical groups share interests which are narrow enough to be limited predominantly to the groups members. Conversely, members of social groups do not necessarily share a specific common interest, therefore their favoriting behaviour is more varied and with higher chance to have an echo also outside the group. On the geographical dimension instead the difference is almost negligible, with slightly higher values for geo-wide groups for both metrics. This might be related to a better capacity of geo-wide groups to spread information in general.

More evident trends are obtained for the time dimension. On average, the evergreen groups have more coverage than the short-lived or the bursty, whereas the bursty groups are the ones with most external spreading. Evergreen groups are always active, so they get a lot of attention from their members, partially explaining why photos published in them get more coverage. On the other hand, bursty groups are often related to major events with broad scope whose photos can be of interest to a large audience in the Flickr community not restricted to the members only.

5.10 Are Groups the Missing Link Between Atomic Interactions and Emergent Social Phenomena?

Social networks fall into the category of complex systems, where relationship between atomic components give rise to an emergent behaviour that cannot be inferred or modeled directly from the composition of the individual parts. Complex processes in networks have been studied in several fields including physics, biology, and computer science. Also social scientists have been discussing the so-called *micro-macro* problem for long time. That refers to the duality (and often the incoherence) between the behaviour of an individual actor or of its interpersonal dyadic relations and the behaviour of the masses. In his book [11] Peter Blau, commented on this challenge:

> The problem is to derive the social processes that govern the complex structures of communities and societies from the simpler processes that pervade the daily intercourse among individuals and their interpersonal relations.

Later, in an updated introduction to the same book, he states:

> I thought that this microsociological theory could serve as a foundation for building a macrosociological theory; I no longer think this is true. The reason is that microsociological and macrosociological theories require different approaches and conceptual schemes, and their distinct perspective enrich each other.

Groups fall exactly in between the micro and macro scales, being manifestation of a collective identity that emerges from a limited number of individual motivations. The important role of groups in bridging different scales motivates even more the need for a nuanced characterization of their multiple facets.

We have contributed to fill this gap by proposing a set of general metrics to capture the spatial, temporal, and socio-topical dimensions of groups, which are the three aspects about groups that have been informally identified in the previous literature but never formalized and studied in conjunction. We identify two main classes of spatially-characterized groups (geo-narrow and geo-wide) and discover three major patterns of their temporal activity (evergreen, bursty, and short-lived). By transposing the concepts of the common identity and common theory into metrics of reciprocity, activity, and topical diversity we are able to accurately tell apart social from topical groups. The analysis of the three dimensions in combination allows us to show interesting correlations between different classes. In particular, we find that groups that manage to spread on geographically-large scale are usually more long-lived than "local" groups, that topical groups tend to have a constant activity behaviour, being tolerant to the churn of their users, and that social groups have bursty activity traces, with all the members joining at first and then interacting with each other from time to time, after relatively long periods of inactivity. We have also discussed the structural effect that group size in shaping the amount of activity within members, thus giving to groups of different sizes different relevance to the aspect of the construction of a social identity versus being vehicles of social bond construction. Last, inspired by previous work that puts in relation communities and information cascades and relying on a well-established model of information diffusion on Flickr, we study the dependency between group type and volume of information spreading inside or outside a group. We find that social and bursty groups allow the information to spread crossing the boundaries of groups more than topical and evergreen groups, that instead tend to retain more information within them.

Besides carrying on detailed studies about all the facets of groups' structure and dynamics, it is equally important, as Blau wisely suggests, to corroborate and comple-ment the findings of studies focusing at the group level by doing research on related social structures or dynamics. Especially, the socio-topical dichotomy coming from the principles of the common identity and common bond theory has been spotted also at the level of social link, without the need of fixing any apriori classes. In our recent work [4] we focus on dyadic conversations in Flickr (represented by mutual com-menting on photos), trying to interpret individual conversational exchanges under the light of Blau's social exchange theory [11], stating that every dyad is a repeated set of exchanges of different types of *non-material resources* such as knowledge, social support or manifestation of approval. To associate each message to those non-material resources, we developed a method that combines topic detection with the analysis of reciprocation in conversations, motivated by the assumption that con-versations might touch upon several topics but tend to exchange the same type of resource all along. This assumption has been derived as a theoretical necessity in the exchange of status [24], has been shown to exist in the case of social support [5]. The interesting aspect of the method is that, differently from classic classification approaches, the number of resources is not specified in input, allowing the discovery of the main non-material resources exchanged in any conversation network.

The application of the method on the Flickr conversation network finds two well-distinct domains, namely the ones of *status exchange* and *social support*, the first being associated to expression of appreciation or esteem for each other's work (e.g., "very nice shot, you are a good photographer!") and the second one representing everyday minute exchange or chit chat with some emotional evaluation (e.g., "how is your dad? I hope he is feeling better now"). The parallel between the socio-topical partition of groups is striking and, although the outcomes of the two different methods have not been directly compared yet in a quantitative way, it is surprising to get concordant results from an unsupervised method focused on atomic dyadic interactions and a supervised classification of groups.

Future work aimed at understanding social structures, either online or offline, should tap right into this direction: different social phenomena such as formation of groups and diffusion of information should be studied no longer in separation, as they are manifestations of the same complex entity. In this setting, groups might represent a key tile to bridge between the micro and macro scales of social interactions.

Acknowledgments We thank Przemyslaw Grabowicz, David Martin-Borregón, Rossano Schifanella, Bogdan State, Alejandro Jaimes, and Ricardo Baeza-Yates for the research work they have conducted jointly with the author and that is summarized in this chapter. This work is supported by the SocialSensor FP7 project, partially funded by the EC under contract number 287975.

Appendix

Correction Parameter for Standard Deviation

Standard formulation of standard deviation is:

$$\sigma^2 = \sqrt{\frac{1}{N-1} \sum (t - \mu)^2} \tag{5.15}$$

Given a list N values t that can assume in $[0, 1]$, with a given mean μ the greater possible standard deviation would be achieved under a Bernoulli distribution with $t = 1$ with probability p and $t = 0$ with probability q. Under these circumstances we can write:

$$\sum (t - \mu)^2 = N \cdot p \cdot (0 - \mu)^2 + N \cdot q \cdot (1 - \mu)^2 \tag{5.16}$$

which, under a Bernoulli distribution, can be rewritten as:

$$\sum (t - \mu)^2 = N \cdot (1 - \mu) \cdot (0 - \mu)^2 + N \cdot \mu \cdot (1 - \mu)^2 \tag{5.17}$$

$$= N \cdot (1 - \mu)\mu^2 + N \cdot \mu(1 + \mu^2 - 2\mu) \tag{5.18}$$

$$= N\mu(1 - \mu) \tag{5.19}$$

Therefore, being $N\mu(1 - \mu)$ the maximum value for $\sum(t - \mu)^2$, we use it as normalization factor in Formula 5.2.

Correction Parameter for Skewness

Under a Bernoulli distribution with that assumes value 0 with probability $p(0)$ and 1 with $p(1)$, the mean μ is equal to $p(1)$, while the median is given by:

$$median = \begin{cases} 0 & if \quad p(0) > p(1) \\ 0.5 & if \quad p(0) = p(1) \\ 1 & if \quad p(0) < p(1) \end{cases} \tag{5.20}$$

In case $p(0) = p(1) = 0.5$ the normalization factor is not relevant so mean and median are equal and the difference would remain the same. In other cases, one can define the maximum difference (max_{diff}) given the mean μ as follows:

$$maxdiff = \begin{cases} 1 - \mu & if \quad p(0) < p(1) \\ \mu & if \quad p(0) > p(1) \end{cases} \tag{5.21}$$

Under a Bernoulli distribution taking values 0 and 1, the mean is equal to $p(1)$. Also, $p(0)$ is equal to the remaining $1 - \mu$. Given that, we can rewrite the equation as:

$$max_{diff} = \begin{cases} 1 - \mu & if \quad 1 - \mu < \mu \\ \mu & if \quad 1 - \mu > \mu \end{cases} \tag{5.22}$$

that can be finally rewritten as:

$$max_{diff} = \min(1 - \mu, \mu) \tag{5.23}$$

which we use it as normalization factor in Formula 5.3.

References

1. Aiello LM, Barrat A, Cattuto C, Schifanella R, Ruffo G (2012) Link creation and information spreading over social and communication ties in an interest-based online social network. EPJ Data Sci 1(12):1–31
2. Aiello LM, Barrat A, Schifanella R, Cattuto C, Markines B, Menczer F (2012) Friendship prediction and homophily in social media. ACM Trans Web 6(2):9:1–9:33
3. Aiello LM, Deplano M, Schifanella R, Ruffo G (2012) People are strange when you're a stranger: impact and influence of bots on social networks. In: Proceedings of the 6th AAAI international conference on weblogs and social media, ICWSM'12. AAAI, pp 10–17

4. Aiello LM, Schifanella R, State B (2014) Reading the source code of social ties. In: Proceedings of the 2014 ACM conference on web science, WebSci'14. ACM, New York, pp 10–17
5. Antonucci T, Fuhrer R, Jackson J (1990) Social support and reciprocity: a cross-ethnic and cross-national perspective. J Soc Pers Relatsh, 7(4):519–530
6. Backstrom L, Huttenlocher D, Kleinberg J, Lan X (2006) Group formation in large social networks: membership, growth, and evolution. In: Proceedings of the 12th ACM SIGKDD international conference on knowledge discovery and data mining—KDD'06. ACM Press, New York, p 44
7. Backstrom L, Huttenlocher D, Kleinberg J, Lan X (2006) Group formation in large social networks: membership, growth, and evolution. In: Proceedings of the 12th ACM SIGKDD international conference on knowledge discovery and data mining, KDD'06. ACM, New York, pp 44–54
8. Backstrom L, Kumar R, Marlow C, Novak J, Tomkins A (2008) Preferential behavior in online groups. In: Proceedings of the international conference on web search and web data mining—WSDM'08. ACM, New York, pp 117–128
9. Baldassarri A, Barrat A, Capocci A, Halpin H, Lehner U, Ramasco J, Robu V, Taraborelli D (2008) The Berners-Lee hypothesis: Power laws and group structure in flickr. In: Alani H, Staab S, Stumme G, (eds), Social web communities, number 08391 in Dagstuhl seminar proceedings, Dagstuhl, Germany. Schloss Dagstuhl - Leibniz-Zentrum fuer Informatik, Germany
10. Barbieri N, Bonchi F, Manco G (2013) Cascade-based community detection. In: Proceedings of the sixth ACM international conference on web search and data mining, WSDM'13. ACM, New York, pp 33–42
11. Blau PM (1964) Exchange and power in social life. Transaction Publishers, New Jersey
12. Butler B (1999) When a group is not a group: an empirical examination of metaphors for online social structure. Ph.D. thesis, Carnegie Mellon University, Pittsburgh
13. Cha M, Mislove A, Adams B, Gummadi KP (2008) Characterizing social cascades in Flickr. In: Proceedings of the first workshop on online social networks—WOSP'08. ACM, Seattle, pp 13–18
14. Cha M, Mislove A, Gummadi KP (2009) A measurement-driven analysis of information propagation in the Flickr social network. In: Proceedings of the 18th international conference on world wide web—WWW'09. ACM, Madrid, pp 721–730
15. Collins NL, Miller LC (1994) Self-disclosure and liking: a meta-analytic review. Psychol Bull 166(3):457–475
16. Cox A, Clough P, Siersdorfer S (2011) Developing metrics to characterize Flickr groups. J Am Soc Inf Sci Technol 62:493–506
17. David E, Jon K (2010) Networks, crowds, and markets: reasoning about a highly connected world. Cambridge University Press, New York
18. David M-B, Aiello LM, Grabowicz P, Jaimes A, Baeza-Yates R (2014) Characterization of online groups along space, time, and social dimensions. EPJ Data Sci 3(1):8
19. De Choudhury M (2009) Modeling and predicting group activity over time in online social media. In: Proceedings of the 20th ACM conference on hypertext and hypermedia, HT'09. ACM, New York, pp 349–350
20. Dunbar RIM (1992) Neocortex size as a constraint on group size in primates. J Hum Evol 22(6):469–493
21. Dunbar RIM (1998) The social brain hypothesis. Evol Anthropol 6:178–190
22. Gloor PA, Zhao Y (2006) Analyzing actors and their discussion topics by semantic social network analysis. In: Proceedings of the conference on information visualization, IV'06. IEEE Computer Society, Washington, pp 130–135
23. Goncalves B, Perra N, Vespignani A (2011) Modeling users' activity on twitter networks: validation of Dunbar's number. PLoS ONE 6(8):e22656, 08
24. Gould RV (2002) The origins of status hierarchies: a formal theory and empirical test. Am J Sociol 107(5)
25. Grabowicz PA, Eguíluz VM (2012) Heterogeneity shapes groups growth in social online communities. Europhys Lett 97(2):28002

26. Grabowicz PA, Ramasco JJ, Moro E, Pujol JM, Eguiluz VM (2012) Social features of online networks: the strength of intermediary ties in online social media. PLoS One 7(1):e29358
27. Grabowicz PA, Aiello LM, Eguiluz VM, Jaimes A (2013) Distinguishing topical and social groups based on common identity and bond theory. In: Proceedings of the sixth ACM international conference on web search and data mining, WSDM'13. ACM, New York, pp 627–636
28. Holmes P, Cox AM (2011) Every group carries the flavour of the admins, leadership on Flickr. Int J Web Based Commun 7(3):376–391
29. Hric D, Darst RK, Fortunato S (2014) Community detection in networks: structural clusters versus ground truth. arXiv:1406.0146
30. Kairam S, Brzozowski M, Huffaker D, Chi E (2012) Talking in circles: selective sharing in Google+. In: Proceedings of the SIGCHI conference on human factors in computing systems, CHI'12. ACM, New York, pp 1065–1074
31. Kairam SR, Wang DJ, Leskovec J (2012) The life and death of online groups: predicting group growth and longevity. In: Proceedings of the fifth ACM international conference on web search and data mining, WSDM'12. ACM, New York, pp 673–682
32. Krackhardt D, Porter LW (1986) The snowball effect: turnover embedded in communication networks. J Appl Psychol 71(1):50–55
33. Laine MSS, Ercal G, Luo B (2011) User groups in social networks: an experimental study on Youtube. In: 2011 44th Hawaii international conference on system sciences (HICSS), January 2011, pp 1–10
34. Lancichinetti A, Fortunato S, Radicchi F (2008) Benchmark graphs for testing community detection algorithms. Phys Rev E 78:046110
35. Lancichinetti A, Radicchi F, Ramasco JJ, Fortunato S (2011) Finding statistically significant communities in networks. PLoS One 6(4):e18961, 04
36. Ludford PJ, Cosley D, Frankowski D, Terveen L (2004) Think different: increasing online community participation using uniqueness and group dissimilarity. In: Proceedings of the SIGCHI conference on human factors in computing systems. ACM, New York, pp 631–638
37. Miller AD, Edwards WK (2007) Give and take: a study of consumer photo-sharing culture and practice. In: Proceedings of the SIGCHI conference on human factors in computing systems, CHI'07, ACM. New York, pp 347–356
38. Mislove A, Marcon M, Gummadi KP, Druschel P, Bhattacharjee B (2007) Measurement and analysis of online social networks. In: Proceedings of the 7th ACM SIGCOMM conference on Internet measurement—IMC'07, ACM. San Diego, pp 29–42
39. Negi S, Chaudhury S (2012) Finding subgroups in a Flickr group. In: Proceedings of the 2012 IEEE international conference on multimedia and expo, ICME'12. IEEE Computer Society, Washington, pp 675–680
40. Negoescu RA, Gatica-Perez D (2008) Analyzing Flickr groups. In: Proceedings of the 2008 international conference on content-based image and video retrieval, CIVR '08, ACM. New York, pp 417–426
41. Negoescu RA, Gatica-Perez D (2008) Topickr: flickr groups and users reloaded. In: Proceedings of the 16th ACM international conference on multimedia, MM '08, ACM, New York, pp 857–860
42. Negoescu RA, Gatica-Perez D (2010) Modeling Flickr communities through probabilistic topic-based analysis. Trans Multi 12(5):399–416
43. Nov O, Naaman M, Ye C (2010) Analysis of participation in an online photo-sharing community: a multidimensional perspective. J Am Soc Inf Sci Technol 61(3):555–566
44. Park N, Kee KF, Valenzuela S (2009) Being immersed in social networking environment: Facebook groups, uses and gratifications, and social outcomes. Cyberpsy Behav Soc Netw 12(6):729–733
45. Negoescu RA, Adams B, Phung D, Venkatesh S, Gatica-Perez D (2009) Flickr hypergroups. In: Proceedings of the 17th ACM international conference on multimedia, MM'09. ACM, New York, pp 813–816
46. Pelleg D, Moore AW (2000) X-means: extending k-means with efficient estimation of the number of clusters. In: Proceedings of the seventeenth international conference on machine learning, ICML'00. Morgan Kaufmann Publishers Inc, San Francisco, pp 727–734

47. Pissard N, Prieur C (2007) Thematic vs. social networks in web 2.0 communities: a case study on Flickr groups. In: Algotel conference
48. Porter CE (2004) A typology of virtual communities: a multi-disciplinary foundation for future research. J Comput Med Commun 10(1)
49. Prentice DA, Miller DT, Lightdale JR (1994) Asymmetries in attachments to groups and to their members: distinguishing between common-identity and common-bond groups. Personal Soc Psychol Bull 20(5):484–493
50. Prieur C, Cardon D, Beuscart J-S, Pissard N, Pons P (2008) The strength of weak cooperation: a case study on Flickr. CoRR, arXiv:0802.2317
51. Prieur C, Pissard N, Beuscart JS, Cardon D (2008) Thematic and social indicators for Flickr groups. In: Proceedings of ICWSM
52. Ren Y, Kraut R, Kiesler S (2007) Applying common identity and bond theory to design of online communities. Organ Stud 28(3):377–408
53. Kai S (2002) Common bond and common identity groups on the internet: attachment and normative behavior in on-topic and off-topic chats. Gr Dyn Theory Res Pract 6(1):27–37
54. Santo F (2010) Community detection in graphs. Phys Rep 486(3–5):75–174
55. Spertus E, Sahami M, Buyukkokten O (2005) Evaluating similarity measures: a large-scale study in the Orkut social network. In: Proceedings of the eleventh ACM SIGKDD international conference on knowledge discovery in data mining, KDD'05. ACM, New York, pp 678–684
56. Tajfel H (1981) Human groups and social categories. Cambridge University Press, Cambridge
57. Tajfel H (1982) Social identity and intergroup relations. Cambridge University Press, Cambridge
58. Tajfel H, Billig MG, Bundy RP, Flament C (1971) Social categorization and intergroup behaviour. Eur J Soc Psychol 1:149–178
59. Tang L, Wang X, Liu H (2011) Group profiling for understanding social structures. ACM Trans Intell Syst Technol 3(1):15:1–15:25
60. Turner JC (1985) Social categorization and the self concept: a social cognitive theory of group behavior. In: Lawler EJ (ed) Advances in group process. JAI, pp 77–122
61. Utz S, Sassenberg K (2002) Distributive justice in common-bond and common-identity groups. Gr Process Intergr Relat 5(2):151–162
62. Van House NA (2007) Flickr and public image-sharing: distant closeness and photo exhibition. In: Extended abstracts on human factors in computing systems, CHI'07. ACM, New York, pp 2717–2722
63. Van Zwol R (2007) Flickr: who is looking? In: IEEE/WIC/ACM international conference on web intelligence, WI'07. IEEE Computer Society, pp 184–190
64. Yang J, Leskovec J (2012) Defining and evaluating network communities based on ground-truth. CoRR, arXiv:1205.6233
65. Wang J, Zhao Z, Zhou J, Wang H, Cui B, Qi G (2012) Recommending flickr groups with social topic model. Inf Retr 15(3–4):278–295
66. Welser HT, Gleave E, Fisher D, Smith M (2007) Visualizing the signatures of social roles in online discussion groups. J Soc Struct 8(2)

Chapter 6
Privacy Issues in Discovering Communities in Social Networks

Bin Zhou

Abstract In this chapter, we review the literature on privacy issues in social networks, with a special focus on communities in social networks. We consider two scenarios: privacy breach in social network data publishing and privacy breach in online social networks. We discuss various aspects of privacy issues in social networks, and summarize several representative studies on privacy protection techniques for social networks.

6.1 Introduction

A *social network* is used to model complex social structures which involve many participants. Generally, social networks capture their participants and various social relationships by *graph* structures using a set of vertices and direct/indirect edges between vertices. Vertices model individual social actors in a network, while edges model relationships between social actors. Nowadays, more and more social networking sites are available online. The fast development of Web 2.0 applications makes building social connections much more convenient than ever before. As a result, the research and development of social networks have received dramatic interests in recent years.

There are different kinds of social networks existing in our daily life. Popular examples of such social networks include *friendship networks*, *telephone communication networks*, and *academia co-authorship networks*, to name a few. Most recently, the rapidly increasing popularity of online social networking sites (OSN) such as Facebook and Twitter makes people around the world all connected. A recent survey study conducted by Social Networking Watch,[1] a popular news website for social media industry, revealed that more than 80 % of the world's internet population use at least one such online social networking site. For those *online social networks*, teens

---

[1]http://www.socialnetworkingwatch.com.

B. Zhou (✉)
Department of Information Systems, University of Maryland, Baltimore County,
1000 Hilltop Circle, Baltimore, MD, USA
e-mail: bzhou@umbc.edu

© Springer International Publishing Switzerland 2015   135
G. Paliouras et al. (eds.), *User Community Discovery*, Human–Computer
Interaction Series, DOI 10.1007/978-3-319-23835-7_6

and young adults are the heaviest participants. Specifically, 83 % of 13–17 years old people and 74 % of 18–29 years old people visit at least one online social networking site on a daily basis.[2]

Social networks contain rich information. Users in online social networks often share detailed user profiles. Various social relationships between users are usually beneficial to entrepreneurs and commercial companies. In many cases, those social networks can be served as a customer relationship management tool for companies selling products and services. For example, retailers such as Amazon is widely reported to use social networks to promote specific merchandise and expand their customer bases.[3]

6.1.1 Community Detection in Social Networks

With the rapid growth of social networks, *social network analysis* [36, 42] has emerged as an important technique in modern sociology, economics, geography, and information science. Due to the complex social structures in social networks, many interesting knowledge is hidden underneath the graph structures. The fundamental objective of social network analysis is thus to discover those hidden social patterns.

Early studies of social network analysis have focused on analyzing attributes of individual social actors. However, recent development of social network analysis has shown that the complex social relationships between social actors are often more important and informative than the attributes of individual social actors. Many different types of social network analysis techniques have been developed in the literature for discovering interesting knowledge from social networks. Among them, *community detection* in social networks is one of the most important social network analysis techniques.

People naturally tend to form groups, within their working environment, family, or friends. *Communities* in social networks, sometimes referred to *clusters* in social networks, are groups of social actors which probably share some common properties. Based on different modeling of properties, communities in social network may have different representations.

For example, Fig. 6.1 represents a simple social network which contains 9 individuals. Each vertex in the network corresponds to an individual, and two vertices are linked using an undirected edge if the two individuals are close friends. By analyzing the graph structure, two communities can be identified, one containing vertices in grey color, and the other containing vertices in white color. Individuals in the same

---

[2]http://www.priv.gc.ca/information/social/index.asp.
[3]http://www.internetretailer.com/2011/12/27/amazon-had-most-social-media-influence-holiday-season.

Fig. 6.1 A simple friendship network with two communities. One community contains vertices in *grey color*, and the other community contains vertices in *white color*

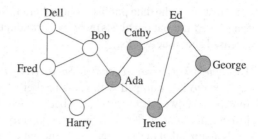

community tend to be connected more closely than those from different communities. As an exception, the individual "Ada" can be considered in either of the two communities.

6.1.2 Privacy Threats in Social Communities

Identifying communities in social networks can be useful for some concrete applications. For example, in the network of purchase relationships between customers and products of many retailers such as Amazon, identifying groups of customers with similar interests enables those retailers to provide efficient recommendation systems to promote specific merchandize and enhance their business opportunities. There are many other important applications of communities in social networks, such as prediction of social relationships, classification of user behavior, fraud detection, and data visualization.

On the other hand, as more and more personal data are shared in social networks, privacy becomes a serious concern in social network analysis. Data privacy is usually considered as "freedom from unauthorized intrusion" [40]. A privacy breach occurs when a piece of private information about an individual is disclosed to an adversary, someone whose goal is to compromise privacy [45]. In online social networks, individuals join voluntarily, and different types of information, most of which are accessible to many other members of the network, are stored.

To protect their private information, users in social networks may decide to hide certain types of information, limit the information access to a selected set of users, or even simply do not share those personal data in social networks. At first glance, those strategies may be sufficiently enough to protect individual's privacy in social networks. However, partly due to the power of many social network analysis techniques, a bunch of recent research studies indicate that even if a well-educated individual discloses little information in social networks, malicious users may still utilize community structure to infer additional information about the target individual.

A common scenario of privacy breach considered in the social network privacy research community is when social networks are released to the third-party data recipients. In this scenario, the publisher of social networks (i.e., the Twitter company) is trustworthy and social network users are willing to provide their personal information to the data publisher; however, the trust is not transitive to the data recipients (e.g., the data analysts) who will conduct various data analytical tasks on the released social networks.

Example 6.1 (Privacy Breach in Social Network Data Publishing) The attackers are assumed to be equipped with some background knowledge. For example, consider the social network in Fig. 6.1, the background knowledge could be some pieces of information that an attacker knows in advance about the individuals in the network. Let's assume that the attacker knows the names of each individual in the network. The attacker also knows that the individual "Ed" lives in Washington, DC. When the social network is released to the third-party data recipients, some pieces of information may be removed due to privacy concerns. For example, the individual "George" thinks his location information is private and thus removes his location in the released social network.

Can the location information of George be inferred from the released social network? In fact, if the attacker conducts a community detection task on the data, the attacker may find out that George and Ed are in the same community. According to the assumption that users in the same community may share some common properties (e.g., live close to each other in this case), the attacker may easily conclude that George lives in Washington, DC with a high probability.

In the scenario of publishing social network data, attacker's background knowledge plays a vital role to develop countermeasures. Based on different assumptions, many privacy protection techniques have been developed in the literature. Some representative studies about privacy protection of social network data publishing will be reviewed in Sect. 6.3.

A different scenario of privacy breach considered in the social network privacy research community focuses on those popular online social networking sites. Once users join those websites, they are able to publish and share their information such as personal user profiles and various daily activities with their friends in the network. To enhance privacy protection, those popular online social networking sites such as Facebook, Twitter and LinkedIn provide users with different privacy settings. These access control-based privacy settings enable users to place restrictions on who may view their personal information shared in the networks.

At first glance, privacy settings provide intuitive ways to categorize users into different groups. Information access in online social networks can be limited to certain trusted groups of users. However, there are some practical issues when adopting access control-based privacy settings. One common issue is that privacy settings in many online social networking sites are often very complex, sometimes even have contradictions among different privacy rules. Users often find hard time to set up proper privacy settings. Moreover, several recent studies indicated that some vulnerabilities exist in those privacy settings. Attackers may abuse those vulnerabilities in those privacy settings to breach private information.

Example 6.2 (Privacy Breach in Online Social Networks) The default access control-based privacy setting in many online social networking sites is to make information access restricted to directed friends. For example, consider the simple social network depicted in Fig. 6.1, Ed may only allow his directed friends Cathy, Irene, and George to view his social activities shared in the network.

However, some popular online social networking sites are continuously reported to have vulnerabilities in their privacy settings. For example, the introduction of open APIs to those online social networking sites creates a new way to circumvent access control settings. A real-life case is Facebook. Facebook released its social networking API for third-party developers to design various kinds of applications. However, once a user installed those applications in his/her private profiles, the third-party developers immediately obtain the privileges of the profile owners and can query the API for the personal information of the users and members of the users' groups. It is reported in [37] that many users' hidden dates of birth can be exposed in Facebook.

Some recent studies also showed that user's private information protected by the privacy settings of those online social networking sites can be easily compromised [35]. It is mainly due to the fact that the privacy setting policy provided by those social networking sites is intrinsically vulnerable. For instance, in many online social networking sites such as Facebook, Twitter, and LinkedIn, the friend list can be set to be "protected" which means only direct friends can access the friend list. However, users in those online social networking sites can configure their privacy settings independently. As shown in Fig. 6.1, Ed and George are mutual friends. If George sets his friend list to be "protected" but Ed sets his friend list to be "public", an attacker, who does not establish any connections with Ed or George, is still able to conclude that Ed is one of George's friends. The friend list of George is not protected as it claims to be.

There are several other privacy breach scandals of online social networks reported up to date [20–24, 31]. The above mentioned privacy threats not only apply to celebrity but also apply to millions of regular users, among which nearly 20 % individuals are teens and young adults whose self-protection consciousness is relatively weak. The current privacy settings provided by those online social networking sites are fragile. Several research efforts have been devoted to enhance access control settings in online social networks, which will be briefly reviewed in Sect. 6.4.

Privacy issue is a broad term in the society. The scope of this chapter focuses on privacy issues for user communities in social networks, with an emphasis on understanding potential privacy threats in social networks and practical privacy protection techniques. It is worth mentioning that there are also some other studies related to privacy issues in social networks. For example, Frikken and Golle [15] studied the problem of constructing a graph from individuals who are vertices in the graph without intruding the privacy of the individuals. Wang et al. [41] proposed using description logic as a knowledge representation in social network data publishing. Leskovec and Faloutsos [27] proposed a method to generate a graph fitting the graph properties of a give graph. The graph generated can be used as a perturbed anonymization of the original graph. Another broad research area of privacy issues in social networks is related to legal compliance [12]. Interested readers may refer to a few recent survey studies [45, 48] for broader coverage of privacy research in social networks.

The remainder of the chapter is organized as follows. In Sect. 6.2, we discuss different types of information that could be considered as privacy in social networks. In Sect. 6.3, we focus on the privacy threats when social networks are published to third-party data recipients, and review a set of representative studies on privacy protection data publishing of social networks. In Sect. 6.4, we provide a discussion on recent development of enhancing access control-based privacy settings in online social networks. Finally, Sect. 6.5 concludes this chapter and provides a few emerging directions for future studies.

6.2 Modeling Privacy in Social Networks

Rich information is contained in social networks. Some may be public and no privacy concerns, but some may lead to serious consequences if they are compromised. To battle privacy attacks and develop preservation techniques in social networks, we first need to identify the *private information* in social networks which may be under attack. In this section, we first discuss a general graph representation of social networks. Then, we emphasize various models of privacy in social networks.

6.2.1 Graph Representation of Social Networks

Generally, we model a social network as a simple graph $G = (V, E, L, \mathscr{L}_V, \mathscr{L}_E, H, \mathscr{H}_V)$, where V is a set of vertices, $E \subseteq V \times V$ is a set of edges, L is a set of labels, and H is a set of groups. There exist a labeling function $\mathscr{L}_V : V \to L$ which assigns each vertex a label and a labeling function $\mathscr{L}_E : E \to L$ which assigns each edge a label. There also exists a group assignment function $\mathscr{H}_V : V \to H$ which assigns each vertex to some groups in the network. A group of vertices can be regarded as a community in social networks. For a graph G, $V(G)$, $E(G)$, $L(G)$, $\mathscr{L}_V(G)$, $\mathscr{L}_E(G)$, $H(G)$, and $\mathscr{H}_V(G)$ are the set of vertices, the set of edges, the set of labels, the vertex labeling function in G, the edge labeling function in G, the set of vertex groups, and the group assignment function in G, respectively.

In addition, users in online social networking sites are able to publish and share various social activities such as posting a message or uploading a photograph. We use A to denote all the possible social activities in online social networks. There is a mapping function $\mathscr{A}_V : V \to A$ which indicates which individual does what social activity.

6.2.2 Definition of Privacy in Social Networks

The privacy issue in relational data has been well studied in the past decade [2]. For most existing research about privacy protection on relational data, the attributes in a relational table are usually divided into two categories: non-sensitive attributes and sensitive attributes. The values of those sensitive attributes are often considered to be privacy for specific individuals. However, due to complex structures and rich information in social networks, modeling privacy in social networks could be much more challenging. In many large-scale social networks, much more pieces of information can be considered as privacy of some individuals.

Some existing studies about social network privacy [25, 28, 30, 45, 48] provided different coverage on modeling privacy in social networks. In this chapter, we follow our previous work [48] and summarize several common types of information that can be modeled as privacy in social networks.

- **The existence of an individual in the network**. In some social networks, whether a target individual appears in the network or not can be considered as privacy of the individual. For example, suppose a social network of millionaires is released where each vertex in the network represents a millionaire. If a target individual can be determined appearing in the network, an attacker knows that the target individual must be a millionaire. As another example, a disease infection network is valuable in public health research. However, if an attacker can determine that a target individual appears in the network, then the target individual's privacy of having the infection is breached.
- **Properties of an individual in the network**. In many social networks, some properties of a vertex such as *vertex degree*, that is, the number of edges associated with a vertex, can be considered as privacy of the individual. For example, if an adversary knows the degree of a target individual in a financial support network, the adversary knows how many support sources the target individual has. As another example, if an adversary knows the distance between a target individual to the center of a community in a social network, whether the victim is a community leader can be easily derived.
- **Sensitive labels of an individual in the network**. In some social networks, vertices may carry labels (i.e., there exists a vertex labeling function $\mathscr{L}_V : V \rightarrow L$). Similar to relational data, labels of vertices in social networks can also be divided into two categories: non-sensitive vertex labels and sensitive vertex labels. Therefore, the values of sensitive vertex labels in social networks are considered to be privacy of the individuals. For example, in a disease infection network, each individual may be associated with a sensitive label disease. The disease of a target individual can be identified by adversaries once the target can be uniquely linked to a vertex in the graph or a group of vertices having the same sensitive label in the graph.
- **The existence of a relationship in the network**. In social networks, an edge between two vertices indicates that there is a relationship between the two corresponding individuals. The relationship between vertices can be considered as privacy of individuals. For example, in a finance transaction network, two vertices

are connected by an edge if there is a finance transaction happens between them. An adversary may detect whether two target individuals have any finance transactions by examining whether there exists an edge between the two individuals in the network.

- **Weights associated with a relationship in the network**. Some social networks may be weighted. The weights of an edge can reflect affinity between two vertices or record the communication frequency between the two individuals. For example, a social network about telephone communications between friends may be weighted such that the weight of an edge is the communication frequency between two individuals, which may be considered as privacy for some individuals.

- **Sensitive labels of a relationship in the network**. In some social networks, edges may carry several labels as well (i.e., there exists an edge labeling function $\mathscr{L}_E : E \to L$). Similar to the above case of sensitive labels of an individual, the labels of relationships may be divided into non-sensitive edge labels and sensitive edge labels. The values of sensitive edge labels are considered as privacy for the corresponding two individuals. For example, edges in a social network about communications may be associated with labels such as `duration`, `time`, and `communication location`. Some labels of the communication could be categorized as the privacy of individuals.

- **Properties of social network structure**. In social network analysis, many graph metrics have been proposed to analyze the social graph structures, such as *betweenness centrality* (that is, the degree an individual lies between other individuals in the network), *closeness centrality* (that is, the degree an individual is close to all other individuals in the network directly or indirectly), *degree centrality* (that is, the count of the number of relationships to other individuals in the network), *the length of a path* (that is, the distances between pairs of vertices in the network), *reachability* (that is, the degree any vertex of a social network can reach other vertices of the network), and so on. As all of the above mentioned metrics of the graph structure indicate the fundamental properties of the individual in the network, they may be considered as privacy for some individuals.

- **Participation of an individual in a group in the network**. Users in social networks may participate in different communities/groups (i.e., there exists a group assignment function $\mathscr{H}_V : V \to H$). On one hand, the groups in some online social networking sites may be explicitly listed. For example, a celebrity or an organization can create a Facebook page. Users can join those pages to participate in the groups of similar users. On the other hand, several community detection methods in social network analysis are able to identify hidden communities in social networks. In many real-life situations, users may not want to disclose the information that they participate in certain groups in social networks. Thus, the participation of an individual in some groups may be considered as privacy.

- **Unauthorized disclosure of certain social activities in the network**. Many social network users actively publish their social activities. For example, Facebook users can post their status updates, upload photographs to the website, click the "like" button, or comment on others' activities. Some users may only allow certain trusted friends to view their social activities. Thus, if unauthorized users obtain access to those restricted social activities, we could consider that as a privacy breach for those users in social networks.

Many online social networking sites are continuously under development and new privacy breach scenarios may arise. Thus, it is important to emphasize that the categorization of modeling privacy in social networks may need to be evolved accordingly. The above-mentioned list of modeling privacy captures the majority of well-known privacy breach scenarios studied in the literature. Modeling privacy is important since it sets up the goal of privacy protection in social networks. Different privacy concerns may lead to different problem definitions and accordingly different privacy protection techniques.

Liu et al. [30] and Zheleva and Getoor [44, 45] proposed different categorizations of modeling privacy in social networks. They classified different types of privacy in social networks into *identity disclosure* (that is, the identity of an individual who is associated with a vertex is revealed), *attribute disclosure* (that is, the values of sensitive attributes associated with each vertex is compromised), and *link disclosure* (that is, the sensitive relationship between two individuals is disclosed). Zheleva and Getoor [45] also described *affiliation link disclosure* which models the scenario when an attacker is able to identify whether an individual joins an affiliation group. The different categorization schema captures similar sets of privacy breach scenarios. The categorization presented here provides detailed and more extensive categories comparing to other categorizations [30, 44, 45].

6.3 Privacy Protection in Social Network Data Publishing

To battle privacy attacks in social networks reviewed in Sect. 6.1.2, a bunch of privacy protection techniques have been developed in the literature. Generally, different privacy breach scenarios require different privacy protection techniques. In this section, we will focus on the privacy breach scenario when some social networks are published to third-party data recipients. In Sect. 6.4, we will discuss some recent developments regarding privacy breach scenarios in those online social networking sites.

When social networks are published to third parties, the data recipients have full access to the released data. As many effective techniques of social network analysis are available to discover interesting knowledge from data, the published social networks need to be sanitized to remove certain sensitive and private information. One common strategy that data publishers can sanitize the data is by conducting a *data anonymization* process [2]. The goal of data anonymization is to transform the original data to an anonymized version such that the identifying information is removed and privacy information of individuals is preserved. Meanwhile, the anonymized data should still be useful for various data analytical tasks.

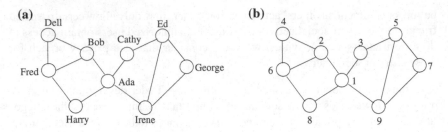

Fig. 6.2 A simple anonymization technique to replace the identifying attributes such as name using meaningless integer identifiers. **a** The original social network. **b** The anonymized social network by replacing names with integer identifiers

However, *is it sufficient to protect privacy in social networks by simply replacing the identifying attributes such as* name *and* SSN[4] *of individuals using meaningless unique identifiers?* For example, Fig. 6.2b shows the anonymized network where vertices are associated with some meaningless integer identifiers. At first glance, we may think privacy is preserved pretty well since the ananymized network only contains a set of vertices and edges without any identifying information. Unfortunately, several previous studies showed that an adversary may intrude privacy of some victims using the published social networks and some background knowledge about the victims [4, 6, 18, 28, 47]. As an illustration, we assume that an adversary knows that Ada has four friends in the network. Since the vertex with degree 4 is unique in the anonymized network (the one with identifier 1), the adversary can determine that vertex with identifier 1 must correspond to Ada. Thus, all the private information related to this individual could be easily obtained by analyzing the released social network.

6.3.1 Adversary's Background Knowledge

The background knowledge of the adversary is an important factor in many privacy protection research about social network data publishing. Being equipped with different background knowledge, the adversary's strategy to breach user's privacy is different. Due to the complex graph structures of social networks, the adversary's background knowledge may be modeled in different ways. Following our previous study [48], we summarize some different models of adversary's background knowledge in social networks.

---

[4]Social Security Number, which is unique for individuals in USA.

- **Values of attributes for an individual in the network**. In social networks, a vertex may be linked uniquely to an individual based on some attributes. Here those attributes may serve as a role similar to *quasi-identifier* in relational data [10]. Attributes of vertex are often represented as labels in social networks. An adversary may know some values of those attributes of certain victims.

- **Degrees of a vertex in the network**. The degree of a vertex in social networks captures how many other people the corresponding individual is connected to in the network. Such information is often easy to collect by adversaries. For example, the neighbor of a target individual may easily estimate the number of friends the victim has. An adversary equipped with the knowledge about the degree of the victim can re-identify the target individual from the networks by simply examining the vertex degrees in the released network.

- **Relationship between individuals in the network**. An adversary may know that there are some specific relationships between some target individuals. For example, in a social network about friendship relationship, edges may carry labels recording the channels people use to communicate with each other such as telephone, email, and/or instant message. An adversary may try to use the background knowledge that a victim uses only emails to communicate with her friends in the network to link the victim to certain vertices in the network.

- **Neighborhood structure of an individual in the network**. An adversary may have the background knowledge about the neighborhood of some target individuals. For example, an adversary may know that a victim has four close friends who also know each other. Using this type of background knowledge, the adversary may re-identify the victim by searching vertices in the released social graph whose neighborhood structures contain a *clique* of size at least 4. Generally, we can consider the d-neighbor of a target vertex, that is, the vertices within a distance d to the target vertex in the network, where d is a positive integer.

- **Certain subgraphs embedded in the network**. An adversary may inject certain well-constructed subgraphs into a social network before the network is publicly released. After collecting the released network, it is possible for the adversary to re-identify the embedded subgraph if the subgraph is unique. As shown in [4], the creation of 7 vertices by an adversary can reveal an average of 70 target vertices in a large network.

- **Properties of graph structure in the network**. In social network analysis, the graph structures have many important metrics, such as *betweenness centrality*, *closeness centrality*, *reachability*, and so on. Those properties of graph structure can be used as background knowledge for the adversaries to breach the privacy of target individuals.

- **Group participation of an individual in the network**. Groups are available in many social networks. An adversary may know the list of groups that a target individual has participated in. The list of groups can be regarded as a signature for an adversary to re-identify the victims from the released social networks.

Many existing studies about privacy protection of social network data publishing make assumptions that the adversary's background knowledge is limited. When social networks are anonymized, the privacy protection techniques can only ensure that the adversaries with specific background knowledge cannot breach user's privacy from the anonymized data. However, there is no guarantee that other adversaries with different background knowledge cannot breach victim's privacy. Due to such weak and sometimes unrealistic assumption, anonymization techniques are often criticized as not being able to provide strong protection on data privacy. Recently, the *differential privacy* model [11, 33] removes the assumption of adversary's background knowledge. In general, the differential privacy model ensures that the addition or removal of a single data item does not substantially affect the distributional information for data analysis. It provides a much stronger privacy protection guarantee on the data. The differential privacy model was originally introduced for relational data. Recently, the model has been studied in social networks as well [19, 39]. There are still many challenging issues in the differential privacy model such as its complexity and applicability. We do not provide discussions on differential privacy model in this chapter.

6.3.2 Privacy Protection Models and Anonymization Techniques

Several anonymization techniques have been developed for social networks in the past several years. As this chapter focuses on user community in social networks, we need to emphasize that there are few research which directly addresses how community information can be used to guide the anonymization techniques. Alternatively, the anonymization techniques usually assume that the anonymized networks may be used to analyze the global network structures. In some other situations, the anonymized networks may be used to analyze the micro-structures. The golden rule of data anonymization is to anonymize the data such that privacy is preserved and the utility of the data is retained as much as possible.

In general, if an attacker cannot uniquely distinguish a target individual from other vertices in the anonymized social networks, the individual's privacy can be considered in secure. In this section, we first briefly review several representative studies on anonymizing social networks, and then discuss whether the anonymized social networks can still be used for community detection.

To protect the privacy, one common solution is to guarantee that any individual cannot be identified correctly in the anonymized social network with a probability higher than $\frac{1}{k}$, where k is a user-specified parameter carrying the same spirit in the popular k-anonymity model in relational data [38]. There are some anonymization methods based on this idea.

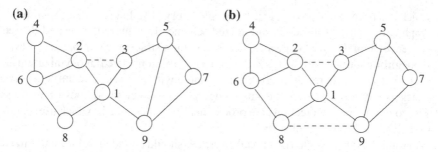

Fig. 6.3 Anonymized social networks using k-Degree Anonymity and k-Neighborhood Anonymity. *Dashed edges* are added to the networks to achieve privacy requirement. **a** The 2-degree anonymous network. **b** the 2-neighborhood anonymous network

- **k-Degree Anonymity.** Liu and Terzi [28] studied the k-degree anonymization problem in social networks. The networks are assumed to be without any vertex or edge labels. They considered the privacy breach scenario where the identities of individuals associated with vertices are revealed.

  To model the background knowledge of an adversary, the authors considered possible re-identification attacks against individuals by an adversary using the prior knowledge of the degree of a target vertex. An adversary is assumed to know the degree of a target victim. By searching the degrees of vertices in the published network, the adversary may be able to identify the individual, even when the identities of the vertices are removed before the network is published. For example, vertex 1 in Fig. 6.2b is under attack since its degree is unique in the network.

  In order to battle degree-based attacks, Liu and Terzi [28] proposed the notion of *k-degree anonymity*, which mimics k-anonymity in relational data. Specifically, a graph is said to be k-degree anonymous if for every vertex v in the graph, there exist at least $k-1$ other vertices in the graph with the same degree as v. An adversary with degree background knowledge can identify some target individuals with the probability at most $\frac{1}{k}$. For example, the network in Fig. 6.3a is 2-degree anonymous. An additional edge connecting vertices 2 and 3 is needed to achieve this privacy requirement.

  For a graph $G(V, E)$, the degree sequence of G, denoted by **d**, is a sequence of vertices in the degree descending order. A degree sequence is k-degree-anonymous if, for each vertex, there are at least other $k-1$ vertices having the same degree. By providing a privacy parameter k, the anonymization method proceeds in two steps. In the first step, starting from the original degree sequence **d**, Liu and Terzi [28] developed a dynamic programming method to construct a new degree sequence $\hat{\mathbf{d}}$ that is k-degree-anonymous and minimizes the degree anonymization cost $D_A(\hat{\mathbf{d}}-\mathbf{d}) = L_1(\hat{\mathbf{d}}-\mathbf{d})$. In the second step, they constructed a graph $\hat{G}(V, \hat{E})$ such that $\hat{\mathbf{d}}$ is the degree sequence of $\hat{G}$ and $\hat{E} \cap E = E$. The graph construction problem is related to the problem of realizing degree sequence with constraints, which has been studied extensively in graph theory [17]. In general, the method of graph construction follows a randomized scheme. To achieve the desired degree sequence, a randomized edge swap transformation strategy was adopted in [28].

- **k-Neighborhood Anonymity**. Zhou and Pei [46] considered anonymization in social networks where each vertex is associated with non-sensitive attributes. An attacker may have background knowledge about the neighborhoods of victims. The goal of privacy protection is to protect neighborhood attacks which use neighborhood matching to re-identify vertices.

  Zhou and Pei [46] assumed that no fake vertices should be added to the anonymized graph. This assumption is often desirable in applications since introducing fake vertices may often change the global structure of a social network. Moreover, they assumed that the original connections between vertices in G are retained in the anonymization.

  To battle neighborhood attacks, Zhou and Pei [46] extended the k-anonymity model in relational data to social networks. For a social network G, suppose an adversary knows the neighborhood structure of a vertex $u \in V(G)$, denoted by $Neighbor_G(u)$. If $Neighbor_G(u)$ has at least k isomorphic copies in G' where G' is an anonymization of G, then u can be re-identified in G' with a confidence of at most $\frac{1}{k}$. For example, the network in Fig. 6.3b is 2-neighborhood anonymous. Two additional edges connecting vertices 2 and 3 and vertices 8 and 9 are needed to achieve this privacy requirement.

  Zhou and Pei [46] introduced a practical greedy method to anonymize a social network to satisfy the k-neighborhood anonymity requirement in two steps. In the first step, the algorithm extracts the neighborhoods of all vertices in the network. To facilitate the isomorphism tests among neighborhoods of different vertices which will be conducted frequently in anonymization, a simple yet effective neighborhood component coding technique based on minimal DFS code [43] was proposed which represents neighborhoods in a concise way. In the second step, the algorithm greedily organizes vertices into groups and anonymizes the neighborhoods of vertices in a group to the same, until the graph satisfies k-neighborhood anonymity. Due to the well recognized *power-law* distribution of vertex degrees in large social networks, a heuristic of starting with those vertices of large degrees is adopted. The intuition is that in real social networks, those vertices with large degrees are the ones vulnerable to neighborhood attacks.

- **k-Anonymity in Social Networks**. Campan and Truta [6] modeled a social network as a simple undirected graph. Moreover, vertices in the network are associated with some attributes, which are classified into three categories, *identifying attributes* such as name and SSN which should be removed in data publishing, *quasi-identifier attributes* such as zipcode and sex which may be used by an adversary in certain re-identification attacks, and *sensitive attributes* such as diagnosis and income which are assumed to be private information. Furthermore, in [6], edges are not labeled.

  To protect privacy in social networks, Campan and Truta [6] advocated the k-anonymity model. Every vertex should be indistinguishable with at least other $k - 1$ vertices in terms of both the attributes and the associated structural information such as neighborhood of vertices. The anonymization method disturbs as little as possible the social networks, both the attribute data associated with the vertices and the structural information.

The method for anonymizing vertex attributes uses *generalization* [2], which has been well studied in the relational data. For anonymizing structural information, the proposed method partitions vertices into clusters in anonymization. To anonymize edges, vertices in the same cluster are collapsed into one single vertex, labeled with the number of vertices and edges in the cluster. The edges between two clusters are collapsed into a single edge, labeled by the number of edges between them.

There are some other social network anonymization techniques based on the well-known k-anonymity principle. For example, Zou et al. [49] proposed a k-automorphism framework to anonymize social networks. Given an original network, the algorithm in [49] converts the network into a k-automorphic network, which is then published. Cheng et al. [8] developed the k-isomorphism model which performs data anonymization by forming k pairwise isomorphic subgraphs in social networks. For other relevant studies on privacy protection of social network data publishing, readers may refer to some recent survey studies [45, 48].

Anonymization methods change the original network structure in one way or another. Some pieces of information may be lost during the anonymization process. One question people may wonder is *how useful the anonymized networks are for various social network analysis tasks*. Campan et al. [7] studied how well anonymized social networks can preserve community structures from the original social networks. To anonymize social networks, the two models, k-anonymity for social networks [6] and k-degree anonymity [28] were considered. Campan et al. [7] focused on a specific community detection methods named *Louvain method*. This community detection method is a heuristic algorithm which is based on modularity optimization. In a nutshell, the modularity is a quality function that can be computed for a graph partitioned into communities.

Campan et al. [7] identified communities from the original network and the anonymized networks based on the k-anonymity for social networks [6] and the k-degree anonymity [28]. To compare the results of community detection, they counted how many vertices from the original communities are remained in the same community in the anonymized networks. Several real social networks were adopted for evaluation, including *Enron* (an email exchange network) and *YouTube* (an online video sharing network). The results indicated that when k is set to be small (e.g., 5 or 10), the community information for more than 70 % of vertices in fact does not change in the network. The results verified that the anonymized networks actually preserve the community information pretty well.

6.3.3 Anonymizing Group Participation in Social Networks

In social networks, users can participate in different groups/communities. If the groups information is explicitly known, the participation between users and groups can be modeled as a bipartite graph. The edges in such a bipartite graph may be considered as privacy. Bipartite graph has different properties comparing to the general graph representation discussed in Sect. 6.2.1. In this section, we discuss some existing studies on anonymizing bipartite graphs.

Generally, a bipartite graph $G = (V, H, E)$ consists of $|V|$ vertices of one type and $|H|$ vertices of the other type, and a set of $|E|$ edges $E \subseteq V \times H$. When a bipartite graph is published, the graph structure is retained. The vertices are clustered into groups and the mapping between groups in the original graph and groups in the published graph is released. For example, the mapping table may state that vertices $\{x_1, x_2, x_3\}$ in the original graph are mapped to $\{a_{20}, a_{31}, a_{206}\}$ in the published graph. By devising the mapping properly, privacy of individuals such as whether a user participates in a group/community can be preserved.

Cormode et al. [9] focused on the problem of anonymizing bipartite graphs. To model the background knowledge of adversaries, Cormode et al. [9] considered both *static attacks* and *learned link attacks*. If a group of vertices $X \subset V$ only connect to a group of vertices $Y \subset H$, a static attack can immediately obtain the vertices that those in X connect to. Generally, if very few edges exist between vertices in X and vertices not in Y, then a learned link attack can obtain the vertices that those in X connect to with a high confidence. The data utility is measured by the accuracy of answering aggregate queries, such as the average number of groups participated for each user in social networks.

Cormode et al. [9] proposed the safe grouping mechanism to protect privacy. A safe grouping of a bipartite graph partitions vertices into groups such that two vertices in the same group of V have no common neighbors in H and vice versa. To control the anonymization granularity, a (k, l)-safe grouping ensures that each group on V contains at least k vertices and each group on H contains at least l vertices.

A greedy algorithm is developed in [9], which may or may not always find a safe grouping. The vertices are processed one by one. For each vertex, the algorithm checks whether it can be put into an existing group without breaking the safety. If yes, it is added into a group. Otherwise, a new group is created. After all vertices are processed, there may be some groups with fewer than k vertices. Those vertices are collected and the algorithm continues to run on the collection with a larger group size threshold, say $(k + 1)$. The iteration continues until either a safe grouping is found or the group size threshold exceeds the number of vertices in the collection of vertices to be partitioned. In the latter case, the algorithm fails.

6.4 Privacy Settings in Online Social Networks

As elaborated in Sect. 6.1, privacy breaches may also exist due to improper privacy settings in those online social networking sites. In recent years, the development of user-friendly, fine-grained tools for protecting personal information is an emerging problem in online social networks [1, 34].

Users in online social networking sites can easily share their information with others. Meanwhile, many users typically do not want to disclose all of their information with everyone else. As a result, the access control-based privacy settings become a popular method adopted by many online social networking sites. Users are able to customize their own privacy settings to meet their privacy protection expectations. For example, Facebook has a specific "Privacy Settings" page for each user. Individuals in Facebook can specify which pieces of information each friend is permitted to view. Facebook also provides a functionality to allow users to partition their friends into different groups. The privacy settings can specify whether pieces of information are visible to all of their friends or only a selected groups of friends.

Although the privacy settings provide intuitive ways to customize users' different privacy protection expectations, there are some important issues which need to be considered thoroughly. Grandison and Maximilien [16] broadly categorized the privacy settings and access control issues in the current online social networking sites as follows.

- **Data partitioning**, that is, how should user's data be partitioned into exchangeable granular pieces? To address this issue, we need to consider requirements from both end-users as well as different applications in online social networks.
- **Privacy settings**, that is, what level of granularity is required for privacy settings? Data should be partitioned and privacy levels should be set up properly so that the privacy settings are easy and effective. Moreover, multiple applications may share privacy settings on the same set of user's data. Then, the communication among applications should be effective so that no privacy is violated.
- **Management**, that is, how privacy settings and data are managed? This involves three different operations. The first one is monitoring the changes of data and privacy settings. The second one is enforcement. For example, how privacy settings are enforced in different applications? The last one is sharing. For example, how are settings shared amongst users of a group?

In reality, people always find they struggle to express and maintain proper privacy settings in those popular online social networking sites. Some survey studies indicated that the user interfaces of privacy setting pages are complex and not user-friendly [34]. Creating groups of friends and assigning different privacy settings for different groups are often a manual process. If a user has many friends in those sites, the process of such manual privacy settings is very time-consuming.

Some recent studies developed machine learning methods to automatically create groups of friends and set up proper privacy settings for social network users. For example, Fang and LeFevre [13] proposed a privacy wizard for those online social networking sites. The goal of the privacy wizard is to ease user's burden and automatically customize a user's privacy settings. The privacy wizard is based on the intuition that users often conceive their different privacy settings using a set of privacy preferences. Specifically, the framework of the privacy wizard takes a limited amount of user input which describes user's privacy preferences. In the most general case, this is in the form of questions and answers. Users can assign privacy labels such as "allow" or "deny" to selected friends. Then, a machine learning model such as *classification* can be constructed to automatically assign privacy privileges to the remaining friends in the network.

In specific scenarios, even though an individual has set up proper privacy settings, the adversary may rely on some other techniques, such as *information inference*, to obtain private information from online social networks. A concrete example of such inference privacy attack is illustrated in Example 6.1. The inference privacy attack is a challenging problem. The *PrivAware system* [5], which is a Facebook application used to score the privacy configuration for a user's profile, provided some initial analysis toward quantifying the risk of privacy inference. As a possible solution, the authors [5] suggested that it is necessary to remove certain relationships in social networks to reduce the inference risk.

In addition to privacy settings, some other functionalities provided by those online social networking sites may bring privacy concerns as well. For example, some online social networking sites allow a functionality called "lookahead", that is, a user can reach the neighbors of her/his neighbors, and so on. To understand the side-effect of lookahead on privacy breach, Korolova et al. [26] considered attacks aiming at knowledge of a significant fraction of the links in the network. It has been shown that if an attacker can subvert some user accounts, and look ahead using those accounts, she/he can use the information obtained from a small number of accounts to intrude privacy of a large number of links in the network. To protect the link privacy of users, a social network should have to be very careful in managing lookahead operations. Probably only 1 or 2 steps lookahead are allowed.

In recent years, several reports also revealed that privacy may be breached in online social networking sites due to unappropriate design of social networking APIs. Social networking APIs integrate third-party content into the social networking site and give third-party developers access to user's data. These open interfaces enable popular site enhancements but at the same time pose serious risk on privacy by exposing user data to third-party developers. Felt and Evans [14] explored the privacy risks associated with social networking APIs. They presented a privacy-by-proxy design for a privacy preserving API that is motivated by an analysis of the data needs and uses of Facebook applications. Their study of 150 popular Facebook applications indicates that nearly all applications can achieve their functionalities using a limited interface that only provides access to an anonymized social graph and placeholders of user's data. Most recently, there has been a flood of malicious Facebook apps that steal user's personal information for various malicious purposes such as *spam* and identity attacks. Rahman et al. [32] analyzed more than 100 K apps in Facebook and found out that 13 % of those apps are in fact malicious. The fighting with malicious apps in many online social networking sites is emerging.

There are some other recent privacy studies related to graph structures of online social networks and user communities. For example, Liu and Terzi [29] proposed a methodology of privacy score for quantifying the risk posed by a user's privacy settings. The privacy score indicates the potential privacy risk caused by his partic-ipation in the network. Liu and Terzi [29] considered two dimensions to define the privacy score: whether the information revealed by a user is sensitive, and whether the disclosed information is visible to a large amount of users in the network. Akcora et al. [3] proposed a risk measure for those online social networking sites. The goal of the risk measure is to provide a quantifying way to evaluate whether it might be risky to disclose certain information with others. The proposed risk measure considers user's risk attitudes and some user behavior measures.

6.5 Conclusion

In this chapter, we briefly reviewed several privacy issues for communities in social networks. Two privacy breach scenarios, one for social network data publishing and another for privacy settings in online social networking sites, were studied. For the first scenario, we examined the privacy protection techniques based on several important dimensions: the definition of privacy, background knowledge, privacy protection model, and utility of the anonymized data. For the second scenario, we discussed some recent developments on enhancing privacy settings in online social networks.

The current research and development of privacy protection in social networks is still far from perfect. As reviewed in the chapter, many existing techniques have their limitations and cannot be generalized to address all types of privacy threats in social networks. As social networks contain rich information and the graph structure is much more complicated comparing to the relational data, privacy protection in social networks is much more challenging and needs many serious efforts in the near future. Particularly, modeling adversarial attacks and developing corresponding privacy protection strategies are crucial.

References

1. Acquisti A, Gross R (2006) Imagined communities: awareness, information sharing, and privacy on the Facebook. In: Privacy enhancing technologies, pp 36–58
2. Aggarwal CC, Yu PS (2008) Privacy-preserving data mining: a survey. In: Handbook of database security, pp 431–460
3. Akcora C, Carminati B, Ferrari E (2012) Privacy in social networks: how risky is your social graph? In: Proceedings of IEEE 28th international data engineering (ICDE) conference, pp 9–19
4. Backstrom L, Dwork C, Kleinberg J (2007) Wherefore art thou r3579x?: anonymized social networks, hidden patterns, and structural steganography. In: Proceedings of the 16th international conference on World Wide Web (WWW'07). ACM Press, New York, pp 181–190
5. Becker J, Chen H (2009) Measuring privacy risk in online social networks. In: Web 2.0 security and privacy workshop
6. Campan A, Truta TM (2008) A clustering approach for data and structural anonymity in social networks. In: Proceedings of the 2nd ACM SIGKDD international workshop on privacy, security, and trust in KDD (PinKDD'08), in conjunction with KDD'08. Las Vegas, Nevada
7. Campan A, Alufaisan Y, Truta TM (2014) Community detection in anonymized social networks. In: EDBT/ICDT workshops, pp 396–405

8. Cheng J, Fu AW-C, Liu J (2010) K-isomorphism: privacy preserving network publication against structural attacks. In: SIGMOD conference, pp 459–470
9. Cormode G, Srivastava D, Yu T, Zhang Q (2008) Anonymizing bipartite graph data using safe groupings. In: Proceedings of the 34th international conference on very large databases (VLDB'08). ACM
10. di Vimercati SDC, Foresti S (2011) Quasi-identifier. In: Encyclopedia of cryptography and security 2nd Ed, pp 1010–1011
11. Dwork C (2008) Differential privacy: a survey of results. In: Proceedings of the 5th international conference on theory and applications of models of computation. Lecture notes in computer science. vol 4978, Springer, Berlin, pp 1–19
12. Elefant C (2011) The power of social media: legal issues & best practices for utilities engaging social media. Energy LJ 32:1
13. Fang L, LeFevre K (2010) Privacy wizards for social networking sites. In: WWW, pp 351–360
14. Felt A, Evans D (2008) Privacy protection for social networking APIs. In: 2008 Web 2.0 security and privacy (W2SP'08)
15. Frikken KB, Golle P (2006) Private social network analysis: how to assemble pieces of a graph privately. In: Proceedings of the 2006 ACM workshop on privacy in the electronic society (WPES'06), ACM, pp 89–98
16. Grandison T, Maximilien EM (2008) Towards privacy propagation in the social web. In: 2008 Web 2.0 security and privacy (W2SP'08), Oakland, California, May 2008
17. Gross J, Yellen J (1999) Graph theory and its applications. CRC Press Inc, Boca Raton
18. Hay M, Miklau G, Jensen D, Towsley D (2008) Resisting structural identification in anonymized social networks. vol 1, VLDB Endowment, pp 102–114
19. Hay M, Li C, Miklau G, Jensen D (2009) Accurate estimation of the degree distribution of private networks. In: Ninth IEEE international conference on data mining ICDM'09, IEEE, pp 169–178
20. http://en.wikipedia.org/wiki/2012_LinkedIn_hack
21. http://mobility.oodja.com/a/detail.do/id-5dd10021-ddd7-4d8e-9066-7869b0fb4b18, (2012)
22. http://www.blogherald.com/2010/05/21/social-media-privacy-scandal-revealed/, (2010)
23. http://www.itworld.com/it-managementstrategy/234649/biggest-privacy-scandal-2011
24. http://www.sexysocialmedia.com/odnoklassnikiru-privacy-scandal/
25. Kleinberg JM (2007) Challenges in mining social network data: processes, privacy,and paradoxes. In: Berkhin P, Caruana R, Wu X (eds) Proceedingsof the 13th ACM SIGKDD international conference on knowledge discoveryand data mining (KDD'07), San Jose, California, USA,12–15 August 12–15 2007. ACM, pp 4–5
26. Korolova A, Motwani R, Nabar SU, Xu Y (2008) Link privacy in social networks. In: Proceedings of the 24th international conference on data engineering (ICDE'08), IEEE, pp 1355–1357
27. Leskovec J, Faloutsos C (2007) Scalable modeling of real graphs using Kronecker multiplication. In: Proceedings of the 24th international conference on machine learning (ICML'07). ACM, New York, pp 497–504
28. Liu K, Terzi E (2008) Towards identity anonymization on graphs. In: Proceedings of the 2008 ACM SIGMOD international conference on management of data (SIGMOD'08). ACM Press, New York, pp 93–106
29. Liu K, Terzi E (2009) A framework for computing the privacy scores of users in online social networks. In: Proceedings of ninth IEEE international conference on data mining ICDM'09, pp 288–297
30. Liu K, Das K, Grandison T, Kargupta H (2008) Privacy-preserving data analysis on graphs and social networks. In: Kargupta H, Han J, Yu P, Motwani R, Kumar V (eds) Next generation data mining. CRC Press
31. Poulsen K (2008) Pillaged myspace photos show up in massive BitTorrent download. In: Wired, January 2008
32. Rahman M, Huang T, Madhyastha H, Faloutsos M (2012) FRAppE: detecting malicious facebook applications. In: Proceedings of the 10th international conference on emerging networking EXperiments and technologies, Sydney, Australia. ACM

33. Rastogi V, Hay M, Miklau G, Suciu D (2009) Relationship privacy: output perturbation for queries with joins. In: Proceedings of the twenty-eighth ACM SIGMOD-SIGACT-SIGART symposium on principles of database systems (PODS'09). ACM, New York, pp 107–116
34. Rosenblum DS (2007) What anyone can know: the privacy risks of social networking sites. IEEE Secur Priv 5(3):40–49
35. Ruan X, Yue C, Wang H (2013) Unveiling privacy setting breaches in online social networks. In: Proceedings of the 10th international conference on security and privacy in communication networks, Beijing, China
36. Scott J (2000) Social network analysis handbook. Sage Publications Inc, London
37. Sophos (2008) Facebook privacy breach exposed user's hidden date of birth. In: Global security mag, July 2008
38. Sweeney L (2002) K-anonymity: a model for protecting privacy. Int J Uncertain Fuzziness Knowl-Based Syst 10(5):557–570
39. Task C, Clifton C (2012) A guide to differential privacy theory in social network analysis. In: 2012 IEEE/ACM international conference on advances in social networks analysis and mining (ASONAM), IEEE, pp 411–417
40. Vaidya YZJ, Clifton C (2006) Privacy preserving data mining. Springer, Berlin
41. Wang D-W, Liau C-J, Sheng Hsu T (2006) Privacy protection in social network data disclosure based on granular computing. In: Proceedings of the 2006 IEEE international conference on fuzzy systems, Vancouver, BC, Canada, 16–21 July 2006, pp 997–1003
42. Wasserman S, Faust K (1994) Social network analysis: methods and applications. Cambridge University Press, Cambridge
43. Yan X, Han J (2002) gSpan: graph-based substructure pattern mining. In: Proceedings of the 2002 IEEE international conference on data mining (ICDM'02). IEEE Computer Society, Washington, p 721
44. Zheleva E, Getoor L (2007) Preserving the privacy of sensitive relationships in graph data. In: Proceedings of the 1st ACM SIGKDD workshop on privacy, security, and trust in KDD (PinKDD'07)
45. Zheleva E, Getoor L (2011) Privacy issues in social networks: a brief survey social network data analytics. Springer, Berlin
46. Zhou B, Pei J (2008) Preserving privacy in social networks against neighborhood attacks. In: Proceedings of the 24th IEEE international conference on data engineering (ICDE'08)
47. Zhou B, Pei J (2011) The k-anonymity and l-diversity approaches for privacy preservation in social networks against neighborhood attacks. Knowl Inf Syst 28(1):47–77
48. Zhou B, Pei J, Luk W-S (2008) A brief survey on anonymization techniques for privacy preserving publishing of social network data. SIGKDD Explor 10(2):12–22
49. Zou L, Chen L, Özsu MT (2009) K-automorphism: a general framework for privacy preserving network publication. PVLDB 2(1):946–957

Printed in the United States
By Bookmasters